I0616219

WINTER KILLS

DEATH LURKS IN PARADISE

M.C. PEAK

HANGAR 1 PUBLISHING

Copyright © 2025 by M.C. Peak

All rights reserved.

No part of this book may be reproduced in any form or by any electronic or mechanical means, including information storage and retrieval systems, without written permission from the author, except for the use of brief quotations in a book review.

I would like to dedicate this book to all the great people of Paradise, Michigan, who made our lives there a true Paradise in every sense of the word. Especially Jodie and Doug Laub, John and Rhonda Smit, Mike and Joanne Cook, Sarah, Bill and Jan Dohm, Dan and Lori Maxwell, Jack and Renee Grimes, Adele and Crit Holland and their daughter, Greta, Mark and Mel Ricki and the Haunted Trail crew, Rob Harbaum, Debbie Shooltz Brown, Paul Bella, The Colonel and his wife, Ron Rix, Dave and Jane Fisher, Ken, Sonny and "Wendy", our snow plow man, Brian, and the "Bored Bachelors", and all the people whose names I didn't get that make that town a great place to live, even in the harshest of weather conditions!

Thank you, ALL!

PROLOGUE

The Upper Peninsula of Michigan holds nearly thirty percent of the state's land mass, but only three percent of the population. Winters in the Upper Peninsula, or the UP, can be brutal. With snowfall reaching as much as 390 inches, almost 39 feet, and 200 inches in a normal winter, mobility can be an issue. Add to that the winds coming off Lake Superior and the other Great Lakes, which can reach sixty-five miles per hour or more, and the wind chill can feel like sixty below zero. And those winds blow the snow into enormous drifts, burying buildings and closing roads. This is the main reason the population of the UP is such a small part of Michigan's total, and why the number of residents who choose to live there year-round drops by two thirds once winter starts to show, usually around Halloween.

Year-round residents need to be a hearty, resilient sort, able to survive these conditions with little or no help from authorities. In many towns and rural areas, there are no local police, fire department, or rescue squads. And those that could be sent to an emergency might be an hour or more away. Enter the Yooper, a play on

UPer. That is what Michiganders call those who live in the Upper Peninsula. Most are native to the peninsula, but there are some transplants. Yoopers are uniquely capable of not only surviving but thriving in those environs. For the most part, they are friendly, helpful to a fault, and have some think-out-the-box ingenuity.

There's a story about one such Yooper, Bobby Bosley. He lived several miles down an unmaintained road. Snow piles up quickly in the Upper Peninsula, but people still need to get to the store, keep appointments, etc. Bobby had a plow that mounted to the front of his Ford F-250 pickup truck. But the mounting bracket broke, and he had lent his welder to a friend, and there was eighteen inches of new snow on the ground. He did have a small snow blower attached to his riding lawn mower for clearing the walkways around his house, but it didn't have enough weight to clear his road. But Bobby figured out that, if he could rig up something to attach the mower with the blower to the front of his truck, the weight of the truck might give it enough backbone to move the snow from his road. Two hours later, Bobby's contraption was roped and bungee-corded to the winch of his truck. He could raise and lower the mower and blower setup, and away he went, snow-blowing his road. It worked, but no one else would ever think of attaching a mower to a truck to move snow. That's how Yoopers think. Out of the box.

Another reason the population of year-round residents is so small, is that there just aren't very many jobs available that far north for a full-time resident. Many of the Yoopers are retired, but most work two or three part-time jobs to be able to live the Yooper life. Large corporations tend to stay away from smaller communities. Not enough return on investment. Tourism is the biggest business in the UP, especially for outdoor-minded people. Snowmobiling, cross-country skiing, ice fishing, and snow shoeing are big attractions. Most of the UP is forests and wetlands, not to mention the Great Lakes and all they have to offer. It's ideal for those looking to escape the busy city life many Michiganders are familiar with.

There are over 3,000 miles of snowmobile trails in the UP. With over 200,000 snow mobiles just in Michigan, sledding is by far the biggest boon to small towns all through the peninsula. These towns live and die by the snow season. With all those people visiting the UP each year, and many unfamiliar with the area and it's hazards, it's no wonder so many people go missing. Over 550 people disappear each year in Michigan. That is five missing for every 100,000 people. Most of those are lost in the UP. Authorities will tell you it's because they rode their snowmobile on thin ice and plunged through, never to be found. Lake Superior's waters are so cold that bodies don't decompose, so the gases associated with decomposition, the main reason they float to the surface, don't occur. "Gichigami never gives up her dead," a popular song once told.

Ice fishing is also popular. People take snowmobiles out to their fishing shacks, sometimes a couple of miles from shore. Some of those simply disappear. There are vast swamps and wetlands scattered all over the UP. People can get turned around pretty easily in those swamps. Add to that the risk of exposure and the very nature of swamps—they tend to "suck up" bodies. They sink in the mud. They are eaten by predators and birds, and the swamp smell may mask the smell of a rotting body. Again, authorities will say they most likely went through the ice and drowned, or succumbed to snowmobiling injuries, and with no evidence of anything else as the cause, most people don't give it a second thought, but some raise an eyebrow to all those official explanations.

There are stories of supernatural happenings in places with names like the Delirium Swamp, where it is said that forces in the swamp confuse a person into wandering aimlessly into the swamp, where they meet their demise somewhere within the vast bogs and pine thickets.

The lakes have their own stories filled with tragedy and horror. With over 350 shipwrecks in Lake Superior, it is said the ghosts of those who perished beneath the lake's frigid waters lure unsuspecting souls to their own watery death. Still others believe those missing people may have been taken by Mishipeshu, the water panther, the Frankenstein of mysterious creatures. It is said to have horns on its head, cat-like facial features and claws, snake-like scales covering its body, and a spiny back and tail. It stands eight to nine feet tall with a heavy build, like a bear but with broader shoulders. Legend says it lives in Lake Superior, and when winter freezes the lake over, Mishipeshu leaves the lake and prowls the shores along Whitefish Bay and the surrounding woodlands and wetlands, searching for those who don't respect the laws of nature—to leave no trace and take only what you need. Not exactly the mantra of some who come to play in nature's winter wonderland. Most vacationers are respectful of the area. They pack out their trash. They don't mar the wilderness with thoughtless graffiti or wildly riding snowmobiles or four-wheelers. They respect the rules and obey the laws. Others believe that Mishipeshu is simply a hunter stalking the sparsely populated area for easy prey. In any case, there is no shortage of mysterious and ghastly legends in the culture of many UP towns. After all, many people do go missing each year, tourists and locals alike. Some say this is why most people vacate the Upper Peninsula during winter.

The town of Paradise, Michigan, is nestled along the shore of a section of Lake Superior called Whitefish Bay. And Paradise lives up to its name. Close to the Shipwreck Museum is the final resting place of the Edmond Fitzgerald, a cargo ship that sank just outside

Whitefish Bay in the 1970s. Paradise offers four-wheel enthusiasts and snowmobilers a vast system of woodland trails and wetland access, mixed in with local history and several lighthouses that can be toured. But there is little nightlife. One restaurant, the Wheelhouse, and it's bar side, the Goat Locker, offer live music most nights. And they host role-playing games like murder mystery night. It's a gathering place for locals and tourists alike to play cards, get a good meal, and have a few adult beverages. During the tourist seasons, summer through winter, it's packed almost every day, all day. If anything's happening, it'll be the buzz at the Goat Locker.

It's quiet in Paradise. Even the sound of snowmobiles is muffled by the snow. It's rare to see any law enforcement in Paradise, as there is very little crime. Not that crime would be tolerated by those who live there. They watch out for their neighbors and step up when there's trouble or someone needs help. In fact, about the only time any law enforcement agency is in town, it's because of an ATV, snowmobile, or boating accident, or someone's gone missing.

The weather is divided by four distinct seasons. Spring comes late, and summers are mild but short, with highs rarely exceeding the upper eighties. Perfect for wild blueberries. One of the main summer activities in the UP is wild blueberry picking, and they are everywhere. The colors of fall explode in Paradise, and the trails are filled with four-wheelers who come to view the spectacular colors. But winter is king in Paradise. It can, and usually does, start to show in late October and holds on into April or May. It averages ten feet of snow each year, and it takes a while for the snow to melt off. Winter is when most of the missing person reports occur. It's difficult to find evidence of where someone went unless there were witnesses to an ice breakthrough or other accident. This is due to the nearly ever-present wind. The wind blows the snow into drifts and erases footprints and snowmobile tracks as if they were never there. It would also erase any evidence of the Mishipeshu.

Native lore tells of the Mishipeshu living in the cold waters of Lake Superior. Those cold waters keep it from coming to the surface close to shore as it can't survive water temperatures above 40°F for more than a few minutes. The main lake averages temperatures of 47°F. But Whitefish Bay can reach 65°F or more in the summer, with winter temps around 32°F. Plenty cold enough for Mishipeshu. Lore says that Mishipeshu comes out of the lake through the ice holes that form along the shore.

These ice holes, or volcanoes, as they are known, are due to the cone shape that forms as water is pushed up and out of these holes and freezes, creating the classic cone-shape that resembles a volcano. The volcanoes form along the ice mountains that form when ice accumulates along the shore and sandbars, creating a dam of ice. Waves crash on these dams and the water freezes along the top, building up the height of the dams. It looks very much like a miniature mountain range. Waves crashing into this carve weak spots in the ice, and the water bores holes into the dam. Viola! Ice holes are formed. The Mishipeshu could easily utilize these holes to exit and enter the lake without leaving any trace. No unusual holes in the ice to draw attention to its presence.

Mishipeshu is just a theory, of course. No one has claimed to see it, at least not publicly. But Yoopers are a pretty tight-lipped sort. They don't want any of that type of notoriety. It's more of an unspoken understanding that there just might be something lurking in the shadows. There is at least a little truth in every folktale, after all. For this reason, Yoopers rarely travel alone after dark. People don't disappear in groups; it's always one here and there.

1

CHANGE OF PACE

"Twenty-two miles to Paradise."

Mike and Sarah Perkins had been on the road for almost seven days. They were moving to the Upper Peninsula of Michigan to be closer to family. They had lived in Northern Idaho for the last twenty-eight years, where Mike was a sergeant with the Coeur d'Alene city police department. But there were grandchildren in the family now, and with the huge influx of people escaping the bigger cities in California, Washington, and Oregon, the city was feeling more and more like a big city. And it was getting big city problems, too. There was a lot more gang activity, and drugs were becoming more prevalent. It just didn't feel the same anymore. So, after many late night discussions, they decided to move. Mike put in for his retirement, put the house on the market, and loaded up the U-Haul and headed east. They chose Paradise because of the slower pace of life there. With the sudden growth in real estate, they could sell their home for substantially more than they paid. They hoped to pay cash for their dream home on Lake Superior. Plus, they would be close to family, but not too close. The rest of the family lived four or five hours away. An easy commute, but far enough away that they wouldn't get those frequent, unannounced visits family is known for. They bought a house without seeing it in person first. They relied on the photos in the posting and the inspection report. It was a fixer-upper, so the price was right, and Mike had some DIY skills, so he would be kept busy in his first few months of his retirement.

As they pulled into their new driveway, it looked like the perfect setup. A modest-sized home with a large detached garage and separate shop. The house sat on a small bluff above the lake, offering spectacular views of Whitefish Bay. There were constant views of the large cargo ships that used the lakes until it froze, sometime between late December and January.

"It's beautiful." Sarah didn't even wait for the U-Haul to come to a stop before she opened the door to get out. "We have a garage, so we can park out of the weather. I'm so excited."

Mike was more of a realist. The first thing he noticed was that the roof was in worse shape than he thought. It would need to be completely replaced. Then there was the fact that the plumbing and electrical would have to be reworked for year-round use, as the cabin had been a seasonal home for an older couple from Traverse City. To call it rustic would be kind. It needed a lot of cosmetic and mechanical upgrades. There was only one bath, and it was a shower and tub combination. Sarah wanted a jetted soaker tub, so a whole master bath would have to be added. The list seemed endless and kept growing. But the price was right. A home, a two-car, two-story garage, and a large workshop all sitting on a half-acre of prime lakefront real estate was almost impossible to find. And at under $200,000, it was a steal. Most homes like this would be sold for over $350,000, even as a fixer-upper. They didn't question the deal; they were just happy to find it. Maybe if they had looked into the history of the cabin, they might have passed on it.

In the winter of 2019, Stan Bromley, the previous owner, made a rare winter trip to his cabin to open it for some snowmobilers who wanted to rent it for a week. Bromley didn't normally rent out their cabin; it was just for family to use. But with the pandemic, the Bromleys could have used the income. So he made the 3.5 hour trip to Paradise to turn the water back on, make sure the generator was operating, and hand over the keys to the renters. He went a day ahead of them so he could get the cabin warmed up. When the renters arrived, Bromley's truck was in the garage, but there was no sign of Bromley. The front door was open and two windows were broken. The authorities were called and an investigation was done, but Stan Bromley was never found. It was assumed he died somehow, but there was no blood, no body, and no one saw anything. That wasn't unusual, as the closest year-round neighbor was a quarter of a mile down the road. The family hadn't been able to bear going back to their cabin with this hanging over it.

"Let's go dip our toes in the lake, Mike." Sarah was already planning out where their garden would go, what color they were going to paint the cabin, and the landscaping layout. But, first things, first. Get the toes in the lake and make it official.

"You know, it's only June. The lake's still pretty cold." The air temperature wasn't even very warm. It was only in the upper 60s. Whitefish Bay's water temperature is normally in the upper 50s to low 60s in the summer and only occasionally makes it to the upper 60s. But toes in the lake was a must.

"Holy crap! That's some chilly water."

"Yeah, but look at how clear the water is. It's beautiful." Sarah always had a way of looking at the bright side of things. They made a good couple. Mike was more of a realist, with the ability to see possibilities in his head. And Sarah was a romantic without the word *can't* in her vocabulary.

"I've got an idea, babe. Let's not worry about unloading the truck today. I say we run into town, grab some hot dogs and stuff, and cook our dinner over a campfire by the lake. Just have a few beers and chill. What say you?"

"Aye!"

Sarah was road weary, so kicking back by a fire on the lake sounded great.

"While we're there, I'd like to stop in that hardware store and see what kind of supplies we can get there. We got a lot of work to do, and the more we can get in town, the better. It'll take forever if we have to run into the Soo every time we need building supplies." Mike was right.

The Soo, Sault Sainte Marie, was over an hour away, and there was nothing between Paradise and there but a couple of gas stations. The Soo was the closest city that had a variety of large stores and restaurants. The town of Newberry was closer in miles, but speed limits were lower, and the road was riddled with bends and twists that made the trip just as long a drive as the Soo, and the selection for shopping was not as varied. So, most Paradise residents preferred the Soo.

"Okay, but don't spend all afternoon in there. I know how you like to visit. Mike did like to talk. Especially when trying get the lay of the land, so to speak. It was just in his nature. Call it a cop thing. Always curious. Always wary. Always looking for options.

"Yes, dear. I'll keep it short and sweet."

The Falls Building Supplies name was a reference to Tahquamenon Falls, just a few miles away. Tahquamenon Falls is a favored destination for tourists and locals alike. It is one of the attractions that brings people to Paradise, providing the local economy with much-needed revenue.

Mike was anxious to see what type and quality of building supplies they might have, so he made that their first stop. Sarah, however, had no interest in building supplies. She opted to visit the Piece of Paradise gift shop next door to see what they had to offer.

Always one to make an entrance, Mike boldly entered the store with a smile and his trademark greeting. "Hola, everybody! How's the day going?"

Roger Armstrong and Donna Harper were sitting behind the counter. Roger was the only full-time, year-round, employee. Donna usually got laid off around Christmas, as the hardware store business really slows down in winter. But she would be brought back in around April, when seasonal cabin owners made their way back to the UP to make sure their cabins had survived the winter. Many would need repairs from snow loads, frozen pipes, and damage from falling trees.

"Good! How can we help you?" Donna had an air of toughness about her—most Yooper women did—like nothing could phase her. Not much did. The same could be said about Roger. Built like a linebacker, Roger was one of those Jack-of-all-trades types. He knew a lot about most things construction related. And what he didn't know, he could quickly figure out. He was a good fit to run the hardware store.

"I'm Mike Perkins. My wife, Sarah, and I just bought the old Bromley place, and it's gonna need some work. I was just wondering about what kind of building materials and such you guys have."

"You planning on living up here full-time?" Roger's voice had a touch of concern. He'd seen so many people who had moved to Paradise, planning on making it their year-round home, only to pack up and leave after one or two winters. Most simply said the winters were too rough. Others wouldn't give a reason, just saying they didn't like the area, or something along those lines. There were a few who said the area felt "off," or that they had a bad feeling sometimes, an uneasiness they couldn't quite explain. Cabin fever, or some such excuse. But Roger wasn't new to Paradise, or its stories. "Winters can be pretty rough up here. Most people can't handle it."

"Oh, I think we'll be okay. We moved here from North Idaho. Winters get pretty rough up there too. Plus, my wife's family lives down state, so we have support if it gets too bad." Mike had to chuckle at the "winters can get rough" line. He'd seen his fair share of winter in Coeur d'Alene, Idaho. And there could be ten to fifteen feet of snow on the ground where his family's home was up in the higher elevations.

"Well, we've got most everything you might need in stock. And if we don't, we can get it from our sister store in Pickford. Usually in about a week."

"Sounds good. I'll be back in a few days for some tools and supplies, once I know what I'm into. Nice meeting you guys."

"Good to meet you. Welcome to Paradise."

As Mike left the hardware store, Roger and Donna looked at each other and, at the exact same time said, "The Bromley place." They knew the story of Stan Bromley and his mysterious disappearance. Everyone in town knew the story. Everyone except the Perkins.

Mike went over to meet Sarah at the gift shop and head to the grocery store. The Paradise store was great for picking up things you might've forgotten or ran out of, but selection was limited, and items cost a little more than the stores in the Soo or Newberry.

The price of living in the boonies. Not exactly where one would buy their monthly groceries. Still, the people who ran the store were friendly, and if they didn't have what someone needed, they would order it for them. And they had the basic necessities: beer, booze, sodas, and a good selection of meat products from a local farm, even hotdogs. Just what the doctor ordered for FF—fanny fatigue, from driving.

"Find anything interesting, babe?" Sarah already had a pile of clothes stacked up on the counter.

"You know me. I love my comfy clothes." Sarah was being helped by the shop owner, Julie Ward. Julie was as outgoing as they come, and her personality bubbled over. She never met a stranger and had a strong business sense. In a small town like Paradise, there was always one or two people who kept the town running. Julie Ward was that person in Paradise. If there was a committee or board, she was on it. She knew everyone and everything in town. A good contact to have for new arrivals like Mike and Sarah.

"Your wife says you bought the Bromley place and plan on living here year-round. I hope you like winter." Julie let out a nervous, high-pitched giggle. She knew the Bromley story. Probably better than anyone else. There were details that weren't released to the public, but Julie knew the first police officer to arrive at the Bromley home the night Stan Bromley went missing. His name was Jimmy Sullivan, but everyone called him Sully.

Julie and Sully knew each other all through high school and even went to prom together. Sully had been a Chippewa County Sheriff's office deputy for fifteen years, since graduation. He would stop by Julie's shop whenever he was in town just to say hi and get out of his cruiser for a few minutes. The night Stan Bromley disappeared was no different, except Julie could tell he was a little shaken. He had told her that, when he first arrived, everything was just as stated. Stan's vehicle was in the garage. The front door was open. And there were two windows that had been broken. What was *not* released was that the windows were broken from the inside, like someone broke them to get *out* of the house. The other thing not reported was the footprints in the snow. At least, Sully thought they might be footprints. But they were extremely large and not shaped like a human foot. They were more rounded. But the wind had been blowing, and any defining edges or imprints were erased, so they were deemed unimportant by the lead investigator. How could they be connected, after all? They looked more animal-like in their shape. But no animal that inhabits the UP makes tracks that big.

Sully recalled the stories he was told as a kid about the Mishipeshu. They were much like the boogeyman stories told around the campfire. The thought of this myth coming to life sent an uneasy, almost sickening feeling throughout his soul. He told Julie about the tracks and how they seemed to skirt the edge of the tree line surrounding the Bromley cabin, like it was watching or staking something.

There was something else. A large, fish-like scale. Just one. It was on the front porch by the open door. Fish scales were not an unusual thing to find around the cabins on the lake. Fishing leads to catching leads to cleaning. Fish scales can end up almost anywhere. Again, the investigator dismissed it as just a large fish that had been caught and cleaned. The scale being unusually large made little difference. After all, there would be no logical reason to think a fish scale had anything to do with Bromley going missing, unless he fell through the ice while ice fishing. So, it was never collected into evidence. Time and the ever-present coyotes and other scavengers made sure it would never be seen again. But that didn't explain the broken windows and open door. Plus, there was no ice fishing shanty out on the ice. It was all just a little too weird for Sully. But there was no way in hell he was going to say anything about the Mishipeshu. He would be the laughing stock of the department. But he told his friend, Julie, what was on his mind.

Julie knew Sully was not one to make up crazy stories or be scared over a ghost story. So when he told her what he saw and how it reminded him of the Mishipeshu stories, she listened and took him seriously. She, too, had been told the stories of the Mishipeshu, and truth be known, Julie and several others in town were intimately aware of the legend and how it would drag its victims into the lake and devour them, never to be found. The thought of it scared her, but not enough to leave Paradise. She couldn't help but wonder if poor Mr. Bromley had fallen victim to it. It gave her a sick feeling in her stomach.

There were many in town, mostly those with some Native American in them, who claimed every mysterious disappearance was due to the Mishipeshu. For that reason, those who believed steered clear of the lakeshore, especially at night. And they always traveled in at least pairs. Because they also believed the Mishipeshu only took those who disrespected the lands around Lake Superior or its waters, they would take special care to abide by the natural law of waste not, want not, and of only taking what you need and leaving nothing behind. Better safe than sorry, was their motto. They also lived by the World War II mantra, "Loose lips sink ships." People in town may be friendly, but they weren't going to share everything with strangers. Best let them figure things out for themselves. Even so, sometimes words slip out, unintentionally.

"Shame about what happened to Stan Bromley." As soon as the words left her lips, she knew she had over-shared. In her head, she yelled, *Fuck!* She also knew she would have to tell them at least part of the story if the Perkins' asked. She hoped they didn't catch on, but sometimes there is no hope.

Mike picked up on it right away.

"What do you mean? What happened?"

"Oh, well, it's really nothing to worry about. It's just, well, kinda weird, that's all. You see, Stan had gone to the cabin last December to meet some snowmobilers who were going to rent his cabin for a week. Only, when the renters got there, Stan's truck was there, but he was nowhere to be found. They never did find out what happened to him. He just disappeared. Folks think he may have fallen through the ice. It can be pretty treacherous out there, you know. Well, after that, the family couldn't bear to ever stay at the cabin again. Too many memories, and one big mystery."

"Man, that is weird. Never found him... at all?" Mike's police instincts kicked in. He felt Julie was leaving something out but didn't want to push too hard.

"Nope. Just up and vanished. People go missing all the time up here. Usually in winter, and usually ice related. People don't respect the ice. It may be a foot thick in one spot, and only three inches just a few feet away. That lake is cold. Doesn't take long to go into hyperthermia. Once you sink, you don't come back up. Gitchigumi never gives up her dead."

"I wonder why no one said anything about this to us. I mean, if someone died in the house, shouldn't we have been told?" Mike was visibly pissed and saw that Sarah had gone white as a sheet, so he moved away from the subject.

"Well, you said they never found him, so there's no proof that he died anywhere, let alone in the house. Maybe he just disappeared on purpose. A lot of people went off the deep end, during the lockdowns. Could be he just left." Mike didn't believe that theory but wanted to settle Sarah's nerves. It seemed to be working, as her face didn't have that just-saw-a-ghost look anymore.

Julie was eager to minimize her slip of the tongue, so she tried to make light of the subject.

"Well, Stan was a little quirky. A lot of people up here are. Me included. Quite the introduction to Paradise, huh? You got plopped into the middle of a mystery. Well, welcome to Paradise." They all chuckled. It was an uneasy laugh, but a laugh just the same.

"You about ready, babe? I'm ready to kick back a bit." Mike's curious mind was already working on the information Julie had given them. He wanted to get home, not just to relax; he wanted to get online and see if he could find anything out about the Bromley story. Plus, he was ready for a beer.

"Yep. Just let me pay for my stuff, and we'll head over to the grocery store."

They were both a little preoccupied by their thoughts; Mike wanted to dig deeper, and Sarah wanted to forget it. They picked up their supplies and headed home. Mike knew better than to discuss it unless Sarah brought it up. She had to process things in her own way. So Mike would do most of his research without Sarah knowing. He had to admit, though, that it felt kind of good exercising his police brain. Once an officer, always an officer. It gets in the blood and never really goes away. Not even retirement can cure it.

"I see they had a small fire ring set up, but I'm not crazy about where it is. What would you say to moving it out to that little point that overlooks our beach?"

"Good idea, Mike. I'll get our goods ready. Just let me know when you're ready for the dogs."

Their new home sat on nearly an acre of lakefront property on an elevated bluff about twenty feet above the lake. This gave them some protection from the waves that get worked up from the occasional gale. It also allowed for great views of the lake and the large freighters that used this inland sea to deliver a myriad of goods and supplies to the numerous ports along its shores. Their property was also heavily wooded in spots, so grabbing a few logs for the fire wouldn't be a problem, and it wasn't long before Mike had a pretty good fire roaring.

"Perfect. I just love it here. Just look at the view. Kinda makes the lakes back in Idaho look tiny. It's spectacular." Sarah seemed to have put the Bromley disappearance out of her mind and was back to being excited to be in this house.

"Not bad, if I do say so myself. I know my bonfires. Time to pop a cold one. You know, babe, it's kinda funny how everyone we've met so far seems surprised that we plan on living here year-round. Almost all of 'em said, 'You know, winters can be tough up here.' It's almost as if they think we're stupid or something."

"I get what you're sayin', Mike. But I just think these folks up here aren't used to newbies moving in full-time. They don't know who we are or what our backgrounds are. In my opinion, I just think they're worried they're gonna have to come save us or something."

"You know, you've got a point there. I mean, they've got enough to do dealing with winter without having to help some rookies out, right? Good thing I know how to operate a snow blower and shovel. But I will say, we have a lot of work to do to get this place ready for winter."

So began their adventure. And it would be an adventure. Unexpected house repairs, high costs of building materials due to supply chain issues, the remoteness of their home, and the short amount of time they had to accomplish everything all worked to keep them so confined to the property that they didn't really have an opportunity to make new friends. They met some of the townspeople, but many of them had left for their homes down south in the mitten of

Michigan. And those they met who did stay for the winter were not very close to where they lived. It gave them a feeling of isolation. Oh, there were lots of people going by their place, and there were many family visits to their new home that summer, but they still didn't feel like part of the community, something they were not used to.

Back in Idaho, they had been plugged in, so to speak. They knew a ton of people and had great neighbors. They would all chip in to fix things, help with issues around the properties, and keep the roads clear of snow.

For the most part, they would be on their own in Paradise. One of Sarah's sisters, Cathy, and her husband, Jared, had a cabin they used occasionally throughout the year a little over a mile from Mike and Sarah. Jared was a farmer downstate, and Cathy had recently retired, so they mostly visited their cabin after planting season and once harvest was over. Winter was when they spent most of their extended stays at the cabin. So the Perkins' would be able to rely on them if anything should happen that they weren't prepared for.

Another sister, Leslie, and her husband, Pete, had a cabin in the opposite direction about three miles away. But they were busy with careers and only came up for brief stays to fish or snowmobile. But Pete owned a construction company, something Mike was happy about; if he got stuck on one of his projects, Pete might be able to help or offer insight.

And that was about it for contacts for Mike and Sarah. The only people they could guarantee would be there were themselves. It might be June, but that's only four months from October. And winter often showed in October. They would have to hustle to be ready, but would they really be ready for the winter? There would be events this winter that there was no way to prepare for. There was no reason to even consider these events, as they were way outside the expected. Outside the norm. Hell, outside of the wildest nightmares one could conceive.

For now, Mike and Sarah would enjoy the peacefulness of a quiet fire by the lake. Drinking beer and cooking hotdogs, as if their life was going to be one long vacation by the lake. Funny thing about life, sometimes, just when it all looks laid out and planned, it throws in a pitfall, a monkey wrench, or a tragedy or two, just to shake things up.

2

AUGUST

Enter monkey wrench number five.

"What? You can't get here until *next* year? I need this electrical done *now*. I need the generator wired in before winter. I don't trust this old piece of crap generator to make it much longer."

Contractors—reliable contractors—were almost impossible to find in Paradise. The pandemic had made things worse. Many of the workers had gotten used to the stay-at-home unemployment pay and decided they didn't need as much income to live and hadn't come back to work. This created horrendous worker shortages and backlogs of jobs. Contractors were choosing to do the most profitable and simplest jobs first. Add to that, Paradise was well out of the way for most contractors, whose businesses were in more populated areas. Simply, it was too far to go for the money. Many of them added a surcharge to work there, making the price of doing business too steep. Mike had contacted every electrical contractor who was willing to work in Paradise. They were either booked up for the year or claimed to be short-handed. Mike would either have to do the work himself, or rely on the generator that came with the home to provide power when the power got knocked out.

Power outages were all too common in Paradise. Gales blew up from the lake in every month of the year, but most were late fall and winter. Add heavy snow to the winds, and power could be out for days. Mike had purchased a new dual-fuel generator with increased wattage over the gas-only generator that came with the house. That old generator had seen better days. Mike had plenty of do-it-yourself skills, but electrical work was not in his wheel-house. If he couldn't find an electrician to redo his generator setup, he and Sarah would be stuck with Ol' Rusty. The old red generator was faded and rust-covered. But it ran. For now.

"Well, thanks anyway. If something changes, please call me." Mike was starting to wonder if moving to Paradise had been a good idea.

"Well, Sarah, I'm done. I've called every damn electrician in the book, and even the ones Julie told you about. Not one single electrician can get here until next year, if they're willing to come to Paradise at all. Looks like ole Rusty's gonna have to do until next year. Shit."

"It'll be okay, hon. It's not that big a deal. We'll have the wood stove for heat, and we can cook on the grill and the flattop if we have to. It's gonna be fine."

There it was. Sarah's never-ending, optimistic outlook on everything. Except, she left out that the wood stove wasn't even at the house yet. And someone was going to have to install it, as the wood stove company said they wouldn't guarantee installation in October, the stove's scheduled arrival from the manufacturer. The reason? The Perkins' had a metal roof and, in October, those roofs tended to have frost or snow on them, making them dangerous to work on. Sarah was right. They wouldn't need the generator rewired if the wood stove was in. It would keep them plenty warm if they lost power.

"I know. But it just seems we keep hitting roadblocks at every damn turn. First, the septic goes out. Thank God our realtor knew of someone who could do it fast. Then, the damn plumbing needs to be redone. Completely. I don't even want to bring up the damn roof. But, holy shit—twenty-five thousand dollars! It's a small damn house. Smaller than our Idaho house. That roof was only seven thousand. Fuckin' supply chain bullshit. Then, we had to increase the size of our water heater, add floors, *and* a complete new kitchen, which they couldn't deliver, so we had to pick it up *and* put it in. *Again*, the damn worker shortage. We picked a great time to move *and* buy a fixer-upper, didn't we?" Mike was pissed. Everything seemed to be falling on his shoulders to get done, and he wasn't sure if he had it in him to do it all.

"I know, babe. But it's coming together. It'll be fine. You'll see."

The workload wasn't the only thing wearing on Mike. He had been looking into the disappearance of Stan Bromley. He looked on the web, and he went to the Chippewa County Sheriff's Department and asked for any information on the case. The Sheriff's Department wasn't much help. They claimed it was an ongoing investigation so they couldn't release any information. They wouldn't even consider Mike's law enforcement background. Mike found that unusual. Usually, law enforcement agencies gave up bits of information to other law enforcement personnel, even if they weren't active anymore. It was considered a common courtesy extended to those in the "brotherhood."

The internet wasn't much better. He found the newspaper report on the incident. There was nothing new, but the reporter had interviewed several locals, including Joseph Makwa—an Ojibwe tribal name meaning bear. A comment Makwa made to the reporter when asked about the Bromley disappearance stuck in Mike's head:

"I don't think he disappeared. I think the Mishipeshu got him. Someone was stealing fish from the native fishing nets in the lake. Maybe it was him. That might bring the Mishipeshu up from the lake."

The reporter left this in to add color to an otherwise bland story. Putting a little Native lore in the story added a larger sense of mystery to an already mysterious case. Gotta love folklore. Bigfoot, Dogman, and now the Mishipeshu. Mike wasn't prone to putting stock in folklore. His time in Idaho had had its share of Bigfoot stories. He even had one 911 call regarding a supposed Bigfoot encounter.

A man named Ben Walden, who lived up a fire service road off-grid, had set up trail cameras around his cabin for hunting purposes. Ben had found one of his cameras smashed and quite far from its mount. When he looked at the photo card, there was something in two of the frames that prompted him to call the police. It was a large, hairy something. It stood on two legs and, by his best estimates, was over eight feet tall.

Mike got the call as a possible trespasser. When he got to the Walden cabin, Ben came running out in a panic, photo card in hand, screaming something about Bigfoot. At the time, Mike had absolutely no inkling of belief in Bigfoot, and he rolled his eyes at Walden's claims. But when he looked at the pictures, even the skeptic in him had to admit there was something strange. He came up short of admitting it was Bigfoot, but one thing he knew: It wasn't a man, and it wasn't a bear. He took a report and advised Mr. Walden to contact Fish and Game. It was more up their alley.

Mike never really thought about those pictures much. But the hint of an unknown creature roaming the waters and woods around his home brought back those thoughts and the question,

"What if it were real?" For a second, a cold wave coarsed through Mike. But, being an ex-law enforcement officer, someone who was supposed to be grounded and not prone to baseless fears, Mike shook it off and put it in the back of his mind. But he had a nagging feeling about Walden's story. He may have to look into it, even if just to eliminate the possibility. He had a contact at the University of Idaho in the forensics department who might be interested in seeing the photos Mike took at the scene. So he sent them to him for his input, but not even his esteemed contact could make sense of what he was looking at. So much for concrete answers.

"I'm sorry, babe. I guess everything's just catching up to me. And once the snow comes, we're done until spring. And winter comes in about two months or so." Sometimes it was best if Mike just blew off a little steam to restore his sense of balance, something Sarah never really got comfortable with.

"I've got an idea. Let's make a couple drinks and take the side-by-side up Wildcat. We could go for a walk on the beach down there. You know, take a break and clear our minds a bit." Sarah was hoping Mike would accept that plan. She loved walking on the beach and picking up rocks. One of the great things about beach combing on Lake Superior was all the different gemstones and other interesting rocks that washed up on the shore. Not to mention, with all the shipwrecks in the lake, an artifact might just wash up too.

"Yeah, that might just be the best thing to do. One day isn't going to kill us. Make mine a double."

Sarah was excited because a double meant she was driving. And she loved going off-road.

"You got it, mister. We might even find some wild blueberries along the way."

As Mike maneuvered their off-road vehicle down the narrow,

winding curves and deep sand of Wildcat Road, his thoughts went to the vastness of these woods. They were thick and filled with large pines and maples, with a smattering of birch trees. There were ferns, lots of ferns. It was a primeval scene. And here it was, the height of the summer tourist season, and the town's hotels and rentals were full. The restaurants were packed, and all manner of off-road vehicles filled the roads on their way to their own off-road adventures. And yet, Mike and Sarah had yet to see another four-wheeler on the trail. Oh, there was evidence of their passing. All different sizes of tire tracks made their impressions both on the trail and, although discouraged, some made their own trails that crisscrossed Wildcat. There wasn't even the sound of distant engine noises. It was as if Mike and Sarah were the only ones on the trail.

All along the right side of Wildcat Road was Lake Superior were miles of rock covered beaches that ran the entire length of the two-track road. It seemed strange that they didn't see anyone on the trail. It was eerie. There was no cell signal out here, so if they were to break down or get stuck, it might be a while before someone passed by. Mike's motto was, prepare for the worst, but hope for the best. So they had provisions and supplies to stay the night out in the woods. The only thing that concerned Mike was the bugs. The insects were relentless, especially at night. Mosquitoes, biting flies, and gnats could make an overnighter a miserable experience. But staying on the beach would minimize the bugs. Lake breezes, or more like winds, helped to keep the mosquitos and biting flies away.

His thoughts went to Joseph Makwa's statement in the paper: "I think the Mishipeshu got him." It got him wondering why the reporter thought it necessary to put that in the story? After all, it was a serious story about one of their regular, seasonal residents disappearing. Adding a quote about some creature from Native folklore seemed strange to Mike. He knew that most Native folklore had some basis in actual events or people. So what was the Mishipeshu based on? Looking into the woods, Mike could see how an animal, even known animals, could exist in great numbers and not be seen. After all, there were deer, moose, wolves, and one of the highest populations of bear in these woods. Tracks were everywhere, but few people ever saw them. A moose could be just feet off the trail and be virtually invisible. He would have to look into this Mishipeshu thing.

"You okay, Mike? You're awful quiet."

"Huh? Oh, yeah, I'm good. Just enjoying the scenery. Hey, feel like walking along the beach?" Mike knew Sarah wouldn't turn down an opportunity to look for rocks.

"You know it. I brought the bucket just in case."

Ah, the bucket. A five-gallon bucket that Mike would have to carry. That bucket got heavy when the rocks started filling it.

It was almost dark when they pulled back into their driveway, and they were startled to see a car parked there.

"Who the hell is that?" Mike was irritated that someone would drop by unannounced at such a late hour. Being the prepare-for-the-worst type, he always carried his firearm on him, so he parked in such a way as to have the Kawasaki Mule's headlights shining into the vehicle.

"Stay here, hon. I'll check it out and let you know if it's okay." Sarah had no intention of getting out unless everything checked out.

"Hello? Can I help you?" Mike was using what he called his "police voice." It wasn't a loud voice like a yell; more of a firm lower-pitch that exuded confidence but not arrogance. He had always said the proper tone of voice, delivered with firmness, could end most confrontations before they escalated. Add to that, using his headlights to a secure his position gave him the upper hand.

He could see a man and a woman in the car. The man seemed nervous or scared, he kept fidgeting in his seat, and he didn't make eye contact with Mike. Body language is the language of the subconscious and is virtually impossible to hide, and their body language was showing that they were uncertain, nervous, or submissive. The man got out of the vehicle to greet Mike, still not really making eye contact with him. When he went to shake Mike's hand, he glanced downward, indicating that he was uncomfortable or unsure. This indicated to Mike that the stranger was not confident in approaching him. That gave Mike the edge if things got dicey.

"We're sorry to bother you. We weren't even sure if we should come. I'm Dave Bromley. Stan Bromley was my dad."

Mike was taken aback. Why would Stan Bromley's son show up out of the blue, just a couple of months after the sale of his dad's cabin? His first thought was there was some family issue, where selling the cabin might be contested or something along those lines. Just what they needed, another unexpected cost. But Mike didn't like to assume anything in situations like this, preferring to let the younger Bromley explain what he was up to before making judgements.

"Nice to meet you. What can I do for you?" Mike's voice indicated slight irritation, and that's exactly what he intended. Put Bromley on defense.

"I know it's a little late. I should've waited until tomorrow, but I really wanted to talk to you. My wife and I—that's her in the car. Paula. We wanted to meet you and see if you've heard anything about, well, how my dad disappeared. It's been wearing on us. The police haven't been very helpful, and we know the townspeople know more than we've been told by the authorities. Didn't know if you've heard anything, or what."

Mike thought this was weird. He had gone over the whole thing again and again in his head. And now, here was Old Man Bromley's son in his driveway doing the same thing.

"Oh, sorry. That's my wife, Sarah, in the four-wheeler." Mike motioned to Sarah that all was okay. Sarah got out and started towards the group.

"Honey, this is Dave Bromley and his wife, Paula. Stan was his father. They're wondering if we've heard anything about Mr. Bromley's disappearance."

Sarah thought, *Great. Just what we need. More mystery hanging over this house.* She knew Mike had been digging into things but didn't want to know what he found, if anything. It made her nervous. What if it turned out he was buried somewhere on the property? That would freak her out.

"Oh. Nice to meet you." She was trying to sound friendly and welcoming, but Mike could tell she wasn't so sure of the premise.

"Well, to be honest, we were a little put out that this wasn't brought to our attention before we bought the place. We didn't find out about your dad disappearing while at the cabin until after we moved in. And that was an accident. It just sort of popped out in a conversation with a local. Why weren't we told about it?"

Dave shifted nervously.

"I get it. You should've been told why the cabin was being sold. Our attorney advised us not to mention it. He said there was no proof that anything actually happened at the cabin, so we didn't have to disclose it. He felt it would affect the sale either by delaying it or greatly reducing the amount we would be offered. I'm sorry for that."

"I appreciate that." Mike was a little less put out about the whole thing, now. Dave's attorney was right. There really wasn't any evidence that something bad happened to Stan Bromley at the cabin. At least, no evidence presented showed foul play.

"That said, not knowing what really happened to Dad has really been on my mind. I'm losing sleep trying to figure it out. Have you guys heard anything? Is there any gossip?"

Mike was hesitant to bring up Joseph Makwa's theory about the Mishipeshu, so he decided to bring it up almost jokingly.

"The only thing I've heard, other than the official police report, is something about some Native American lake monster called the Mishi-something-or-other. Some sort of creature that's supposed to live in the lake and comes out during winter." Mike was a little embarrassed that those words even left his mouth. But when he mentioned a lake monster, Mike noticed Dave and Paula both got a strange look on their faces, it showed that they were uncomfortable at the notion of this.

"What? You guys look like you just saw a ghost."

"Sorry. It's just that one of the last things Dad said to us was that there was some strange stuff going on at the cabin."

"Really? Like what kind of stuff?" Mike was surprised that these two people seemed to think something out of the ordinary may be the explanation, instead of run-of-the-mill foul play.

"Well, Dad had come up for a few days to get the cabin ready for some people who rented it. He said there was a strong odor of rotting fish a couple of nights, but he couldn't find where it was coming from. He wrote it off as maybe some raccoons had gotten under the cabin and left some scraps there. But he checked. No raccoons. Plus, there was almost two feet of snow on the ground and no signs of critters getting under there. And the lake was frozen out about three hundred yards. The only thing fishing out there would be otters, and they're pretty rare on this part of the lake. He said that one night, he thought he saw someone walk by the kitchen window, but when he checked, there was nothing except for what looked like some unusually large footprints. But they were largely distorted from the wind blowing the snow all over. He figured it might've been a moose passing through. He said the tracks didn't really look like moose, but it was hard to tell."

"A moose? Really? I mean, I see the watch-for-moose signs, but we've never seen one."

"Well, they're up here. Not many of them, but there are moose. But I've never heard of them hanging around people's cabins. But a moose is tall enough to see pass by that window. It's kinda high."

"Well, it was the next night Dad disappeared. It was another windy, snowy, night. So any evidence of a prowler or something would be quickly erased. You'll see what I mean once winter really sets in. There's a lot of snow and a lot of wind. And the snow moves all over the place. You might have grass showing in part of the yard and six feet of snow in other parts. And it's never the same. Visibility can be almost zero. It's just weird that all these strange things happened right before he vanished.

"It's kinda interesting someone thought it might be the Mishipeshu. That's usually relegated to campfires and bedtime stories. I know the Natives put quite a bit of stock in it, but most everyone else considers it a myth. Still, there are a few up here who claim they've seen it. Some say that's why so many people don't stay up here all year. Not the winter. I mean, the county does a great job keeping all the snow plowed off the roads, and there are a bunch of folks who'll plow you out for twenty-five or fifty bucks. I've always thought it was weird so many people live here six or seven months, only to leave in October and not come back until spring. I even asked Dad why he left for winter. He was in good health. No reason to leave. Between the snowmobiling, snowshoeing, and ice fishing, there's plenty to keep active. He would just say, "Winter kills." We thought that was funny. And yet, here we are, wondering what happened to Dad. And it's winter. Weird, huh?"

Mike was just thinking the same thing. The whole damn thing was weird. The way Bromley just vanished without a trace. The weird things Dave Bromley had just shared. The fact the realtor had never shared anything about the disappearance. How everyone they had met acted almost the exact same way and asked the exact same questions. Like living along Whitefish Bay in winter was reserved for those aware of what happens during winter and who knew what to do. It was as if the veteran residents were part of a special club or click or something. Even the police were reluctant to share information. Even with one of their own, so to speak. It was almost an unwritten rule that police officers could share information with other police officers. Even if they were from other states and localities, retired or not. Providing it didn't interfere with ongoing investigations. And, as far as the Bromley disappearance went, it didn't look like they were really investigating it. Case closed.

"Yeah. It's weird, all right. Feels like there's more to see here. I'm not saying there's some sort of monster out there, but something's going on. I did some looking into this. I came up with zero info. No one knows anything, or they know and won't tell. Either way, there's more to know, and someone knows what that is. Did you know that an average of fifty people go missing in Chippewa County each year? Most of those go missing in winter. Kind of a high number, if you ask me."

"Really? Wow. Funny how you never really hear about these. I mean, I've never read any kind of story on disappearances or theories as to why or anything like that. You'd think with all those people going missing, there would be quite the buzz around town about them. Makes you wonder, huh? Paradise is a small town, and small towns have no secrets. Everyone knows everything about everything. You're right. Someone knows something, but they're not talking. I would guess it's because so much depends on the tourists up here. Don't want to scare them away."

Mike got the feeling young Mr. Bromley didn't know anything either. After all, seasonal residents weren't given the same considerations year-round ones were. Still, there was something he wasn't saying. Something about this lake creature. Mike wondered if Bromley was holding back for some reason; it sounded ridiculous. Mike was glad Sarah and Paula Bromley had wandered towards the lake and not heard any of this story. Sarah was the type to mull these kinds of stories over and over in her head and get herself all worked up. He would have to water it down somewhat before he told her what Dave had said.

"Hey, Dave, do me a favor and keep this lake monster thing under your hat. My wife is a worrier. I don't want her getting all scared or nervous over a fairytale."

"Oh, of course. I mean, it's just stories, right? No need to go any further than that."

Yes, there was something missing from Bromley's story. Mike sensed Bromley wasn't so sure about this just being some campfire story. And that made him more than a little uncomfortable. He would have to delve a little deeper into this Mishipeshu thing. There might be some logical explanation for it.

"Hey, Mike, since it's getting kinda late, and Dave and Paula haven't eaten yet, either, you could just start a bonfire and fire up the grill. We have some burgers in the fridge we can grill up. That is, if you guys wanna stay a bit." Sarah enjoyed having visitors and, since these visitors had a history with the cabin, she wanted to hear everything they knew about it.

Mike was going to grill up dinner anyway, so he had no problem with Sarah's idea.

"Sure. We can do that, if you guys are up for it."

Sarah and Paula agreed to the plan, and Dave knew that look in Paula's eyes. She wanted to hang out at the cabin one last time. Truth was, so did Dave.

"Sounds good to me, if it's no trouble."

"Good deal. I'll get the bonfire going. You know, Dave, we bought the vacant lot next to the cabin, so we moved the bonfire ring over there. Seems a little more private. Plus, it's a better view."

"Nice. Dad talked about buying that lot someday. But, man, it was filled with a bunch of crap. Dad didn't want to have to clean it up."

"Yeah, it was pretty trashy. We hired it out. Some guy did it for the scrap, so it didn't cost us anything."

"Are you kidding me? If Dad had known about that, I think he would've snapped that lot up."

The evening went along without any discussion about Stan Bromley's disappearance, until well into the night, after a few drinks. Alcohol: the grease that opens the most tight-lipped mouth. Dave breached the topic of his dad's disappearance in an awkward stumbling of words, as he had forgotten about Mike's request to not mention anything about lake monsters or tribal myths.

"So, Mike, you haven't heard *anything* about Dad being taken —uh, picked up—by anyone or any theories about that night? I mean, everyone in Paradise seems to know everything about everyone. Hard to imagine people not having any inkling as to what happened. Even if it was an off-the-wall idea, like—what was the Indian's name? Magwa or something? He said it could've been that lake cre— Uh, that the lake ice cracked or whatever."

He knew he almost blurted out the Mishipeshu theory. But he thought he did a good job changing direction. The problem was, Sarah knew all of Mike's facial expressions and could see in his face while Bromley rambled on that Mike was uncomfortable with where Dave was heading. She also knew that now was not the time to ask Mike about it. She would wait until the Bromleys left.

Mike hadn't really talked to Sarah about his looking into the whole thing. It was more of a personal thing, exercising his police skills, so to speak. So he didn't want to bring all that up now. As far as Sarah was concerned, the case was closed.

"Not much, Dave. I mean, I haven't really brought it up to anyone around town. I did see a newspaper article on it, probably the same one you're talking about. But that's about it. And it's not like we've had a lot of contact with people yet. We've been very busy working on this place. But maybe I'll dig around some. You know, casually. I would think the police would let us know if there was anything we should worry about. Maybe we should exchange phone numbers. In case I hear anything, I can let you know."

"Yeah, that would be great. I appreciate that, Mike. I don't want to be a pest about this. It's just that it's tough trying to close this chapter down without some sort of resolution. I mean, who the hell just disappears without any trace? No blood, no footprints in the snow. The damn lake is only a couple feet deep off the property. And even if Dad did fall through the ice, there would be a damn hole in it. And Dad would be visible in the ice. It's like he was snatched up by aliens or something. And the kicker is, not one damn thing was missing from the cabin or shop. There's TVs, power tools, fishing gear... You'd think if someone broke in, and Dad caught 'em, they'd have taken something. It just doesn't add up, and it's driving me nuts."

Sarah didn't buy one word of what Mike said about him not really looking into this. For one, she knew he was a curious man, always up for a mystery to solve, and what better mystery than the strange disappearance of the cabin's previous owner? Mike had also taught her about how to spot when someone's lying or trying to hide something. It was all about the eyes and where they looked when telling the truth or a lie. And Mike was lying, or at least not telling the whole truth. She was going to find out what Mike was hiding but she would have to wait until he was off-guard. If she pressed him tonight, he might be ready for it, and she might not get all she wanted. She would wait a day or two to bring it up. In the meantime, she would keep her ears open for any ammunition she could use to coax Mike into telling her what was going on.

Mike wondered what Bromley's theory was, or if he had one at all, but wasn't going to ask him in front of Sarah in case the whole "lake monster" thing came up. He would wait for the opportune time when they were alone.

"I'm going to grab some more wood from the shed. Let's build up this fire. Hey, hon, do we have s'mores supplies?"

"Absolutely. Always gotta have stuff for s'mores. It just isn't a bonfire with them."

"I'll give you a hand, Mike. I need to move around anyway. Been sitting in the car all day, and I'm getting stiff."

Mike thought this would be a great time to ask Bromley his thoughts. It would be a few minutes before the women got back. Sarah was a compulsive cleaner, and she would want to clean up the kitchen before they came back out.

"So, Dave you haven't really said what you think happened to your dad. Got any theories?"

Bromley seemed hesitant to answer, and for good reason. His thoughts on his dad's disappearance were, well, out there.

"Okay. But before I tell you, you have to know I'm not crazy or on drugs. I'm also gonna lead with, I don't buy into superstitions or mumbo-jumbo crap. That being said, I think there's something to this whole lake creature thing."

Oh, great. Just what Mike wanted to hear. A crazy idea, at best.

"What? Are you nuts? The Mishi-whatcha-ma-call-it? That's just crazy."

"I know. I know. But hear me out. We've been coming up here ever since I was five or six. Mostly spring through fall. But there were a few times we came up in winter. Dad loved ice fishing and would take us with him sometimes when we got old enough. Mom would go snowshoeing or just hang by the fire and knit. It was great. We even spent a couple Christmases up here. Until one winter in 2005. I was fifteen that year. Dad took me and my brother ice fishing out past the river mouth down the road. You know, where the boat launch is, just out of town."

Mike knew the place. He'd been fishing there, right off the dock.

"Yeah, I know where it is."

"Well, Dad's fishing shanty was about a half mile out into the bay and a little south of the river. We always caught walleye there. Well, this year, we weren't catching anything. I mean *nothing*. Our auto tippers hadn't sprung one damn time."

"Auto tippers?" Mike wasn't familiar with ice fishing.

"They're poles that automatically pop up and set the hook when a fish bites the bait. Anyway. Three days and not one bite. Like something scared all the fish out of the area. Then, on day four, we got to the shanty about four in the morning. The moon was almost full and you could see just fine without a flashlight. We were unloading our gear and getting ready for the day. That's when my brother, Charlie, saw something on the ice. We all looked where he was pointing, and about a hundred yards out on the ice, there was something moving. Something *huge*. We couldn't get a good look at it because of all the ice volcanoes and hills out there. It was moving behind them, and we only caught glimpses of it whenever it passed by an opening or low spot between the hills. We must've tried to figure out what we were looking at for five or ten minutes before it disappeared into one of the ice volcanoes."

"Whoa, there, cowboy. What the hell is an ice volcano?"

"Well, when it starts to get cold up here, ice starts to form out on the lake. The wind drives that ice towards shore, and while it's moving, the ice gets bigger and bigger, forming giant balls of ice. When they get heavy enough, they sink a bit and get stuck in the sand. More ice comes, sticks to the other ice, and a mountain range of ice is formed. When the wind really gets blowing, the water slams into these mountains and finds weak spots, where the water shoots out like lava from a volcano. They look just like volcanoes, cone and all. They can get pretty big. We think this thing went into one of those and under the ice."

"Did you guys ever figure out what it was? A bear or something?"

"Not really. For one thing, bears are hibernating at that time of year, and for another thing, it was too big for a bear. It looked like it had a tail too. Anyway, after that thing disappeared, about two or three minutes later, there was a huge surge of water that spewed out of our ice holes, and the ice kinda heaved a bit. Something very large swam right under us. That ice was about eighteen inches thick. Had to be very big. I don't know of any fish that big in the lake. Sturgeon, maybe. But they're rarely seen where our shanty was. Dad loaded up our gear, strapped the shanty to the snowmobile, and closed it down. I think it freaked him out. He never went ice fishing up here again. There was something else. While we were packing up, there was a powerful stench of rotting fish, and it was coming from our ice fishing holes. Whatever was producing that smell was under the ice.

"We came up a couple more winters, but it wasn't the same. After 2007, we closed the cabin for winter every year. I put the whole thing out of my head until Dad mentioned he smelled what he thought was rotting fish just before he vanished. Weird, huh?"

Mike stood there, listening to Bromley's story. He found it an unbelievable tale, most likely a kid's imagination gone wild. But, if it was just imagination, why did Bromley's dad react so strongly to it?

"I'll say it is. If what you're saying is true, then there's an unknown something out in the lake. But I'm finding it hard to wrap my head around it."

"I get it. It's been almost seven months since Dad disappeared, and I've been reliving that morning in 2005 the whole time. What if that thing we all saw, whatever it was, had something to do with Dad's disappearance? Hell, what if it's the reason for so many people going missing up here? Dad said something walked by the kitchen window, and it left some sort of tracks. He said maybe moose tracks. Well, moose tracks, even if the wind was howling, which it was, according to Dad, would still be fairly easy to identify. They're like really big deer tracks. But Dad's seen moose tracks and knows what they look like. He would've been more sure it was moose tracks. Where the tracks were was right through that small covered area in front of your firewood shed. It's pretty protected from the wind. The county sheriff who was sent to investigate took some pictures of the tracks. Before the sheriff's department shut off all access to the case, I got to see those pictures. I'm telling you right now, it wasn't any moose. Most of the tracks were pretty much filled in by snow, but there were two or three that were mostly intact. They weren't hooves. They were more like paw prints. Big paw prints. Like a cat but much bigger."

"Like a cougar or something?" Mike had seen cougars while running the back roads of North Idaho. They sure weren't tall enough to cast a shadow on the kitchen window. It was over five feet off the ground. That would have to be one tall cat. Or it was walking on two legs, but big cats don't usually do that.

"They were too big for a cougar. Best I could figure, they were close to twelve inches across."

"Twelve inches? Holy shit! They had to have been distorted by the wind or something. I don't know of anything up here that leaves tracks *that* big. Bears don't even get that big in the UP."

"I know. I know. It's unimaginable that something that could leave tracks that big could go unnoticed around here. But there is a lot of wild country. I guess it's conceivable something could hide. But, sooner or later, tracks would show up or someone would catch it on a game camera or something. But I keep going back to that morning with my dad and brother out on the ice. We all saw *something* out there. Add to that the missing fish and something large enough to force eighteen inches of ice to heave up a good six inches, and there's a very large animal of some sort living in and around the lake. And what the hell is up with this winter exodus thing? I can see a few people leaving, but over half the population? Seems kinda high considering most people, at least in Paradise, are retired. And didn't you say most of those people that go missing, go missing in winter? There's definitely something going on with winter up here."

Mike was more of a realist and not likely to just blindly accept any theories, especially one as far-fetched as a lake monster. Loch Ness of Lake Superior just didn't seem plausible.

"Well, yeah. What I read was that most, maybe seventy-five percent, disappear in winter. But, if winters are as weather-filled as everyone keeps saying, I'm thinking a lot, if not all, of them can be attributed to that. One thing all my years as a police officer in a high winter-tourist area is this. People unfamiliar with the hazards of the weather in an area they don't live in, made up almost all accidents my department worked. And we had emergency services close by. Not so here. Most rescue or law enforcement is at least forty-five minutes out. Cuts that golden hour down quite a bit."

"Golden hour?"

"Yeah. Most accidents or life threatening situations can be survived, provided the victim is alive and can get treatment or surgery within an hour of the injury. After that, chances of surviving drop dramatically. Add to that the remoteness of where some of these people go missing, and chances aren't too good they would be found in an hour. Cold can be deadly and quick."

"You might be right, but my gut's telling me you might want to keep your eyes peeled for anything out of the ordinary. Especially when winter gets here. You know, better safe than sorry."

"Hey, what are you two doing? Fire's almost out. I thought you guys would've had that thing blazing by now. What's better safe than sorry?"

Mike had lost track of how long he and Dave had been talking. Sarah and Paula had finished putting everything away and getting the s'mores ready. They had expected a rip-roaring fire when they got back out. Instead, embers.

"Sorry, hon. We, uh, were just looking for the perfect logs to crank things up. Guess we kinda lost track of time. You know me—too particular about my fires, I guess."

"Yeah, that's you, all right. Mr. Fire Master. Still haven't said what's better to be safe than sorry."

"Oh, well, Dave and I were wondering how many logs to bring. You know, to add the right amount of flame. He said we should bring a wheelbarrow full. Better safe than sorry that way."

Mike knew his firewood story was lame, but it was the best he could do.

The rest of the evening was fairly uneventful. A few more drinks, several s'mores, and a series of reminiscences of their times at the cabin by the Bromleys made for a more relaxed second half of the night. No one brought up anything about the disappearance until the Bromleys were leaving. It was just a short, "If you hear anything..." type of comment. Nothing too heavy. As they watched the Bromleys head down the driveway, Mike's thoughts were on Dave's story. It was too fantastic to be true. But he was so sure they had seen something on the ice. And why did his dad act so strangely if there wasn't anything out there? And, if whatever it was was explainable, why abandon his prime ice fishing spot? Why quit coming up in winter? What was it about the winter that seemed to freak everyone out? Mike knew he'd be doing some more digging into things. But the thing he would be looking at the most was the Mishipeshu—what exactly was it, and was there an explanation for it?

"Okay, Mike. What exactly did you and Dave talk about? I know it was about his dad, but what is it that you don't want me to hear? I know you all too well, and you can't get anything over on me. So, spill it."

Mike knew he would have to let Sarah in on the conversation about what he and his dad and brother saw in 2005, and how Bromley thought it might have something to do with his dad disappearing.

"I'm not sure where to begin. It's kinda out there, babe. As a matter of fact, it's far enough out there that it may not even be worth mentioning." Even Mike wasn't buying what he was selling. He couldn't completely discount Bromley's theory, and he couldn't commit to it either.

"Out there or not, I can tell whatever it is has you upset or distressed. What *is* it?"

"Well, seems young Mr. Bromley thinks some kind of lake monster or mythical creature may have had something to do with his dad disappearing. And before you say anything, hear me out."

Mike shared the story about the fishing shanty and how Stan Bromley reacted to the incident. Then he shared the information on the strange things that happened at the cabin in the days leading up to Bromley's disappearance. Sarah listened with that deer-in-headlights look, which Mike knew meant she wasn't believing this was coming from him, Mr. Level-headed. They had wandered over to the fire by the time Mike finished with the newspaper story about the Bromley disappearance and the bit about the Mishipeshu. Sarah turned to look nervously out at the lake. It was dark and suddenly seemed ominous instead of awesome.

"You don't actually believe this creature story, do you? It just seems like something out of some sci-fi movie. It *can't* be a real thing, right?"

"Of course not, honey. But I will say this. Most myths have some basis in truth or fact. There may be some logical explanation for the Mishipeshu. A misidentified, known animal. And, believe me, I'm gonna look into this, if just for my own curiosity. I really don't think there's a monster, but there might be an animal. Maybe a mutated bear or cougar. If there is some animal like that, it's harder for them to hunt normal prey, and humans are easy pickings. That might explain the 'monster' theory. Still, people around here act kinda funny when winter's brought up. And then there's the local police. I get a sense that they know more than they're saying, and my question is, why? But there is one silver lining here."

Sarah was still staring out at the lake.

"Yeah? What's that?"

"Seems like we don't have anything to worry about until winter. So, we have a few months to noodle this out and prepare. One thing's for certain. I'm loading up on some of those wireless game cameras to put around the property. That way, if something comes nosing around, we should get a picture."

Sarah turned her gaze from the lake to the fire.

"Do you really think there might be some kinda animal responsible for Dave's dad disappearing? That really bothers me. Besides you and me, we have the cats, and what about the grandkids when they come to visit?"

"Well, first of all, if it is an animal, it's covering an awful lot of ground. I've looked into this a little over the last couple of months, and *a lot* of people go missing every year up here. Not just Paradise, but the whole county. Chances of having it come here again are pretty slim, if not zero. Personally, I think Bromley may have wanted to disappear. You know, fake a death or something. Maybe he has a girlfriend nobody knows about. Maybe he owed a bunch of money. That is a more logical explanation than a lake monster. And, hell, maybe someone took him out and hid the body in one of these swamps around here. They would never find a body in there. I don't think there is anything to stress over. Besides, I'm going to put up some wireless game cameras all around. We'll have this place so secure, a mosquito won't be able to sneak in without us knowing."

"You're probably right. But the thought of someone, and not something, taking Bromley doesn't necessarily make me feel better. And what's this about people going missing up here? I thought we were moving into a safe, fun-filled town. Not death central."

"Babe, I think it's just the nature of things. There's a huge lake with unexpected weather, ice, winds that pop up suddenly, combined with some adrenaline junkies pushing the edge, and you're bound to have accidents. You've seen how remote these trails are and how few people we actually come across on those trails. These woods are full of bears, cougars, bobcats, wolves, and coyotes. If you're injured and can't get out, those guys might just finish you off. There would be no trace left.

"Remember, back in Idaho, we had that missing hunter case? An experienced hunter, who knew his hunting area very well, disappeared, and we had search parties out there for weeks, until the weather kicked us off the mountain. Turns out, two years later, another hunter hunting the same area finds this skeleton sitting against a tree, rusted rifle in hand. It was our missing hunter. He had broken his leg and pulled himself up to this tree for shelter. No cell signal, just like in these woods. And when the snows came, it just covered him up. We could've walked right over top of him and not known it. The snow gets up to thirty-five or forty feet deep on that mountain. He was missing some body parts because the animals had got to him. If that hunter hadn't stumbled upon him, we never would have found that guy. I think it's just that simple."

Mike wasn't completely sold on his own theory, but he had to keep Sarah from getting too worked up. Once something got into her head, she would mull it over and over and over, until she'd get so focused on that one thing that she couldn't get it out of her mind. It was that way on good things, and it was worse on not-so-good things. This was a not-so-good thing, and Mike needed to put it to rest.

"You really think it's something like that?"

"No. I think ole Mr. Bromley disappeared himself. It's the most logical choice. I didn't tell Dave and Paula that, though. No one wants to hear that their father wanted to abandon the family. But it happens more often than people care to admit. Sometimes life just pushes people to their breaking point, and vanishing seems like a good solution. I bet, sooner or later, Bromley turns up in some tropical beach resort or Vegas, or someplace like that."

"Now, that's just an awful thing to do to a family. But I hope you're right."

It looked as if Mike was able to move Sarah into "rational mode" with his explanation. But he wasn't buying it. Most people who try to disappear from life make stupid mistakes almost from the start, like using credit cards linked to their names. Or using their cellphone. That's a big one. It's easy to track someone from their cellphone use. But they've become so much a part of people's lives, they forget to toss them and get fresh ones under a different name or, better yet, switch to those prepaid cellphones that don't require credit cards or addresses. When they've reached their usage limit, they throw it away and get a new one.

But it was going on eight months since Stan Bromley met an unknown fate, well past most people's ability to stay voluntarily "disappeared." That only left two or three options. Bromley was killed, more than likely somewhere else, as there was no blood found at the scene, but Mike had found no evidence of anyone else being there. The only tire tracks at the cabin were from Bromley's truck and the renter's truck. So, if he was abducted, it was by space aliens.

Or, maybe he just fell into the lake and died from hypothermia. This was unlikely, as there was no breaks in the ice. Plus, the water was no more than five feet deep out to 200 yards. With no real currents, the body would've been pushed under the ice by the wave action, and he would've been found in the spring when the ice melted.

That left only one other explanation. The lake monster got him. Mike was not happy with where this was going, but there were a couple of things for certain. Mike would be digging into this with more purpose, and he was ordering those wireless cameras tomorrow.

3

STAN BROMLEY

The last day of Stan Bromley's life was a bad day, to say the least. The weather had turned ugly. Gale force winds had kicked up off Whitefish Bay, and the snow was flying. Getting the cabin ready for his guests just became a worse pain in the ass. Snow piled up fast in the doorways and walkways and had to be cleared off every twenty or thirty minutes or it would get too heavy to shovel before his renters arrived. Add to that, he had to split enough firewood to last them the weekdays. There was a furnace to heat the house, but everyone wants a fire blazing away at the end of the day.

Stan had a nagging feeling something was lurking around the cabin. He had caught glimpses of a large shadow passing by the windows and smelled a strong, fishy smell, and he'd found large, unusual tracks in the snow around his cabin and in the wooded part of his property. They seemed to circle the property but without beginning or end, as far as Bromley could tell. He wrote them off as moose tracks, even though they were shaped a little weird for a moose, but the wind can make tracks change shape, and the wind had been blowing, especially on this day. The wind blows in the UP like nowhere else. It doesn't wane and come back; it's more like a fan that gets steadily stronger as the storm blows on. That's how the snow piles up so fast; it's constantly being moved across the landscape.

As night engulfed the area, Stan Bromley felt uneasy. He was tired from all the snow shoveling and still had to do one last vacuum and stage everything for his guests, who would be arriving sometime after 9:00 pm. Toilet paper stocked, beds made, ice trays filled, everything placed just so to provide that inviting ambiance everyone wants when they arrive. Not exactly Bromley's forte. That was his wife's strength, but she wouldn't make the trip to the UP with the weather coming in; the Mackinac Bridge closes if it gets too bad, and she didn't want to be stuck.

Bromley couldn't shake the feeling of being watched. He always packed his grandfather's old double-barreled sawed-off shotgun in his truck for security when he came to the cabin. Even though crime was virtually nonexistent in Paradise, Stan was from a larger city where people were less trusting than in the UP. Stan brought his shotgun into the cabin, just in case. It was worn, but the simple break-open breach meant there were few moving parts to cause issues. The drawback was it only held two shells, which was not usually a problem, as two blasts would be more than enough in most instances. So, Stan rarely carried extra shells on his person. Stan had rigged a paracord sling to could carry it hands-free while he worked. This was the case as he went about preparing the cabin.

About 6:30 that evening, Bromley smelled that fishy smell. He turned on the outside floodlights to see if he could see anything lurking in the darkness. As he turned on the lights on the lake side, he thought he caught a glimpse of a large figure just at the edge of the light, but it was gone as soon as he noticed it. He figured it was just a shadow from one of the trees outside the windows but wanted to make sure. So he went out front to investigate.

The wind was blowing steadily at around thirty-five miles per hour, and it was snowing. The wind-blown snow stung his face and eyes, making it hard to keep his eyes open, so he focused towards the ground to protect his eyes. As he stepped around the southern edge of the cabin toward the east side, the lake side, he noticed those strange tracks in the snow. Even though the wind and snow had distorted and partially filled them in, he knew they were fresh because they hadn't been there just two hours earlier. He strained to peer through the blowing snow into the darkness for whatever had made these tracks. That's when he saw it.

He could barely make out a large figure just ten or fifteen yards away. It had to be at least eight feet tall, and it stood on two legs. Stan froze. He hadn't even removed the shotgun from his shoulder, so he was not prepared to shoot. The beast took a step towards him, revealing its face and, more noticeably, large teeth like a saber-toothed tiger's. That step shook Stan back to his senses, and he turned to run and made it inside just before the creature caught up to him, but the hunt was just beginning.

Stan made his way throughout the cabin, switching off all the interior lights to try and hide. This also made seeing outside much clearer, as there was no reflection. It wouldn't help. The Mishipeshu's eyes were used to the darkness of Lake Superior's depths. One other thing about its eyes: in darkness, they saw in infrared. No visible light necessary. Stan stood in the middle of his family room, shotgun at the ready, waiting for the creature to show itself, listening for any sound that might give its position away. It was hard to hear anything but the howling of the wind. Several minutes passed before Stan would move nervously from room to room, peering out each window to see if the creature was still out there. This went on for almost an hour with no further sightings. Stan thought about calling the police but changed his mind. They would probably think it was a prank call or some crazy asshole seeing moonshine monsters or something.

As Stan exited the hallway and re-entered the family room for what would be the last time, he saw it just outside the lakeside window. It was just standing there, staring into the cabin, waiting for its prey to show. Stan panicked. He pointed the shotgun at the creature and gave it both barrels. The blast blew out two of the four windows, allowing the Mishipeshu a way in. The shots had no effect. The shotgun pellets just bounced off the Mishipeshu's scaly armor. But the blasts did make the Mishipeshu react. It quickly entered through one of the blown-out windows and grabbed Stan Bromley by his left shoulder with those large canine-like teeth.

Stan was unable to even put up a fight. His arms were useless, as one was connected to the shoulder that was grabbed, and the other broke when he was taken out the window. There was little blood, as the wounds were filled with the Mishipeshu's teeth. There would be no blood trail. The Mishipeshu hurried across the ice, down one of the ice volcanoes, and into the icy waters of Whitefish Bay. Stan Bromley was alive for most of this. He felt the pain of his wounds as the Mishipeshu ran across the ice. He felt the cold, icy walls of the volcano as he was pulled through and down into the water. He felt the shock of the frigid water taking his breath. He felt the fear of imminent death as they went deeper and deeper into the lake. There was nothing he could do but die. The last thing poor Stan Bromley would be aware of was the darkness of the lake. He would drown in its dark, cold waters, totally alone except for the beast killing him. His family had no idea what horrors he was put through, nor would they ever.

4

MID-OCTOBER

"Wow! Just in time. I can't believe how difficult it was to find someone to install our wood stove, but here it is, and the fire is feeling great."

Mike and Sarah had faced a series of struggles with their home improvements from the very start. Installation of the wood stove, which was to be their primary heat source, was another in a long line of frustrations. The only project that went smoothly was getting their property blanketed with a network of wireless cameras and connected it to their home computer and set up to send alerts to Mike's cellphone if something or someone came within view of a camera. Over the last few weeks, the cameras had caught coyotes, rabbits, squirrels, deer, and even a wolf. Sarah loved seeing all the wildlife, but the coyotes and the wolf made her a little nervous.

"Yeah, thank God Julie knows just about everyone and was able to get someone with experience to get that in. Once snow is on this metal roof, there's no going up there, and snow's coming tonight."

Knowing Julie Tucker made finding contractors and other resources less painful. The pandemic and all the restrictions put on businesses had really put a bind on the construction industry and related contract services. Most contractors lost their employees to the "free money" the government threw at them. After all, why work if they got paid not to? And with tourism being the primary industry in the Paradise area, finding qualified help that was willing to show up for work was proving difficult for most in construction-related professions. Couple that with the fact that Paradise was out of the way for most contractors, and it was almost impossible to find anyone willing to make the trip. And those who would added inconvenience costs. This made every project at least twenty-five percent higher. This was probably why so many Yoopers made do with what they could do for themselves, building codes be damned. With winter right around the corner, Mike would have finished up his final projects the "Yooper way".

"Well, we'll be nice and warm once we get this wood stove installed."

Mike had done extensive research into the Mishipeshu and the numerous missing person reports, trying to find some kind of answer to the Bromley disappearance. And, thanks to Julie's friendship with him, Mike also made contact with Jimmy "Sully" Sullivan, the first officer on the scene the night Stan Bromley went missing. Because of Julie introducing them, Mike spoke with Sully on several occasions, only to confirm that the local sheriff's department didn't consider Bromley's disappearance a homicide or other human-related crime. They had basically closed the case. But Sully did let a couple of things slip. Not about Bromley per se, but about the strange way the other numerous disappearances had been handled. He said the chief and other ranking officers in the department had shown little to no interest in digging too deeply into most of the disappearances. Unless there was irrefutable evidence of how they vanished, like a hole in the ice, a crashed snowmobile, or four-wheeler in a river or swamp, or evidence of a crime such as a bloody weapon, the cases were never followed up on. They would stay missing person cases forever.

Sully had said that, one time, he asked one of the investigators why that was, and he got a strange answer. He was told there was no need to look into some cases any further, because the bodies would never turn up, because the lake never gave up her dead. Sully thought that was odd, because that really only applied to those who drowned in the big lake or the deeper areas of White-fish Bay, and not all the disappearances happened at or on the lake. Also, it would be difficult for most people to get to some the areas where a disappearance had occurred, especially in winter. Sully also said that, when he arrived on scene, there *were* some strange footprints in the snow. They were very large and seemed to circle the Bromley cabin and then head out to the lake. But it was hard to say for sure, because the wind had filled most of them in or distorted them so much that he couldn't tell if some were part of the track line or something else. But when his sergeant got there, he was told not to even mention the tracks, because they were, obviously, moose. Sully had told Mike they were not moose tracks. They were too big and seemed to have toes. So much for hoping the case wouldn't involve lake monsters. Even Sully said there was something "out of the ordinary" about the Bromley case.

Mike also did some extensive research into the Mishipeshu. According to legend, it protected the lake from those who would defile it. If someone took even one fish from the lake without permission, Mishipeshu would seek that person out and dispense justice, and justice was, supposedly, gruesome. This also went for those who would pollute the lake or mar its beauty. This seemed a little out of the realm of reality for Mike—more like science fiction or a boogeyman story to keep kids in line. But there were some records of sightings. Not many, because they were mostly accounts by some of the local Native tribes, and they weren't recent. Not even close.

One such story involved a French explorer searching for gold and other precious metals. Four Ojibwe Tribe members took the explorer to Michipicoten Island. The island, in Lake Superior on the Ontario side, held a vast amount of copper. It was also said to be one of the places the Mishipeshu could be seen on land. They filled their bags with the copper and went to head back across the lake. But as soon as they pushed off, they heard the roar of the Mishipeshu, and they all perished at its hand. Only the French explorer survived long enough to tell the story. Apparently, they took the copper without permission, bringing the full fury of the Mishipeshu upon them.

There were some other similar stories: taking too many fish from the lake, dumping trash or other pollutants into the water— that type of thing. But they all ended up the same way. Mishipeshu got them, and they were never seen again.

It got Mike wondering about Bromley. If these stories were true, and he didn't believe them for a minute, what did Bromley do to bring on the ire of the Mishipeshu? Even though Mike didn't put much stock in these stories, he couldn't help but think about that ice fishing story that Dave Bromley told him. Did Bromley take too many fish? Seems unlikely, since, according to Dave, they weren't catching *anything*. If anything, the vacant lot that Mike and Sarah had bought that was next to the Bromley cabin would be more deserving of a visit by the beast. It was loaded with leaky oil cans, yard chemicals, and all manner of trash. And a lot of that stuff was washed into the lake when some particularly strong storms struck the Whitefish Bay area in 2015. The property lost about fifteen feet of land into the lake, along with a sizable amount of debris. Mike and Sarah had found a pickup truckload of trash buried in the sand from the shore and out about twenty feet into the lake, including parts for some type of motor vehicle. But Bromley didn't own that lot. So that wasn't it.

Mike even made contact with the Bay Mills Tribal Police Department, hoping to get some insight into the legend, hoping to get some information grounded in fact and not legend. The department was in Brimley, Michigan, along the shores of White-fish Bay. Brimley was home to the Native American tribes of Ojibwa or Chippewa, who had been on those shores for hundreds of years.

Mike spoke with Lt. John Wilkins. The twenty-year veteran of the department knew the Native folklore intimately, as he worked closely with the tribal elders on a regular basis. When Mike brought up the Mishipeshu, Wilkins' face went white.

"Why are you interested in tribal lore, Mr. Perkins? Not very many people outside the tribe are even aware of the Mishipeshu."

Mike was a little taken aback by Lt. Wilkins' reaction. He expected a chuckle or some sort of laughing off of even the suggestion of a lake creature. Mike explained the whole Bromley story and how they had purchased his home, his son's story—everything.

"Have a seat, Mr. Perkins."

Wilkins went and closed his office door and returned to take a seat at his desk. He looked Mike over for a minute before saying anything.

"I'm going to share something with you, Mr. Perkins. Only because you have a connection to this and used to be one of us. I hope you'll appreciate what I'm going to share with you and treat it with the respect it deserves."

"No problem."

Mike was a little confused, but he wanted answers; any answer was better than nothing.

"Good. First, you have to realize, Native legends have a way of proving themselves true, and are *not* simply stories. Every day, animals that were once thought to be imaginary are found to be real—just hidden. The mountain gorilla is one such story. Most, if not all, Native stories are based in truth. The Mishipeshu may just be one of those truths."

Lt. Wilkins turned and opened a cabinet.

"You see these files in this drawer? Every single one is a case involving someone who disappeared. No evidence whatsoever of any foul play. Just someone who was here one day and gone the next. Every single one occurred between the months of November and March. Those are the months where the lake's water temps are extremely cold, as cold as the lake is in the deeper parts year-round. Technically, these are classified as missing persons. But many around here call them the 'winter kills.' I don't know if you know the whole story about the Mishipeshu, but legend has it that the Mishipeshu lives in the depths of Lake Superior, where the water temps are very cold. It can't come to shore until the air and water temps there are cold enough for it to be there. Now, I'm not saying I believe in the Mishipeshu, but the people who live in my jurisdiction do. And because they do, I have to approach these cases with that in mind. Do you understand?"

"I get it. But what I really want is your honest appraisal. What do you *really* think? Do I have to watch out for some lake monster or not?"

Wilkins was quiet for a few minutes. He took a sip of his coffee and looked Mike in the eyes. "All I can say is, better safe than sorry. ...One more thing. This Mishipeshu is said to be some sort of protector of the lake. Anyone who disrespects the lake and the animals that call it and its lands home is subject to its vengeance. The people in these files—I would say that eighty percent, if not more, did *not* respect the lake or its creatures. There are backyard mechanics who were known to dump their oil or other auto liquids into the lake. There are litterers, and those that used the wrong material, like engine blocks, to create breakwaters. There are those who caught more fish than allowed, or fished without a license. Every one would be considered a violation and subject to the Mishipeshu's justice, according to Native lore. And there are those who would be called adrenaline junkies and did some ripping in the natural areas on their sleds. But there is about ten to twenty percent where we haven't found any of that type of connection. They just went missing. I'm guessing, wrong place, wrong time. So, if I had to give you my honest opinion, I would say, don't disrespect the lake. ...Obviously, we never had this conversation."

"Have you ever seen anything yourself? Or have you seen any evidence of this Mishipeshu at any last-known location of a missing person? Anything?"

"That's the other thing. There's never been a lot of physical evidence at any of the—for lack of a better term—crime scenes. A few of them had some strange footprints I can't explain, but almost all of those were distorted by the weather or destroyed by human activity. Other than that, nothing. But there are a couple of officers who've claimed to see something weird out on the ice at times. But I doubt they would want to talk to you about it."

"I get it. Hard for me to even be discussing the possibility, let alone claim to see it. But, if you would pass my info on to the officers, just in case they wouldn't mind at least describing what they think they saw, I would appreciate it."

"I can do that, but don't hold your breath. Both of the officers are Ojibwa, and not prone to share these things with outsiders. I hope what I've told you helps you somehow on your quest."

"Well, you've definitely given me something to think about. Still having a hard time wrapping my head around this. I mean, we live right on Whitefish Bay, and in the house someone who vanished without a trace lived in last winter. It's a little unnerving, to say the least."

"I get it. I guess my advice to you is, keep an eye on the ice and pack some big guns."

Mike left the Bay Mills Police Department unhappy about the information Lt. Wilkins had provided. He had fully expected Wilkins to tell him he was crazy for even considering a Native folk monster as the reason for Bromley's disappearance. That didn't happen. In fact, Wilkins all but confirmed that there *was* reason to be concerned. Not only that, but to be ready if it showed up again.

On his drive back home, Mike mulled over what Wilkins had said about all the missing person cases he had and how many of those cases involved some sort of mistreatment of the lake, and his theory about the Mishipeshu dispensing justice on those who did. But that didn't account for the other cases where there didn't seem to be any obvious wrongdoings. So, Mike figured, *if* there was something that hunted the shores of Whitefish Bay during winter, it would be attracted to noises or activities close to the lake. And those who were trying to hide criminal activity or keep from being seen polluting or trespassing where they shouldn't, would probably be alone or few in number. And a hunter would prefer an easier prey, not a large group where getting injured could be a possibility. Less chance of being seen or hurt if it went after loners. At least, that's what made sense to Mike. *Makes sense. That's funny.* Nothing about this made sense. Still, he couldn't help looking out his truck window at the lake all the way home. It was cold enough for ice to be forming on the rocks along the shore.

Sarah wanted to surprise Mike with a nice fish dinner when he got home, but they didn't have any in the freezer. Fortunately for her, the Wheelhouse Restaurant made a great whitefish dinner. So she called in an order and headed out to pick it up. While waiting, she thought she would enjoy a glass of wine in the restaurant's bar, the Goat Locker, a popular hangout for locals and tourists alike. This time of year was the in-between time for tourists. Four-wheelers weren't allowed on the road after November 1, and there wasn't enough snow for snowmobiles yet. So it would, more than likely, be mostly locals and not too busy. She hoped to see someone she knew there so she wouldn't have to sit by herself, and she was in luck.

Julie was there with a couple of her friends having drinks.

"Sarah! Come on over and sit with us."

Sarah could tell they were a little ahead of her on drinks. But hell, it was Saturday, and Julie worked hard at her shop. She always closed up shop for winter, with a few exceptions. So she deserved to cut loose every once in a while, and Sarah was ready for a little "steam-letting session" as well. Her and Mike had been working hard on the house to get it ready for winter, all the while dealing with the whole Bromley thing. Drinks were definitely in order.

"Thanks. I'm not staying long. I just put in an order for a couple of fish dinners for Mike and I. Just didn't feel like cooking tonight."

Sarah kind of wished she had waited until she got here to put her order in. That would've let her get a couple more drinks in before she headed home. Besides, she hasn't had a real chance to get to know anyone from town. This would be a welcomed distraction.

"I don't blame you. You guys have been busting your asses working on that house. Say hello to Joanie Mills and Laura Burke. Joanie lives across from me, and Laura has a cabin just outside of town heading towards the falls. They live up here year-round, so you'll probably run into them from time to time. Laura's the tough one. She lives up here alone. She lost her husband, Danny, a couple years ago in an ice fishing accident."

"Oh my God. I'm so sorry to hear that. How in the world do you manage?"

Sarah was a little taken aback at the introduction including a death announcement, but that's how it was in the UP; everyone knew everything about everyone.

"It's all good. I'm a native Yooper and lived on my own for many years before I got married. I know what to do in just about any situation that can happen up here. Aren't you the ones who bought the Bromley place?"

"Yep. That's us. We love living there, but it sure has been a *ton* of work. It's amazing what people will do without when they only live someplace a few months out of the year. We've had to completely redo most of the plumbing and electrical, not to mention all the other building projects going on. It's been a job."

"Yeah. And it's amazing what some people will do without when they *do* live here all year. You know—convenience, doctors, hairdressers, shopping. The essentials."

The women had a good laugh at that. But Joanie was right; there was absolutely nothing close. No shops for clothing, except touristy stuff. Gas cost about fifteen percent higher in town than anywhere else. No mechanics, no doctors, no dentists, and no traditional fast food restaurants. But there were food trucks in the summer. And the two restaurants that never closed for the seasons were good, so no one really missed fast food fare. Even the grocery store in town closed for the winter.

"Yeah, that's been the biggest adjustment for Mike and I— finding doctors or where the best places to get stuff is. Everything is an hour or more away. Gotta plan every shopping trip to optimize time. I'm not very good at that. I'm more the type of person... I see someplace that looks good, and I want to go there."

The ladies shared stories of Paradise with Sarah so she could get a feel for the lighter sides of things. The drinks went down easily, and before long, they were all acting as if they'd known each other for years, which, of course, Julie, Joanie, and Laura had. But Sarah was fitting in just fine. Then the topic came around to Laura's husband's accident.

"You know, Sarah, I understand Stan Bromley's son came out to visit you guys. Is that right?"

Julie bringing up Dave Bromley's visit made Sarah a little uneasy. She didn't like thinking about the whole Bromley thing. Yet, here it was, the rain cloud on the parade, so to speak. She was enjoying the time with the three women of Paradise and didn't want to ruin it. But it wasn't like she had broached the subject. Plus, a couple of glasses of wine could brighten any discussion.

"Yep, sure did. He and his wife came out two or three months back. Kinda out of the blue. Wanted to know if we had heard anything about his dad's disappearance. Of course, we didn't have any real news, but him and Mike were talking, and there was some crazy crap discussed. Mike's been trying to find out more, but not too many people know or are willing to talk about it. The whole thing's got me a little nervy, if you know what I mean."

Laura's face went pale, and a blank look took over.

"Crazy? Crazy like somethin' from the lake got him? Crazy like there's no reason for them not finding a body? You mean, crazy like there's *nothing* to show for what happened? *That* kind of crazy? Because that's the kind of crazy that happened to my husband, John. The police said he musta' fallen through the ice when he went out ice fishin', but the ice was plenty thick enough to hold his old Ford pickup. It was still on the ice. And there weren't any fresh breaks in the ice, not anywhere. It ain't like he fell into an ice fishin' hole. They're only eight or ten inches across —couldn't even fit his damn leg in one. It's like aliens just beamed him up and off the planet."

The table went quiet for what seemed like an hour but was

only about twenty seconds, before Laura came back from wherever her mind had taken her.

"Sorry, ladies. Didn't mean to piss on our little party. It's just that I still ain't gotten over John being gone and all. Especially the way it happened. Just don't seem fair. He was a good man and a wonderful husband. And nobody, and I mean nobody, knows anything, and here it is two years later. I don't think I'll ever get used to not havin' him around."

Sarah was fixated on Laura's comment about something from the lake getting her husband, and she had to ask her what she meant.

"Laura. You said something from the lake got your husband. What do you mean, some *thing*? Mike said Dave Bromley made some sort of comment about some kind of lake creature. Now you sound like you're saying there's something in the lake. What's going on, here?"

Laura looked around the table at the other ladies' faces before she started to answer Sarah's question. But Julie spoke first.

"Sarah, there's some things you should know about living up here. Not everything is sunshine and lollipops. But it's still Paradise. The people are great, and even if you don't see them, they're looking after anyone who lives here. They check on your place as they drive by. They ask how you're doing whenever they get together. If someone's in trouble, there are any number of people who'll be right there to help any way they can. But there are things about this area that you just can't be prepared for, let alone explain. And what happened to Stan Bromley and Laura's husband are just among the unexplainable. People see UFOs flying over and even into the lake. They swear they've run into Bigfoot on the trails. Hell, I've even seen things in the sky over the lake I can't explain. There are five Native tribes in the UP, and every one of them has stories that go way back into their tribal history about a creature that lives either in the lake or on one of the lake's islands, among other things. But there seems to be something about this lake creature. Some people say they've seen it. There are even some who came upon some strange tracks in the snow that they followed that led out into the lake where they just stopped. Like, whatever made the tracks just up and flew off. Just about everyone who's lived up here most of their life has either heard these stories or had someone they knew go missing. With that said, it's not like there are hundreds of these. It's more like one here, one there. And it's mostly trolls that go missing."

Sarah couldn't believe what she was hearing, and it was really scaring her. But *trolls*?

"What's a troll? Not *another* creature, is it?"

"Oh, sorry. It's what some Yoopers call those folks that live on the other side of the Mackinac Bridge. You know, below the bridge? Trolls? Like *Three Billy Goats Gruff*. Nobody means anything by it. It's just easier to say trolls than down-staters. Anyway, you just need to be careful whenever you're out and about, mostly in the woods or out on the ice. Don't go alone, and always—*always*—respect the lake. You know, give a hoot, don't pollute, and stuff. Do the right thing.

"Seems like most of those that go missing were not respectful of the lake. They were dumping oil or other pollutants into the water. They were fishing illegally or stealing fish from the Native gill nets. And the snowmobilers seem to vanish more than others, and that's not surprising. There are some that race out onto the lake without checking if the ice is safe, or they go off-trail to get their adrenaline fix. That kind of stuff. Doesn't have to be something living in the lake to cause people to disappear when they act like that. Sometimes, it's just Mother Nature being a bitch.

"Still, some of the stories are pretty weird. Bromley's was unique, because it seems he went missing from his cabin. Most happen like I said, out on the ice or in the woods. I don't know if you've noticed, but these woods are pretty vast, and even with hundreds of riders out on the trails, you barely, if ever, come across other riders, do you?"

Julie was right. Only once did her and Mike come across another rider, and that was heading out to visit the Vermillion Lighthouse. That road is heavily traveled by all types of vehicles, because it's fairly easy to drive.

"I don't know what to say. I mean, this seems so unbelievable to me. We moved here to be closer to family and live a relaxed, lake-style life. Fishing, bonfires, canoeing, trail riding. That kind of stuff. We didn't sign up to be bait for some mythical lake monster. There must be some other explanation."

"Could be. Anything's possible. But, if I was you, I wouldn't worry too much about this. If you hadn't bought the house of someone who went missing, I bet you would never had heard about any of this. Look, all of us at this table have lived here most, if not all, of our lives. Yes, we've heard the stories, and some of us have been touched by the mystery. But we're still here. Why? Because it's a great place to live, and you won't find any better people anywhere. Monsters be damned."

That brought out an uneasy laugh from all at the table. All but Sarah. Sarah wasn't laughing. She was confused.

"We're not seriously talking about this, are we? You're just pulling a practical joke, right? Scare the newbie with a monster story kinda thing?"

Julie got a serious look on her face and looked Sarah square in her eyes.

"I wish that were the case, but everything we've told you is the God's honest truth. At least as we know it. Most full-timers up here have at least heard these stories. But I'll go you one better. Have you met the owners of the Wheelhouse, Jim and Rhonda Harrison?"

"No, I haven't. I wouldn't even know them if I saw them."

"Well, that's Jim, sitting at the bar, and Rhonda's probably upstairs in the office. They used to run a tourist fishing boat that traveled all over the world . They've seen lots of strange things on their journeys. Jim grew up down-state but always wanted to live in the UP, so after they saved enough money, they sold the business and built this place about five years ago. But they've always missed the water. So they came up with a plan to start a sightseeing boat trip that leaves from the harbor up the road. I'd tell you their story, but maybe you should hear it from the horse's mouth, if he'll even tell you. ...Hey, Jim. You got a minute?"

Jim looked like a ship's captain. He was a stocky man with the weathered look one would expect of a man who's spent years in the sun and wind. He even wore a faded blue captain's cap. As he walked over to the table, Sarah imagined he would have a New England accent and speak in naval jargon. She was wrong. He sounded more like a lumberjack than a seaman.

"Sure. What can I do you for, Julie?"

"First, I'd like you to meet Sarah Perkins. Her and her husband, Mike, bought the old Bromley cabin."

"Nice to meet you. I heard some people from out west bought that cabin. How you likin' livin' in the UP? Gotta be quite a change for you guys."

"It's been a challenge, but, for the most part, it's been good. At least up to now."

"Oh? Somethin' happen?"

Julie decided that was a good time to bring Jim up to speed.

"Funny you should say that, Jim. Sarah and Mike had a visit from Stan's son a couple months back. Seems young Mr. Bromley has concerns about his dad's disappearance. He even shared one of his theories about, well, you know, the thing. It's got them a little spooked, so we let Sarah know about our, well... for lack of a better term, experiences, with the mystery. And, we all thought maybe you could share your story with her. She's not sure if we're playing a joke on her or not."

Jim took his cap off, scratched his head, and then reluctantly pulled up a chair. He leaned in towards the middle of the table and spoke in a hushed tone, like he didn't want anyone not at the table to hear.

"First, let me tell you, not many folks know about this, so keep it under your hat. These ladies already know because they know every damn thing that happens in this town. And I guess they could've told you the story as easily as me. So, here goes. We first moved up here about five years ago, around October. Bad time of year to move to the UP, especially that year. Winter came early, and it pounded us most of the season. We had six feet of snow on the ground all winter. Great for the snowmobilers, which is great for the town. The bay froze solid almost all the way across to Canada.

"Well, one day, my wife and I decided to take the snowmobiles out on the lake and see if we could get all the way to the Soo. It's a long trip, and we probably wouldn't get back to Paradise until close to dark. We made it without a hitch and headed back home. It was about three in the afternoon when we hit the area called Timberlost. It's just past the entrance to the Curly Lewis. Anyway, there was a long line of ice volcanoes that stretched out along the shore for about a mile. They were huge that year. We sledded between them and the shoreline. The water's pretty shallow there, so the ice is thicker. Don't want to crash through the ice that time of day. No one's out there much after dark.

"We were about halfway along these volcanoes when Rhonda —that's my wife—suddenly veered her sled hard to the shore and came to a stop. She was pointing at the ice volcanoes we were coming up to and screaming about some huge creature she saw heading out from the shore towards the volcanoes. I looked where she was pointing and just caught a glimpse of what looked like a tail disappear into one of the volcanoes. I didn't get the best look at it, but the tail looked to be about five feet long with some kinda spikes sticking out of it. Like a stegosaurus. It was moving very fast. That's why I didn't see what Rhonda saw. It kinda freaked us out. Never seen nothin' like that in all our travels. Rhonda said the skin kinda shimmered like a fish, but not real shiny. More of a dull shine. And it looked like the head had horns too. She said it ran on all fours until it got close to the volcanoes. Then it stood on two legs and ran, diving into one of those holes in the volcano.

"That's when I saw it. After it dove in. It took me a few seconds to grasp what we had just seen. I think it's what the Natives call the water panther, or Mishipeshu. I just call it the Shoo. There's no other thing it could've been.

"Rhonda and I went over to where she saw it running to see if we could see any tracks. We found one damn piece of a track in some fresh snow that the wind had piled up in a little depression in the ice. It looked like a huge cat track, except there was one toe that pointed backwards, like a bird's foot. There were some scratches in a line that we figured were from its claws. But if you weren't looking for them, you'd never see them.

"That was five winters ago, and I haven't seen it since, and, believe me, I look every time I'm out on the ice. We don't talk about it much. Not good for business. There's just a few of us up here that we talk to about this. We call it the Shoo Club. Each one in the club has either seen it or knows someone who thinks they saw it. I'm guessing you already know about Laura's husband, but there are others, including each of the other two ladies at this table. I think it's about fifteen of us all totaled, but I'm guessing there's a whole lot more who just haven't said anything about seeing it. Some of the stories go back thirty years. That's about it. Welcome to Paradise. One thing. If you think you've seen it, and you want to talk to someone about it, keep it limited to those here at this table. Don't need people thinking you're crazy or something. After all, you're new here. Wouldn't want to give people a reason to give you the ole side-eye, if you know what I mean. Yoopers are funny like that. Self-reliant, self-sufficient, and they keep things to themselves or a small group of trusted friends."

Sarah had a hard time believing what she was hearing. After all, this was the twenty-first century. There shouldn't be any unknown creatures lurking about. Especially ones as large as what Jim was describing.

"Are you kidding' me?" Sarah was almost shaking at the the thought of some unknown creature living in the lake.

"Mike's been looking into this whole, Bromley thing, but he hasn't said anything to me about *this!*"

Jim was familiar with just about every business, municipality, or government official in Chippewa and Luce counties. He volunteered as a rescue diver when they had water-related incidents, where there may be drownings or when people don't use common sense and operate vehicles on thin ice. Most of what he did was help recover tourists' toys like four-wheelers or snowmobiles. It was a good thing he was available, as the next closest diver was over an hour away. Water incidents were usually time sensitive, and an hour or more response time was not ideal.

"My guess is he won't get much from them. That's a tribal department. The Native tribes are pretty tight-lipped about their traditions when it comes to outsiders. I think the police stay away from this issue because, if they don't come up with anything, they'll look ridiculous for chasing a myth. And if they do find something and kill it, they will have attacked a sacred Ojibway legend. The Ojibway look at this Mishipeshu as a protector of the lake. Something to be respected, not hunted. If the Shoo takes you, you deserved it. You must've disrespected the lake and it's nature or something. So, for the authorities, it's a political quagmire. Personally, I don't buy the mystical protector crap. I do think there's something out there, but it's just some kind of unknown animal. An animal that needs to eat, so it hunts. And, like most hunters in the wild, the easier the prey, the better. And humans can be a pretty easy prey. And, on that note, I'll leave you ladies to it."

That was it. Confirmation. According to some of the town's most respected citizens, there *was* a creature living in the lake, and it was a hunter. This did not sit well with Sarah. How unlucky were her and Mike to end up in a place called Paradise that may be anything but. Not only that, but the very home they bought may have been owned by one of its victims. That means it knows there's food there. Before, it was a seasonal cabin. No one was there during the winter, so there would be nothing to attract it. But, when Stan Bromley showed up to open the cabin that winter, he might have caught the attention of the Shoo, or maybe he was just in the wrong place at the wrong time. Most carnivores are opportunistic, and Bromley was alone. It made sense in a Bigfoot, space alien, Loch Ness Monster kind of way.

"You doin' okay, Sarah? You look kinda pale."

Julie's words seemed to echo in Sarah's ears, like when people speak in a tunnel.

"Huh? Oh, yeah, I guess. Holy shit! What the hell am I supposed to do now? I can't even begin to believe this. Puts a whole dark cloud over everything. I mean, this is 2021, for God's sake. How in the hell can there be an unknown creature living in Michigan? It's not the damn Amazon or anything. It's fuckin'

Michigan. I'm sorry. I don't usually use the F-word, but, what the fuck?"

The women sat there for a minute without saying anything. They felt Sarah's frustration. Hell, they had felt the same way when they first realized all the stories and rumors about the Mishipeshu may actually be true. When faced with any adversity, people have choices. They can either run from it, or face it. Judging by the sheer volume of people who only stay for the summer, it was pretty obvious which route the majority of those people chose. They ran. But for those with the true pioneering, can-do, Yooper spirit, running is *not* in their blood. Yoopers always faced a struggle head-on, relying on their abilities to handle most anything, and if needed, they knew they could rely on their fellow Yoopers. After all, no one was truly alone in the UP. There was always help available.

"Listen, Sarah. Look at it this way. You lived in Idaho, right? Well, in Idaho, there are moose, grizzly bears, mountain lions, and a bunch of other smaller but potentially dangerous animals. Did you ever feel scared that one of them would get you? Were you worried about this? Or did you just coexist and enjoy your surroundings?"

Julie had a point. Her and Mike would go on hikes into the wilderness where every one of those animals lived. And she never felt scared or even worried about being attacked. But, then again, they were always carrying firearms for protection. Sarah never even considered the need to do that in Paradise. That might just have to change.

"I get it. You're right. We were just prepared in case we met with one of those on the trail. Mike and I had a plan on what we'd do, how we would move, and so on. I guess the difference here is that this is something no one really knows anything about. Or even if it's real or not. I guess we've answered that question, though. How do you prepare for something no one knows anything about? If you come across it, and it attacks, what do you do? Where do you shoot it, *if* you shoot it? You would think that at least one person who was attacked by this thing was armed and may have shot it. Have you heard of anyone doing that? If so, was there blood? I haven't heard that story yet. Have you?"

Joanie had been quiet for most of the Shoo talk. She didn't want to add to the conversation. At least, that's how it seemed to Sarah. But that wasn't really the case. Joanie just wasn't the type of person to talk about something, anything, unless it added something new. And usually, she only gave her point of view or her side of the story if directly asked. But on this question, she had the answer.

"I've heard a couple of stories about someone taking shots at some crazy looking monster. Bullets, at least the kind of bullets they used, had no affect. Seems the Shoo has scales all over it, and they must be pretty thick. One guy said it was like his bullets just bounced off it. Of course, that guy drank a bit. He could've missed.

"But there was this one story about a couple of guys out huntin' in the Timberlost. It was about three years back. They said that when they scouted the area in the summer, there was deer tracks and signs all over. But when they came back to hunt the area in December, they didn't even see one fresh track. There was snow on the ground, but not one deer track. They figured the wolves either scared them out of the area or wiped them out. But they didn't see any wolf tracks either. The woods seemed empty. Like all the animals had left. They hunted for three days and didn't see a thing. But on their way out of the woods on the third night, they said something was blocking their way out. It took up the whole trail. It was pretty dark, so they were using their flashlights. One guy said he shined his light on the animal, and its eyes shone green. Green. Not exactly a normal eye shine. But what was really weird was that it looked like this thing had skin like what a dragon would have. You know, all scaly. He said it had horns on its head and spikes at the end of its tail. He said it was standing on its hind legs and had to be eight or nine feet tall. His buddy shot at it with his deer rifle. Not sure how big, but my brother says most deer hunters up here shoot either a .243 or .30-30.

"Anyway, this guy said this thing let out a very loud roar. Kinda like a lion, only bigger, deeper. He said they could feel the roar in their chests, and that thing was about forty-five yards away. Then the thing took a step towards them, so they just opened up on it. They fired all their ammo at it, and it acted like it was hit but not hurt. It let out one more roar and ran off. When they couldn't hear any more sounds from it running, they reloaded and made their way, slowly, to where the animal was. No blood. Not one drop. But there was one thing. According to one of the hunters, there was this thing that looked like a fish scale, only much bigger. Like the size of a drink coaster. It looked like it had broken off from where it might've been attached to the body, and there was a dent in it. The dent, they figured, was from one of the bullets. It never pierced it, so they were certain, whatever it was, was still out there. So they high-tailed it back to their truck and got the hell out of there. Story is, they never hunted in those woods again. That's all I've heard on someone shootin' at this thing."

Julie had never heard either of those stories. And that was unusual.

"How'd you hear those stories, Joanie? You've never said anything about them before."

"Well, that's 'cause the first one was told to me by my dad when I was about ten years old. He drank a lot, so I didn't really believe him. But the two hunters? One of them was my brother, Rick, and his huntin' buddy, who I'll leave nameless for privacy. But I didn't believe him either till he showed me that scale thing. Never seen anything like it. He only told me about this 'cause he was scared shitless and couldn't stop shakin' when he got home that night. He told me not to tell anyone, so keep it to yourselves."

"Wait a minute. You say you *saw* the scale thing he picked up? Did you ever have anyone look at it? You know, have it tested?"

"Nope. Rick didn't want anyone knowing about this, for a couple reasons. One, he didn't want folks laughin' at him. And, two, he didn't really have permission to hunt in that area. He said that after they couldn't find any fresh signs, they kinda wandered onto some private land. You know, just to see if they could pick up any signs. He knew he shouldn't have been there, but it was their last day hunting, and they really wanted meat in the freezer. He didn't want to get him or his buddy in any trouble."

"Do you still have it? If you do, do you think we could take a look at it? We could have it tested to see what it is. We could just say we found it walking the beach looking for rocks or something."

"I think Rick still has it. But I'm not too sure if he wants anyone looking at it. But I'll ask him."

"Well, let me know, and I'll get Mike to get it over to one of his lab buddies for testing. At least we should be able to find out if it's some kind of mutated known animal or not."

Sarah couldn't wait to get home and tell Mike what she'd found out. But first, she needed to finish her drink and grab her dinner order. She wasn't really much of a drinker—maybe two at a bonfire or special occasions—but she chugged that last one like she was used to it, and she could feel it.

"Whew! Should've sipped that one. I'm really feeling it, if you know what I mean. I'm kind of a lightweight when it comes to drinking. Do you think I could get one of you guys to drive me home? Being a retired cop, Mike's kinda funny about the drinking and driving thing."

Julie was ready to head home too, so she was quick to volunteer. Besides, she hadn't seen the Bromley place since Mike and Sarah bought it and was curious to see the changes.

Mike had been home for an hour. He knew Sarah had gone to the Wheelhouse because they were anal about leaving each other notes on where they were going or what time they should be home. It was something Mike's mother had instilled in him and his siblings when they were kids. They had freedoms, but if things went bad, his mom and dad would know where to start looking for their children. It was something Mike took seriously, especially with his law enforcement experience. There were many times where someone hadn't been home when they should have been. When Mike would ask where they might be, the answer was often no. It made trying to find out what happened difficult. Most times, things worked out. The missing person had simply lost track of time, or there was a car issue—things like that. But dozens of times over Mike's twenty-five-year career, there was a more nefarious reason for the person to not be where they should be.

If there had been a clue as to where they may have gone or who they were with, some of those cases may have been resolved with a much happier outcome. There were a couple of particularly brutal cases where a note would have helped stop a murder or rape. One involved a teenage girl named Nicole Hinch. Nicole, or Nikki as she was known, was raped and murdered, and the body was set on fire in a wooded area near the base of the Selkirk Mountains in North Idaho in attempt to destroy any evidence. It was late July, and the forests were bone dry, as they usually are in that region in late summer. Burning the body set off a forest fire that ended up burning over 5,000 acres before it was extinguished. The plan would've worked if Nikki's body hadn't been found by the fire crew mopping up hot spots. Her body was burned beyond recognition, except for her left hand. It was curled up under her body and survived the fire just out of dumb luck.

Apparently, Nikki put up quite a fight and had scratched her killer with her left hand. The killer stabbed her with a bowie knife several times in the chest. As Nikki lay there bleeding out, she had the foresight to put her hand under her body. This, coupled with the loose rocky soil and no forest litter where she was killed, had slowed the burning long enough to keep Nikki's hand from burning completely. If the fire crew hadn't gotten the fire out as quickly as they did, it would've burned Nikki's body down to bone.

Forensics found skin cells under Nikki's nails and match the DNA to one of Nikki's schoolmates, Brian Fowler. Brian was a good-looking boy of seventeen and in several classes with Nikki. He even took Nikki to the school's ring dance. But when Brian showed up to pick Nikki up for the dance, his Dracula-esque tux and dyed jet-black hair left Nikki's parents a little concerned. But they let Nikki attend the dance with him, as she had been so excited to go. But the day after the dance, Nikki's parents expressed their concern over how Brian looked, and they banned her from seeing him socially. Nikki wasn't happy about that but stayed clear of Brian for the last six months of school. So, when Brian showed up at Nikki's door that hot July afternoon, Nikki was surprised but excited to go for a ride with him. Her parents weren't home, and she must've thought she would get home before them and nobody would be the wiser. Turns out, Brian was stalking her and knew she was home alone.

According to the timeline of the Hinch's last contact with Nikki and the approximate time the fire was started, Nikki's mom had gotten home somewhere between thirty minutes to an hour after she left with Brian. It was a twenty-five-minute drive from Nikki's house to where her body was found. If Nikki had left a note saying she was going for a ride with Brian, her mom could've possibly saved her daughter's life. Police could've been looking for Brian's truck or cellphone pings. That might've made the difference. It was lucky forensics was able to match the DNA to Brian. Ordinarily, there wouldn't be anything to match it with, but Brian fantasized about being a vampire, so he had a habit of biting people whenever he got into fights, which was quite often. That meant there were hospital as well as police records which included his DNA. That's how they were able to put Brian at the scene. If it hadn't been for his biting habit, they may never have caught him.

After this case, Mike was even more adamant about Sarah leaving notes and voicemails, but it still took almost three years for her to finally get on board with it. Better late than never.

Sarah and Julie got home not long after Mike. They gave Julie the grand tour of all the changes they made to the cabin, as well as what renovations were coming. After all the pleasantries, Sarah told Mike about what her, Julie, and the other ladies had discussed, about the mystery of the Mishipeshu and the possibility of looking at an actual scale from what Joanie's brother said had come from a creature he took a shot at.

Mike listened in stunned silence before letting them know what Lt. Wilkins had told him, or, to be more accurate, what he didn't say. It was all adding up to an unknown but known-about lake creature. At least by some of the locals. Even law enforcement seemed to think there was some truth in the legend of the Mishipeshu.

"I'm completely floored by all this. Here we are in 2021, in a town visited by thousands every year, and there's no mention of this damn thing. No newspaper stories. No nickname given to this mysterious lake monster, like the Loch Ness Monster, or other supposed lake monsters. Hell, those towns make a killing off merchandise related to their monster. You'd think some marketing guru would've thought of that and come up with a non-threatening nickname like Miss Mishi or something. It's like that's taboo. I don't get it. I guess Loch Ness doesn't have the whole it's-eating-people thing. Nothing would kill tourism more than having to look out for the man-eating lake monster."

Sarah had seen this from Mike before. It's how he processed things. Mike would often talk out loud to himself about things that confused or confounded him. Hearing his thoughts being spoken helped him focus and see things clearer. This technique, if that's what it was, helped him figure out how crime scene clues might come into play, or whether testimony given by witnesses and suspects made sense or were flat out lies. He would do this with almost everything he wasn't completely sure of. Sarah knew to just let him ramble and not interrupt.

"I'm really just having a hard time believing that there's some kind of lake creature that comes out in winter. It's totally crazy. So, Julie, you really think there's an unknown animal out there?"

"I do. The people I know who claim to have seen it or evidence of it being here are some of the most credible people I know. It's not like they're stoners or prone to making up stories. These are businesspeople, respected members of our community, even law enforcement."

Julie was trying to bring a little levity back into the conversation. She knew Mike was a retired police officer. It seemed to work, at least a little.

"Ha, ha. Very funny. I get it. What about you guys? Have you or your husband ever seen this?"

"I haven't, and I don't think Dan has either. He doesn't talk about things like this much, anyway. So he might not tell me if he has. He's just superstitious that way. Thinks if you talk about things like ghosts, the Devil, or Mishipeshu, they will hear you and pay you a visit. I know, crazy, right? That's just Dan."

So, what's this scale thingy Sarah mentioned? Is it a real thing?"

"I guess so. Tonight's the first I've heard of it. Like I said, most people up here keep things close to the vest. The fact that Joanie told you about it is a sign of acceptance. Looks like you guys are fast becoming Yoopers. Assuming, you know, the winter thing. I'm just messin' with you guys. It'll be fine. You'll see. On that note, I gotta get home. Call me if you guys need anything."

"Will do, Julie. Thanks for giving Sarah a ride home."

"No problem. We all gotta look out for each other up here, you know. We're all we got."

While Mike and Sarah watched Julie pull out onto the road, her "We're all we got" statement hit home. She was right. In case of an emergency, the closest law enforcement or emergency services were at least an hour away. Unless, by some lucky fluke, a police unit happened to be patrolling near town. But those days were few and far between. Especially in winter when the snow covered the roads. Drifts could unexpectedly make miles of highway impassable. Times like those showed how important it was to have good neighbors. And, having those good neighbors might just prove lifesaving once winter really set in. As Mike and Sarah turned to go in the cabin, the first of what would be several winter storms released the first snow of the season.

5

MISHIPESHU

In the depths of the frigid waters of Lake Superior, it could feel the change. The water gets heavier as the colder water sinks and sends the warmer water towards the surface where it is released into the atmosphere, further cooling the lake. Those warmer air masses mixing with the colder air above the lake are what create lake-effect snow. It can be relentless, dumping huge amounts of snow on the land. Lake-effect snow is extremely hard to predict, so those who tend to live in these snow belts, expect and prepare for the worst.

As for the Mishipeshu, it meant its hunting grounds would soon be expanded. Already, it could hunt a little closer to land, cruising the submerged shelves or ledges, where many different species of fish hover in wait for smaller fish to swim by for their meal. Easy pickings for an apex predator like the Mishipeshu, but not nearly filling enough for such a large creature. Hunting takes energy, and hunting for these smaller fish species is almost a negative result. High energy expense with low energy production. To provide enough food for it to survive requires a much easier prey in sufficient numbers to maintain its body's demand.

The Mishipeshu was a holdout, a leftover from the ice age. While many species died off due to the cooling temperatures, others adapted to the cold and survived or found a way to go dormant, waiting for the climate to normalize so they could, once again, roam the earth. Most of the creatures that used dormancy as a survival mechanism were small. This allowed them to make use of numerous hiding spots to keep them hidden from the many predators looking for an ever-dwindling food supply. The Mishipeshu, or its scientific name, *Puma Concolor Abyssi*, as the Canadian scientific community labeled it, adapted to the cold, as well as becoming more amphibious than its predecessors. This allowed it to feed on aquatic life that would not be available to it if it stayed a solely terrestrial hunter. It first grew a thick hide that would eventually be covered in a combination of fur and scales. Fur on the underside and legs, scales over the rest. The scales allowed it to glide smoothly through the water with less friction, conserving energy. The fur helped regulate its body temperature when out of the water. As the ice age receded, and Earth's temperatures rose, its kind couldn't tolerate the higher temperatures, so it adapted once again.

The melting ice formed the Great Lakes, and Lake Superior's depths meant the water at those depths would be cold enough for it to survive. So it adapted to staying under water for greater and greater amounts of time, much like a seal, and eventually, it didn't need to surface at all. It developed specialized gills that breathe both under water and above. Its one big weakness was its size. The bigger the animal, the more food it needs. But the cold depths of Lake Superior allowed the Mishipeshu to store vast amounts of food where it would not decompose. Mother Nature's natural refrigeration. So, when the temperatures dropped low enough for it to hunt on the land surrounding the lake, it would move from the depths to the shallower waters where there was more food, otherwise known as victims. It would take its cache to its under-water lair, an undiscovered subaqueous lake known as Lake Inferior. Its original name, the Lake of Hell, was mistranslated by early French explorers to the region. A lake beneath the lake, the perfect place for it to stay hidden. It was not thought of as an actual geological feature by academics, so it was relegated to legend. The Mishipeshu would need to gather enough food to make sure of its survival and the survival of its offspring until the next season a year away. To ensure it didn't overwhelm the food supply with overpopulation, it only produced one offspring during its lifetime. This was done through parthenogenesis, or reproduction without the need for an opposite sex. It would lay one fertilized egg, and once it hatched, the elder Mishipeshu would show the young Mishipeshu the way of the hunt, how to avoid detection by using the ice volcanoes that formed close to shore, exiting the lake and then re-entering through the vents. By the time the elder passed away, the younger was well versed in survival.

And now, the seasons were changing again. The ice would soon start to form on the lake. It starts off as small balls of ice that move with the wind and waves, coming ever closer to the shores. As the air and water temperatures cool, and the small balls of ice bump and collide with other ice balls, they get bigger and heavier. Some reach the size of a Volkswagen Beetle. It's these car-size ice balls that eventually form the bases of the ice volcanoes. As the balls get heavier, they sit lower in the water. As they get closer to shore, their weight causes them to get stuck on sandbars or in the shallows. Over time, all sizes of ice balls collide with these anchors, creating what looks like an ice mountain range that stretches along the entire shore. Then the winter winds whip up the wave action, and these waves pound those ice mountains, splashing over the tops of the peaks, which, in turn, flash freeze, making the mountains higher and higher. Waves carve gouges into weak spots along the ice and force water into these gouges. The force of this wave action and restricted channels create the ice volcanoes. Once the volcanoes are formed, water spews from their throats, like erupting volcanoes of frozen and frigid water. This cycle could repeat several times over a winter, resulting in rows of ice mountains with hundreds of these volcanoes. Beneath these ice mountains and volcanoes is liquid water between five and eight feet deep—a hidden highway for the Mishipeshu to travel, with hundreds of exits to take. It was a perfect system.

As the ice formed, the Mishipeshu would venture to the lake's surface, using the ice to hide its movements. These were, for lack of a better term, scouting missions. Most years, the Mishipeshu would seek out more secluded hunting locations, areas where unsuspecting victims would venture with few others around. But, last year, one Mishipeshu found success among the houses and cabins in more populated areas, and that's where it would start this year. These killing fields, as it were, were closer to its lair, which meant it was easier to move its food to its cache. Less time, less energy, less exposure. Maybe.

Hunting closer to the residential areas meant more eyes and a greater chance of being seen, or worse, killed or injured. But these were not things the Mishipeshu thought about. Its thoughts we're confined to finding, gathering, storing, and eating its food. It didn't have a moral compass or reasoning mentality. It was reactionary to its environment, and its environment was changing. More people were moving into its territory, which meant more opportunities to find new sources for its meals.

As a solitary being, there had only been one of its kind living in the lake at a time. It has been this way since the great extinction, when food sources became scarce. And so it has been for all this time, due to the limited resources available to it during the winter months. There just hasn't been enough people to support the dietary needs of more than one. But, as always, times change; one day, there may be enough food to support multiple Mishipeshu. It's all about food availability combined with its ability to stay hidden. If the time ever came that more than one could survive, the cycle would produce two eggs, or three, or whatever number nature determined was appropriate. This is observed in other species. When the food supply for deer, squirrels, and other animals is abundant, more young are born. Triplets have been seen in the deer populations during bounty years. But this creates a possible problem if the following years prove less productive. So, as a counterbalance, the young of the predator species in the area also become more numerous. Nature keeps the balance.

But for the Mishipeshu, there has been no known predator to control its numbers; only humans are capable of killing it, and they have not had enough contact with it to understand its weaknesses. Those who have tried to kill it have had no effect on it whatsoever. Oh, sure, it's been scratched and even had pieces of it damaged by these attempts, but no real damage. This is another factor in the Mishipeshu being limited to one. No viable source of predation.

As winter starts its cycle, the Mishipeshu will venture ever closer to the shores of Whitefish Bay, smelling the air, tasting it as predators do, searching for its first hunt, its first winter kill. Although the snow had started and the waters had cooled, the ice —the big ice—had yet to form. But it knew, as did those who lived in Yooperland, that the ice could show overnight. And once the ice started, it wouldn't be long before the ice ranges and volcanoes formed, granting the Mishipeshu close access to the shores.

6

MID NOVEMBER: THE MEETING

Winter storms have pounded the Whitefish Bay area for two weeks, bringing gale force winds and heavy snow. Although Mike and Sarah were used to snow, they were not prepared for the ferocity of winter weather in the UP. In Idaho, snow was fairly predictable. Weather patterns were simple, and accumulation estimates were pretty accurate. If the weather said two feet of snow, they got two feet of snow, give or take. It would snow, sometimes for days, but then the sun would come out, and the landscape was like a glitter-covered Christmas card, all pristine white and sparkling. Not in the UP. It would snow when there was no forecast for snow. Accumulation estimates of three inches could end up as eight, twelve, or even twenty.

And forget about all that beautiful, evenly distributed, pristine and sparkly, snow. The winds drove the snow into drifts—drifts that could close roads down, and often did. It piled up in compacted mounds on every barricade it came in contact with. This was usually doorways and the north- and south-facing walls of every building. There might be bare grass in one part of the yard and four feet piled up in another. And the wind changed direction so much that snow would actually spin in what looked like "snownadoes."

And the sun? Forget about it. It may not shine for weeks. Winter is the dark time. Daylight is short and, most days, was more like gray light. Dismal was the word. But even with all this, there was beauty in the chaos. The wind would shape the snow into curvy, sloped masterpieces of winter art. A beautiful sight for some, but for those responsible for clearing the driveways, walks, and doorways, it was a backbreaking and tedious chore. Walk-behind snowblowers could not remove these tightly packed piles. They would simply climb the drifts and make things worse. The drifts would first have to be loosened with a shovel. Only then could the snowblower rake in the snow and fling it to a new location. Backbreaking.

Then, there was the ice. Once it started to form, it just kept coming, piling up upon itself and building the ice mountains and volcanoes along the shores. This process was sped up considerably by the gales of November. Winds pushed the ice with great force onto the shore and built up on docks, decks, and anything else that extended from the shore. And ice is destructive. There are hundreds of dilapidated, wooden structures all along the coast that were eaten by the ice littering the beaches, with the remnants spit back out by the lake. Yes, winter in the UP can be violent, and often is.

"Holy shit! The damn wind just doesn't let up." Mike was watching the storm rage on the bay through the family room windows. "I can barely see the water with all the damn snow flyin'. How long's this storm supposed to last, anyway?"

Sarah was a weather geek. She checked the reports at least three or four times a day. She even had a NOAH weather radio that gave continual updates.

"It says the winds are supposed to end sometime tonight, but the snow's gonna get heavier before it's all over. Looks like about ten inches or so. I wonder what the ice is going to look like after this storm. It was really coming in, last time I could see out there."

"Yeah, it's kind of amazing to see. I'll have to clean off those security cameras out there. Might even need to put them up a little higher too. All we've caught so far is one lousy deer, a fox, a coyote, and some rabbits. Oh, and let's not forget the delivery driver taking a piss in the woods. Can't blame him, though. Not many places to go on this road."

"I know this isn't the winter weather you're used to, but it is kinda cool, huh?"

"I guess you could say that. It's always amazing to witness nature's power firsthand."

Mike was looking out the window at the storm, mesmerized by the unrelenting, wind-driven snow and how fast it was piling up on the outbuildings. But the weather was not the only thing on his mind. Colder weather meant, if he was to believe everything they'd been told about the Mishipeshu, that it was getting close to time to be more watchful. More cautious. More aware. He hesitated to say anything to Sarah about these thoughts. He didn't want her to dwell on it. But he needed to say something to make sure she put it on her radar. Sarah tended not to be very attentive to her surroundings.

Once, in Idaho, her and Mike were doing some spring cleaning in the yard. Sarah had gone around a shed to do some raking, and Mike was doing the same next to their garden. Mike saw some movement out towards their fence and watched a young moose calf hop the fence and walk right up to him. A calf moose meant a momma moose, somewhere. And momma moose are more dangerous than mama grizzly bears. As the calf approached him, Mike kept moving to position some trees between him and the moose. It may have been a calf, but it was still a 250-pound wild animal. Momma never showed, and Mike figured she may not have survived the winter. Sarah came back from the other side of the shed and walked towards Mike, talking about what she wanted to plant and how she wanted to have the flower beds done. She never saw the moose standing just ten feet from Mike until Mike, for the third time, yelled, "Sarah! Moose!" Even then, she kept walking towards it. Mike had to stop her and remind her not to get close. Being situationally aware was not one of Sarah's strong points. So Mike needed to remind her to be more aware of her surroundings.

"Sarah? I hate to even bring this up, but with this weather coming in, it might be time to, you know, keep our eyes open. Watch the lake and keep an eye on the woods."

"Funny. I was just thinking the same thing. Do you really think it's a real thing?"

"I'm not sure. But it's always better safe than sorry. I'm gonna move a couple of those cameras to the lakeside of the house. If anything comes from the lake, we'll know it. I haven't set up the alerts yet, but I can sync my phone with the cameras so we get an alert when the camera is tripped. That way, nothing's gonna sneak up on us. And just for some added peace of mind, I got some dragon's breath shells for the shotgun."

"What in the world is dragon's breath? Do they smell bad or something?"

Sarah thought Mike was making it up, so she was laughing as she asked about the dragon's breath. But Mike was not joking.

"Laugh all you want, but these shells spray fire. You know, like a fire-breathing dragon. Get it? Dragon's breath? I figure, I'll load the shotgun with alternating shells. Dragon's breath. Slug. Dragon's breath. Slug. I figure, if this thing's for real, it lives in the darkness and won't like the fire. Might give us a shot with the slugs.

And if the slugs don't work, maybe the dragon's breath will scare it off. I might even get a second shotgun to have on hand and load them both like that. That way, if it doesn't scare easily, we can reload while the other's blasting away. Suppression fire, so to speak. What do you think of that?"

"Sounds like a plan. A plan I hope we never have to use."

Sarah wasn't afraid of guns, she just had a hard time with the recoil. Before she met Mike, she lived on top of a mountain in Washington state. There were all manner of animals up there. Cougars, bears, and deer. Just about anything that walked or crawled. She carried a .22 magnum pistol for unwanted encounters, mostly for the bang factor. She never wanted to shoot anything. She just wanted to scare things away. That pistol was loud, but without much recoil. A shotgun was quite a different weapon offering a more effective weapon for someone adverse in the use of firearms. But the shotgun made her nervous. Mike knew this, so he bought her a .410 shotgun when she moved to Idaho after they got married—smaller caliber, bigger bang, little recoil.

The problem was that the dragon's breath only came in twelve gage shells. Way too much for Sarah. But Mike had some skill with loading his own ammunition. He might be able to retrofit the dragon's breath into the smaller shells. Based on what Mike and Sarah had been told about encounters with the Mishipeshu, the smaller-caliber shells probably weren't big enough to do any damage to it. But fire is fire, and maybe loading Sarah's shotgun with all dragon's breath shells could keep it occupied while Mike reloaded his. Mike still wasn't convinced they actually needed these precautions, but something in the back of his mind told him otherwise.

As Mike stood there, looking out at the storm, he made a mental checklist of all the things he wanted to do before the ice was completely set up. Move the cameras, program the phone alerts, work on the shotgun shells for Sarah's gun, and make sure all the spotlights on the house were replaced so they were fresh. Mike's trance was broken by his cellphone ringing; it was Julie with some good news.

"Hey, Julie. What's up?"

Julie never called Mike's phone. It was always Sarah's phone she called, so it took Mike a little by surprise.

"Well, I think you'll like what I have to tell you. Remember Joanie's brother, Rick? The one with the scale thing from that thing he shot at?"

"Yeah, I remember him. I've been trying to get ahold of him ever since I heard about his story. No one ever gets back to me."

"That's just how folks up here are when they don't know you. It takes a bit. Well, he came into the shop the other day wanting to know what I thought about you and Sarah. Basically, if he could trust you guys. I guess Joanie's been buggin' him about it. Anyway, he says he'll talk to you, but it has to be out at his place. It's kinda out there. No one around."

"I'm good with that. Did he say when?"

"He said he'd be around the place the next couple days. But you're gonna need your truck. The road's kinda sketchy, and with this snow, it's gonna be a mess. Might want to bring a come-along and some rope, in case you get stuck. Just give him a call to let him know you're on the way."

"Thanks for smoothing the way, Julie. I'm kinda excited to see this scale thing, if he still has it. Can you text me the address? This storm's supposed to peter out sometime tonight, so I should be able to get out there tomorrow afternoon. I've got a plow blade for my truck and a winch somewhere in one of my shop boxes. Haven't been able to unpack everything yet. Might earn me some points if I plow his road out for him. If he's still got the scale, I've got a buddy at the University of Idaho in the Department of

Biological Studies who can test it. They've got some pretty high-tech equipment out there that might identify exactly what this thing is."

"If he's still got it, I'm not so sure he'd be willing to hand it over and have it sent across the country to someone he doesn't know. Did I mention that folks up here aren't quick to trust strangers? I'll text you his address when we hang up. He lives down Falls Road just before the falls. His place is back off the road about a half mile, so be prepared for an adventure."

"Thanks again, Julie. I owe you one."

Mike knew he would need to rely on his interrogation skills and knowledge of people's body language if he was to convince Rick to not only show him the item, but also allow him to test it. But before he could do that, he had to find his winch and hook up his snow blade, and he didn't have a lot of time; Rick was receptive for now, but that could change. And Julie said he'd only be around a couple of days. For all Mike knew, that was just a timeframe Rick offered before he would change his mind.

"Honey, I'm going out to the shop to find my winch. Joanie's brother is willing to talk about his experience and hopefully show me his trophy. But I only have a couple days. I need to hook it up and attach the snow blade up so I can get to his place. Julie says it's kinda out there."

"Wow. I'd just about forgotten about him. Do you need any help?"

"I might need an extra hand when I put on the blade. I'll come get you when I'm ready."

The storms in the UP can dump large amounts of snow in a very short time, due to the lake affect. That's why it's hard to predict potential snow totals. And this storm was no different. Ten inches had been forecasted, but by the end of the storm, it would be closer to eighteen inches in the areas protected from the winds.

Wind-prone areas would have drifts up to three or four feet. Breaking a fresh trail down an unknown road was going to test Mike's skills, if he could even make it to Rick's place. High winds often blew trees down across roads, blocking access to all but the prepared. Mike was used to riding the trails that zigzagged around the high mountains back in Idaho. During the late fall and winter, high winds would blow trees down across those trails too. Mike always carried a chainsaw just in case. He would do the same when he headed out to Rick's.

"Yeah?"

Mike had called Rick to make sure he was still okay with him coming out and to get any information he may need to help him find his place.

"Rick?"

"Yeah, this is Rick. What can I do for ya'?"

"This is Mike Perkins. I'm friends with Julie. She said you might be willing to talk to me about, well, your experience a while back. I was calling to see if tomorrow afternoon would be good."

"Well, I'll be here, if you can get here. My driveway's close to a half mile long, and it ain't straight. It kinda winds around a bit. Most of it's in the woods on high ground, but about midway down, it dips down and can be kinda tricky, especially with all this snow. It makes it hard to see the dip. Plus, I'm sure there's gonna be trees down."

"I figured as much. I got a plow blade and my chainsaw. Should be able to get to you."

"You must really want to know about what I saw. Why?"

"Well, we bought the Bromley place, so I think you probably know why I'm so interested."

There was a pause before Rick spoke. "Yeah, I guess I do. Tomorrow should be fine. I ain't goin' nowhere. I'll scout the road in the morning to let you know if there's any problems. This number a good one to reach you?"

"Yes, it's my cell. It's on me all the time."

"Okay. When you're comin' down Falls Road—I put a post with a sign on it by the road. You'll see it on the right. You can't miss it. My name's on the post. Towne. The sign actually says *UP-Towne*. Kind of a play on being from the UP. Anyway, it's painted in bright orange, so it's easy to see."

"Thanks. I'll call you when I'm on my way."

"See ya', then."

"Well, looks like I'm meeting with Rick Towne tomorrow afternoon."

"Wow. Just like that, huh?"

"Yeah. Just like that. After a couple months. Gonna be a job gettin' there, though. Might take me most of the day just to reach his house."

"Plow and winch hooked up and working?"

"Yep. And I'm bringing my chainsaw too."

"Good idea. What time are you heading out there?"

"I'm thinking I'll give the road crews a little time to clear the roads. Maybe around noon. That'll give me enough time to dig out of here first. Looks like it's gonna be a snow-moving kinda day."

"You love it, and you know it."

"Yeah, I kinda do."

That night, as the storm subsided. Mike was going over his plan for the next day, making sure he had everything he needed for his adventure. He was always a bit of a planner. Better to have it and not need it than to need it and not have it, was how he did everything. Even when he traveled, he tended to take more things than most thought he needed to. But, on more than one occasion, his overpacking came in handy. For this day trip, he would bring a chainsaw, bar and chain oil, an extra chain, extra gas for the chainsaw, two five-gallon cans of diesel for his truck, a first aid kit, and an extra set of clothes in case he got wet. Not to mention lunch, a gallon of drinking water, some snacks, and "Jenny"—his Smith and Wesson M&P .45-caliber handgun. He never went anywhere without Jenny. Better to have it and not need it than to need it and not have it.

The next day started early—4:30 a.m. Mike wanted to get their driveway and walks cleared and have time for a big breakfast, a warmup on the chainsaw, and one more test of the winch.

"That was fast. Only an hour. Must be some kind of record."

Sarah was used to the three and a half hours it took Mike to clear all their snow in Idaho. Of course, it was a much longer driveway and bigger parking area.

"Coffee's on, and I've got pancakes ready to go. You hungry?"

"Well, duh. I burned up all my stored calories, and I'm going to need all the calories I can get today. Gonna be a busy day."

"I'll make 'em until you tell me to stop."

"I knew there was a reason I married you."

The storm gave Mike an opportunity to practice with the snow blade. In Idaho, he used a snow blower because the snow was so powdery; it blew easily, and blowing kept the snow from encroaching on the drive. But in Michigan, the snow was wetter and didn't blow as well. It would get sticky and required several stops to clear the snow from the blower. Plus, the drifts didn't blow well. In drifts, the snow became compacted and even more difficult to blow. A blade made more sense. Plus, the added weight of his truck made breaking and moving the drifts much easier. Of course, he wouldn't have known this if Julie hadn't warned him. One day, Sarah and Julie were talking about winter weather and what to do about the snow, and Sarah had said something about Mike blowing the snow. Julie told her that wasn't the best option and told her what her husband does and why. So Mike got a snow blade. The timing couldn't have been better for this storm to hit. It gave Mike a chance to practice using the blade before he headed out to Rick's.

"The plows are running. Figures. Just when I get the drive cleared, the plow buries it again. At least with the blade, I can move that plow snow pretty quick. With the plows running, it won't be long before Falls Road is drivable. Should be no issues with leaving by noon. I'll give Rick a call around eleven or so. He said he was going to scout his drive to make sure I can get there. I'm guessing he's going to let me do the plowing as a sort of payment for his info."

* * *

"Rick?"

"Yeah, this is Rick."

"Mike Perkins here. I'll be heading your way around eleven, if that's still good with you."

"Yeah, that'll work. Scouted the drive this morning on the sled. The good news is, there ain't no trees down. But I got about ten inches most places, and that dip I was telling you about has about fifteen. It don't look like it, but it'll grab you if you're not ready. I tied a yellow flag about fifty feet before and two flags at the dip. Take it slow and keep in four-low, and you should be good. Other than that, there are plenty of open slots for pushing the snow off the road, both on the right and left sides. Easy to see those, 'cause there ain't no trees in those spots. If you have any issues, I got my phone on me."

"Thanks. I should be good. See you then."

Moving snow with the snow blade was a bit of a learning curve for Mike, but it didn't take him that long. It was all about feel and knowing the edges of the truck and the blade. That's not to say a few small plants and trees weren't plowed up in the process. But these were native plants and trees that were planted by nature, and Mike had planned on widening the driveway anyway; so, no harm, no foul. Plowing through Rick Towne's drive would be a different story. The road was fairly narrow and had a lot of twists and turns. And what Rick didn't tell Mike was that the edges of the road were kind of soft. Get too far off track, and the tires might spin. It hadn't been cold enough long enough for the ground to freeze yet. This would be a tricky task for an unseasoned plower like Mike.

There were only two ways in or out of Paradise. Michigan 123, or M-123, and Falls Road, which was also M-123. But as M-123 into Paradise was a north-south road, it switched to an east-west road at the only traffic light in Paradise and continued west to Tahquamenon Falls and the town of Newberry, about forty five miles away. A flashing yellow light warned motorists of the intersection. M-123 east and west was the main road into Paradise from down state, and since Tahquamenon Falls was a popular stop any time of the year, the snow plows hit M-123 early and often. Got to keep the tourists happy. People can't spend money if they can't get around. The plow drivers for this route were not only some of the best the transportation department had—they needed to be—but they were also some of the nicest people around. This made for great PR for the area. You rarely heard a complaint about the plow drivers. This was made obvious to Mike as he headed out for Rick's place. When he got to the end of his driveway, the snow plow was approaching his drive on the return trip up Whitefish Point Road. Mike sat in his drive waiting for the plow to pass, but instead of passing, the truck came to a complete stop just before his drive. Mike wondered what was wrong, but it was just Walter Reynold's way. He saw an opportunity to meet the new neighbors, so he stopped his truck and got out with his customary ear-to-ear smile.

"Howdy, neighbor. I'm your snowplow driver, Walter. Just thought I'd introduce myself in case you need anything."

Mike was a little taken aback. His experience with the plow drivers back in Idaho was that they were mostly a pain in the ass. Many times, he'd had to deal with complaints about the plow drivers intentionally damaging property or spraying snow all over someone. Walter looked just like he would imagine a snow plow driver to look. He was wearing a bomber style hat, flannel shirt, and jeans, and had a face full of beard. He was rugged looking but slim, and his smile shone through that beard like sunrise on the lake. He was beaming. He jumped out of that truck like he was a twenty-something, but he had to be pushing sixty. Walter almost ran over to Mike's truck to shake his hand for a formal introduction.

"Just thought you should know who's keeping your road clear up here. Always good to know who's behind the plow. I heard you moved here from Idaho. What brought you all the way from Idaho?"

"Wow, word gets around this town, huh?"

"Well, I'm not only the plow driver for this area. I'm also on a couple of committees with Julie, and you know she knows *everything* about *everyone* in Paradise. It's mostly a good thing."

"Yeah, you got that right. She's helped us out quite a bit with contacts for gettin' things done around here. Anyway, our grandkids moved from Washington State to Michigan, and my wife wasn't going to be happy living a country away from those kids. So, here we are, living the dream in Paradise."

"Well, if you have to move, Paradise is an awful great place to move to. They don't call it Paradise for nothin'."

"We're likin' it so far. Been busy, though, with all the repairs and stuff. Haven't even gone fishin' yet. By the way, how's Falls Road? I'm headin' there now to meet with someone."

"It's good. I hit that about three-thirty this mornin'. It ain't completely plowed, but you can get down it just fine. Who ya' meetin' out there? Not too many people livin' out that way this time of year."

"Oh, just goin' to see a guy named Rick Towne about doin' some work on the cabin. I hear he's pretty handy, and I could use an extra hand here and there."

Mike didn't want to go too deep into his meeting with Rick, but he figured that most of the full-timers in Paradise knew just about everyone who lived there. And since Julie had told Mike she used Rick as a handyman on occasion, sayin he was going to meet Rick about a job seemed believable.

"Rick, huh? Well, he can swing a hammer, all right. And he's got a strong back. But I wouldn't let him do any plumbing or electrical stuff. I could tell you stories about that, but I got to get back at it. Be careful going down his road. It's gonna be a little dicey today, but looks like you got the truck for it. Nice meetin' ya'."

"Good meeting you too. Thanks."

As Mike watched Walter bound back to the plow, he was thinking how strange it seemed to have complete strangers drop what they were doing to make a point to introduce themselves with that seemingly ever-present UP perkiness. Yes, it was different and sometimes inconvenient. But, at the same time, it was comforting to know so many were willing to offer a hand of friendship to a stranger. Like the time Mike was building the firewood shed and one of the seasonal neighbors just walked down the road and came up to him to introduce himself. "They call me the Commander."

What his actual name was, he never said. Just, "the Commander." And while he was just as nice a guy as anyone, he stayed there talking to Mike for almost an hour. And when everything seemed on a tight schedule to get done, losing an hour felt more like losing a half day. Yes, people in Paradise were different; sometimes a little too nosey for Mike's tastes.

But different wasn't necessarily bad. Mike just wasn't used to people being so friendly and accommodating. So, yes, they were different. But it was nice to be surrounded by so many people who seemed genuinely interested in welcoming him and Sarah to Paradise.

Walter wasn't lying. Falls Road had been plowed with one pass heading west and one more heading back east. But that didn't mean the road wasn't covered in snow. It usually took several passes both ways to clear the snow to where it was considered safe. At this point, there was a fairly clear patch of road along the center line with just enough room for two mid-sized vehicles to pass in opposite directions. Mike's truck was *not* a mid-sized vehicle. Thank goodness there was rarely much traffic in the winter when the roads were clear. Mike was unlikely to see any other vehicles on the road at this stage of plowing, but he was one of those better-to-be-prepared types. He kept his speed around thirty-five so, if needed, he could move into the unplowed lane without having to brake. The drive was eerily quiet. He didn't see anyone else on the road. The snowmobile trail that ran next to the road hadn't even been ridden on yet. It was a gray looking day with varying shades of gray and white encompassing his view, with the occasional yellow curve-ahead sign dotting the road.

After what seemed like an hour of driving, it suddenly came into view. Rick was right. There was no way to miss it. There was a post that had to be ten feet high that was painted in safety orange from top to bottom with the placard with *UP-Towne* carved into it. The letters were painted black to contrast against the orange. Mike could see that beacon from 600 yards out. That gave him plenty of time to slow down to make the turn onto Rick's drive.

The first thing Mike noticed was that the road seemed plenty wide enough for him to operate. The second thing was the snow-mobile tracks, which must have been from Rick scouting it out earlier. Those tracks made it a lot easier to see the terrain of the road. Every dip and bump was highlighted by the sled's tracks. This was a good thing, as there were a couple of spots along the drive where Mike might've followed a false road. He figured those must be some kind of access roads to different parts of the property, roads that would end up being much too narrow for a full-sized truck. Hunting access maybe.

Mike took it slow as he plowed the drive. There were several areas where the snow would suddenly change from ten or twelve inches to over twenty. Those change-ups caught him by surprise a couple of times, causing his truck to suddenly slow almost to a stop. To compensate, Mike slowed down even more as he progressed. The snow pushed easily into the carve-outs Rick had made into the woods, and Mike was making good progress. That was, until the big dip. Mike saw the warning flags and thought he was ready. He just wasn't ready for just how big a dip it was. Rick neglected to tell him it wasn't just a dip. It was a place in the road where there used to be a culvert that carried snowmelt down to the river. A couple of years earlier, the snow melted so fast that it caused quite a flood in the lower parts of Chippewa County. That volume of water had washed out the culvert and created a deep gouge in Rick's drive. It wasn't impassable, but it was steep and deep. Hit it too fast, and too fast was almost any speed above a crawl, and the vehicle's front end would bury into the upslope. This could cause some pretty bad damage to the vehicle. When Mike plowed into the dip, he was driving about fifteen miles per hour. The front of his truck suddenly dropped at a steep angle, and his plow bade slammed into the upsloping bank and dug in. The jolt rocked Mike's entire body. He thought he had mangled his blade and truck from the impact. No matter how hard he tried, he was unable to back out of the dip. It felt as if his blade was caught on something. He was right.

When the blade had plowed into to upslope, it dug up a boulder that ended up wedging between the blade and the bumper of Mike's truck. No matter how much he tried to winch the blade out, it wouldn't move. He would have to get out of the truck to see what the problem was. He was aggravated. It was cold and the snow was at least two feet deep in the dip, but this was why he carried a small shovel with him during winter driving or whenever he went off trail. More than once, he had to dig his vehicle out. It didn't take him long to see the problem. The boulder was pinned between the blade and the undercarriage of his truck so tightly that the winch couldn't raise the blade. He tried kicking the boulder free, but it was wedged solid.

"Looks like you found Lucy."

Rick Towne had heard Mike's truck coming down the road and come out to make sure he did okay plowing out the road.

"You must be Rick."

Mike was trying to sound calm, but his first time meeting Rick while being frustrated at his predicament was not the first impression he was going for. Mike's first impression of Rick was that he was quite the mountain of a man. Burly would be the operative word—thickly built but not fat. Rick had to be about six-three and 250 pounds. But it was hard to tell those types of things when the subject is sporting a Grizzly Adams-type beard and wearing heavy winter gear. But Rick was a big man, even without the added padding, and he made the snowmobile he was on look small.

"You got it. Looks like you hit the ditch a little too fast. Everybody does the first time. I heard you comin' and figured I'd head down just in case. It don't look too bad, though. I think we can pry that thing outta there with a tire iron or somethin'."

"That's what I figured, too. I have one in the truck we can use. Lucy, huh? Why'd you name that rock Lucy?"

"Because my ex-wife's name is Lucy, and she was a big, fat pain in my ass. Just like that damn rock. Everything that's a pain in my ass, I call Lucy. Reminds me how lucky I am to be rid of her. Been tryin' to get that thing outta the ditch ever since the culvert washed out. It's in my way for laying a new culvert. When the ditch flooded a couple years ago, it washed out all the gravel and exposed this here boulder. It's gotta weigh five hundred pounds. I've tried ropin' it out, diggin' it out, and I even thought about dynamitin' the bitch. I was gonna rent a backhoe this spring after the melt. You just saved me a few hundred bucks. Thanks. Once we get the damn thing loose, if you could push it off the road, I'd appreciate it."

Better to be lucky than good. Mike made a better first impression than he thought. Might just make it easier to convince Rick to let him have the scale, or whatever it was, tested.

"Sure. Shouldn't be a problem."

It took a little elbow grease to wiggle the blade off the boulder, but between the two of them, they got it loose. Mike pushed "Lucy" where Rick wanted it, and he was back in business.

"Looks like your blade just got a little scratched up. Should be good to go. I'm gonna head back to the house and make some fresh coffee. You've only got a couple hundred yards left. Shouldn't take much time at all."

"Sounds like a plan. I'll see you in a few."

With that, Rick sped off towards his cabin, and Mike went back to plowing. The rest of the drive was pretty straightforward. No more surprises for his plow to face. Fifteen minutes, and he was parked in front of Rick's cabin.

Mike was surprised to see how small Rick's cabin was. It couldn't have been more than 800 square feet. Its minuscule size was amplified by the huge garage or shop that seemed to tower over it. And it wasn't just the size difference in the two buildings that caught Mike's attention. It was the stark distinctions in the styles and quality of the two structures that had Mike doing a double take. Not only as the cabin small; it looked rickety. The roof had a noticeable sag in the center, and the overall appearance of the cabin was one of neglect. Faded and peeling paint, a missing window shutter, a broken step on the front porch... It almost looked abandoned. The garage was beautiful, sided with barn-red steel sheets and two large garage doors trimmed in white. It had to be at least 10,000 square feet. Windows ran along the whole east side of the building, and there was a large lean-to covered area on the north end of the building. It was a nice looking building.

Mike was a little nervous about falling through the steps as he climbed them to the cabin's front door.

"You're at the wrong house."

Mike turned towards Rick's voice and saw him standing in the door of the shop.

"Come on over. I'll open the garage door so you can park out of the weather."

All Mike could think was, *What a relief.* He wasn't exactly comfortable sitting in a cabin with a roof that looked as if it could collapse at any minute. Especially with a foot or more of snow on it.

"Quite the garage, Rick."

"Thanks, but it's much more than just a garage. It's broken up into work zones and living quarters. The first floor is all shop and garage, and the second floor is my home. That small cabin over there hasn't been lived in for ten years or more. Anyway, coffee's ready."

Rick wasn't much for giving tours of his property. There were things in his home that were, well, less than legal. He had an unregistered still. Stills were no longer illegal, as long as the proper fees were paid. Rick wasn't much of a believer in paying the government for letting him make booze for his own personal consumption. He was also quite the gunsmith. There was more than one, legally purchased, firearm that he had modified into a fully automatic weapon. Illegal without the proper permits. Again, Rick didn't accept the government's authority in this area. It wasn't like he was going to use these weapons in a revolt against the government, but after his encounter with the Shoo, he wasn't going to be found wanting for more firepower again. Oh, there were the assorted booby traps and pipe bombs as well, but these too were "just in case" he ever ran into it again.

"Do you like your coffee leaded or unleaded? I'm having mine with some added lead."

With that, Rick poured a significant amount of his homemade hooch into his coffee.

"Leaded sounds good. Thanks."

Mike knew that making Rick comfortable with him was more important than whether he wanted booze in his coffee or not.

"I'm gonna learn ya on somethin'. . This ain't no ordinary whiskey. It's *my* whiskey. I made it, and it's a tad more potent than those weak-ass store-bought brands. So go easy on the sippin'."

Mike had had his share of moonshine during his career. Most of it was crap. Home brew made specifically to get drunk, regardless of quality. This stuff Rick made was special. It was good. Real good. It went down smoothly mixed with his coffee. Too smoothly. Rick was right; he would need to pace himself.

"Wow! Now *that's* good coffee."

"Thanks. But you're not here to sample my coffee. Let's get to it. I don't much like talkin' about that day."

"Okay. Well, I guess just start at the beginning when you, well, you know, saw something."

"Well, my buddy, Pete Harmond, and I were hunting in the Timberlost. It's usually a good spot for deer. But not that year. We got a couple spots in there where we hung some tree stands along some well-traveled game trails. There's always fresh tracks on those trails. But that year, not a one. No wolf tracks, coyote tracks, deer tracks—nothin'. We thought it was pretty weird, so we started walkin' the woods tryin' to cut some tracks. We criss-crossed those woods for two days without seeing one damn track from anything except squirrels and rabbits, and those were few and far between. On the third day of walkin', we came across some deer tracks that were pretty fresh and heading towards the river, so we followed them. There's some private property in there, and those tracks went right smack-dab down the middle of one of those. I knew there wasn't anybody on those during the winter, so we figured it wouldn't be a big deal to keep tracking. Who's gonna know, right?

"Not long after we got onto that property, we came across some kinda tracks we ain't never seen before. Funny lookin' tracks. Big tracks. Bigger 'n any bear tracks I've seen. Plus, these tracks looked like they only had three toes—claw-like toes. Two in front—well, at least what we figured was the front—and one dew-claw lookin' mark in the back part of the track. We didn't know what the hell we were lookin' at, and we figured it was either some kind of injured or mutated bear, or someone was playing a joke. Except, there wouldn't normally be anyone to see those prints, so that would just be stupid.

"Anyway, those tracks went off in a different direction from the deer tracks, and we wanted the deer, so we ignored the weird tracks and kept tracking. We figured those deer were going to angle towards the river and maybe cross over one of the frozen sections. If they made the river, we'd probably lose them, so we decided to try and cut them off. Most deer head pretty much one way in the morning, and another way towards evening as they go to their bedding areas. So we found a trail that might put us in position to get ahead of 'em before it got too dark to shoot.

"As we got closer to the river, I got to tell ya', the woods was quiet. And I mean *dead* quiet. Made the hairs on the back of my neck stand up. I looked over at Pete, but he was just staring straight ahead, not moving. He had that fear look on his face. I turned to look where he was starin', and that's when we saw it. It just kinda appeared in the trail about thirty yards in front of us. It was *huge*. It filled the whole trail, and its head was brushing the tree branches about eight feet or more off the ground.

"It was getting dark, especially in the woods, so I flashed my flashlight on it to see it better. Its eyes shone green. Most eye shine is yellowish, so that was weird. We ain't never seen anything like this thing. Kinda looked like a dragon. But its head was more like a big cat, like a cougar or somethin'. It was covered with some kinda scales, and it had spikes all along its back, and the tail had three spikes on it. It even had horns on its head. We froze for a second, but Pete suddenly took aim with his rifle and shot it.

"He shot it three times. Nothin'. The damn thing turned to us and looked like it might come at us, so I started shootin', too. It seemed to flinch and took off towards the river. We just stood there for a while, listening to it running through the woods. Even after there wasn't any more sounds of that thing, me and Pete just stood there, staring down that trail, for about ten minutes.

"Then Pete says, 'We better reload. Just in case it comes back.' I remember thinkin' *What for? Didn't look like we hurt it.* But we reloaded just the same. We went over to where it was standin' in the trail, and there they were. Those same damn weird footprints, and one more thing. One of its scales. One of us musta' shot if off, 'cause there was what looked like some damage to it. Like a dent or somethin'. I picked that thing up and put it in my pack. Hell, I knew nobody'd believe me if I didn't have anything to show for it.

"Pete and I figured that had to be the thing my dad said he'd seen once. But Dad drank a bit, and nobody believed his story. Figured it was just some drunk figment of his imagination. Anyways, it was gettin' too dark to shoot, and we were pretty much ready to get the hell outta there anyway. So we high-tailed it back to the four-wheelers and got our asses back here. We sat up all night tryin' to figure out just what we saw. That was the only time either of us saw it or its tracks. Not that we want to see it again, but I always look for it when I'm in the woods. That's about it. Answer your questions?"

"Yeah, pretty much. I do have a couple of questions, though. You said the river had some frozen sections?"

"Yep. There's a bunch of shallow areas that freeze solid. You can even drive your snowmobile on 'em, and if it's been real cold, I've seen trucks out on it. Wouldn't trust that though. Moving water is unpredictable."

"Well, that holds true to what I've been told about it using ice as cover. A way to move unseen. Did you notice anything else? A smell maybe?"

"Yeah. There was a pretty strong fishy smell. Not like dead fish. More like a fresh fish smell. You know, like when you catch a fish and you can smell it. Like that."

"Did you happen to take any pictures of the prints or anything?"

"I think Pete did. But he don't talk about this with anyone. And I mean *anyone*. I don't even know if he saved those or not. My guess is no."

"You said you picked up what looked like a scale. Do you still have it?"

"Yep. I keep it put away, though."

"Do you think I could see it?"

"I guess so. I'll be right back."

Mike sat there drinking his "leaded coffee" and looking over the decor of Rick's place. It was definitely a man's home. There had to be fifteen or so deer mounts on the walls, along with metal signs from oil companies, Coke, and several beer companies. And these weren't reproductions of signs. These looked original, rust spots and all. It was quite the collection. The garage was fully stocked but clean. It even had a car lift.

Next to Mikes truck was a fully restored 1979 Ford F-150 extended-cab four-by-four. It was immaculate, painted black with all the original chrome trim. It sat on a four-inch lift and huge mud tires, with custom rims that had a black teardrop design. It didn't appear to be driven much. Next to that, on the other side of the truck, were two off-road vehicles. One was a Polaris Razor, the kind for running the trails at high speed. The other was a more utilitarian side-by-side that looked to be a Polaris as well. It had a deer stand in its bed, and the whole thing was pretty muddy, like it had been out recently. The rest was what one would expect. Tool boxes, tools, shop lights, the whole works. Everything had a place, and everything was in its place. Rick was very neat when it came to his shop. Mike couldn't say if the living quarters of Rick's place was kept the same. Rick didn't invite him in to that world.

It was a good ten or fifteen minutes before Rick returned. Mike was starting to think he might have changed his mind.

"Got it. I forgot I had moved the box it was in last year."

"I was wondering what happened to you. As big as this place is, I was thinking even you might get lost."

"Well, I may not get lost, but I do lose stuff occasionally. I have a habit of moving things around from time to time. Keeps things fresh. Anyway, here it is."

Rick was holding an old cigar box, not the cardboard type that most people are familiar with, but an old wooden cigar box. Mike thought it was appropriate, given the collection of old signs and memorabilia Rick had. This thing must have been special for Rick to keep it in such a unique box. Getting permission to have it tested might be more difficult than Mike thought.

"Wow. That's quite the container. Must not want anything to happen to it, huh?"

"I guess. Mostly, it's just how I keep track of what's in a box without having to open it. You see, this cigar box was made in China and has a dragon inlay on it. The thing we saw in the Timberlost reminded me of a dragon, so I put it in here. That's my little system."

"Makes sense. Let's have a look."

Rick opened the box and, less than gingerly, removed the item and tossed it to Mike. Mike wasn't ready for that and almost didn't catch it.

"Oh, shit! Well, that caught me off guard."

"You can't hurt this thing. I've dropped it, hit it with a hammer, and even put it in a vice to try and break it. It took two or three shots from my 6.5mm Creedmoor to even put that dent or chip in it. I load my own shells, and I can tell you, they weren't no light loads. I believe you hit 'em hard, and they don't go very far after. I don't think they even got past this thing's armor. We didn't find one single drop of blood. Just this."

Mike noticed the "scale," for lack of a better term, felt heavy. It was about six inches long, four inches wide, and almost half an inch thick. He found it hard to believe that the bullets didn't do more damage to it. At the yardage Rick said he shot from, the bullet was traveling at full velocity. Bullets do slow down over distances, but not within thirty or forty yards. It had an iridescence, much like a fish scale. This helped camouflage fish in different light and water conditions, and Mike felt this might be the case with the Shoo as well.

"Feels heavy for its size."

"Yeah, I thought the same thing. I ain't never seen anything like it."

"Have you ever shown this to anyone else? Like maybe, someone in the scientific field? You know, at the University of Michigan or Lake Superior College?"

"No. I don't trust too many folks. It took a lot of convincing from my sister and Julie to let you come out. You being a retired cop made me feel better about it. I'm afraid, if it is something special, I may never see it again."

"Yeah, I get that. But I've got a contact at the University of Idaho's forensics department. I've known this guy for over twenty years, and he's a stand-up kinda guy. If you'd let me, I could call him and see if he could take a look at this. He might be able to give us an idea of what we may be dealing with. He's got all kinds of tech that can determine what something is made of, any unique properties, even how old something is. Could be useful information in case we run into this thing again. I'm sure if I asked him to keep whatever he finds under his hat, and to return it when he's completed his tests, he would."

"I'm not sure I want to do that. I mean, sending this thing all the way out west... I don't understand why it can't be tested here."

"Well, if you knew anyone who could test this, and who you trusted, wouldn't you have had it looked at already? At least we have a contact that I know we can trust to do the right thing. Maybe I could take a pic and shoot it to him. See if he has any ideas on it before you say yes or no. What do you think about that?"

"I'd be good with that."

"Let me give him a call, before we send it—give him a heads up."

Mike kept all his contacts from his years in law enforcement saved on his phone. Never know when one of those contacts could come in handy, like now. Mike's contact, William "Bill" Young, had been Mike's go-to guy for some of his most difficult cases, and he was the person Mike had sent his supposed Bigfoot pics to while investigating a prowler call in Idaho.

"Is my phone right? Could this actually be Mike Perkins? I thought you fell into Lake Superior or something. How in the hell are you guys?"

"We're good. Busy. But good. Sorry I haven't called you since we moved. You just can't believe how crazy it's been ever since we got here. And, it's gotten just a little bit crazier, so, of course, I thought of you."

"What you got going on, Mike? Not another Bigfoot problem is it? I still look over those pictures every once in a while just to see if I pick up anything I might've missed. Especially when we get new tech I think might help."

"Well. It's not a Bigfoot this time. It might just be even stranger than that. The difference this time is there's some actual physical evidence. I'd like to send you some pics and see what you think of it."

"I'd be happy to. But I can only do so much without being able to properly test it."

"I understand. Maybe I can get it to you at some later date. But this *has to* be kept on the down low. This is not my artifact, and the person who obtained it was a first-hand witness to what this thing belonged to. And he doesn't want a lot of attention. There is a more personal reason for my interest in this. Let me fill you in."

Mike sent several pictures with a tape measure to give Bill an idea of its size, then he gave Bill a quick synopsis of the situation so he would have an idea of what Mike was dealing with. This was the first time Rick had heard the whole story of the Bromley disappearance and the input from Dave Bromley. It put a different perspective to what Mike was doing.

"Wow, Mike. That's pretty strange. My first impression is that it looks like a fish scale, only much, much bigger. If this came from a fish, it would have to be the size of a bus, or maybe bigger. I've never heard of anything like this, especially something like this being on land. Are you sure this isn't a fossil or something like that? Maybe manufactured?"

"It's not a fossil, and I don't think it's manufactured. But that's your area of expertise."

"Well, I can tell you it looks authentic, from what I can see. You say it came off some kind of dragon or something like that?"

"According to the guy who shot it and recovered the item, that's what it reminded him of. A dragon. From everything I can find out about the Mishipeshu, it fits the description."

"The Mishi-*what*?"

"The Mishipeshu, or Shoo, as some locals call it. According to the Native folklore around here, it's supposed to be some kind of protector of the lake. Several people have said they've seen it or its tracks. And there are a lot, and I mean *a lot*, of people that go missing without a trace in the Upper Peninsula. More than what the average should be. And from what I've found out, mostly in the winter, after the ice forms along the lakeshore. Listen, I know this sounds nuts. But there is some kind of unexplained phenomenon happening up here. And it all seems linked to this Shoo thing."

"Do you think I could get ahold of that artifact? I'd love to run some tests on it. If it did come from an animal of some kind, there might be a chance to pull some DNA out of it. I could also determine whether it came from a reptile, mammal, or some kind of fish, based on its structure. There's all kinds of tests we could do to try and nail it down. But I can't test it if I can't hold it."

"What if you came out here? Is there a way you could run your tests in a facility in Michigan? I'm just not sure the owner of the artifact is going to let it out of his sight."

"I understand the concern there. It's hard to find people to trust anymore. Everyone wants to get famous for some new discovery that'll make them rich. Let me make some inquiries, and I'll try to get back to you in a day or two. Hell, I'm due for a vacation, and the Upper Peninsula of Michigan might just be the place to be. Especially this time of year."

"Yeah, right. The snow's coming, and in a few weeks, it may be hard to get a flight into out tiny little airport. But I'll look forward to your call, and, in the meantime, I'll try to convince the owner to let you test it. Talk to you later."

"I intentionally put him on speaker so you could hear everything we said. But you heard him. It needs to be tested. Would you be willing to have it tested out here? Maybe in the Soo or someplace close?"

"Yeah, I'd be open to that. But I'm going to be there every step of the way. I ain't lettin' that thing outta my sight."

Mike felt that even with Rick's stipulations, agreeing to let him have someone test the scale was a huge success. His fascination with getting some answers to this mystery was multi-faceted. First, was this thing even real? Was the scale an actual artifact from an unknown creature, or was it a fake? Second, if it was real, what is it, where'd it come from, and where does it go after winter? And third, again, assuming it is real, was there a way to stop it in case it made another appearance at his cabin? With what he had found out about the Shoo, it might have been hunting humans for food for who knows how long. Maybe it's been around for thousands of years. Maybe it's just a man-made monstrosity created from hazardous waste or radioactive byproducts, and it's only been around for some decades. If the first theory proved true, it would be a scientific phenomenon that would need to be studied to know its true origins and biology. If the second were the case, it was an abomination and should be destroyed. In either case, Mike's focus would be to protect his family and, by extension, his community.

"Another coffee?"

"No, thanks. I've got to drive, you know, and the lead in the coffee might not be too good for that."

During this whole time, Rick hadn't so much as hinted he knew how to smile, but Mike's comment made him chuckle. As Mike was thanking him for the coffee and his time, his phone rang. It was Bill Young.

"That didn't take long. Holy crap, what's it been? Like, ten minutes? Just to let you know, I've got you on speaker. I've got the owner of the item right here. I want him to hear what you've got to say. Is that okay?"

"Yeah, no problem. Well, you said the weather's getting dicey, so I wanted to get right on it. Turns out, I met a guy a couple years ago at one of our recertification events for one of the pieces of equipment we use. People from all over the country were there, including Matt Wallace. At the time, he was fresh outta college and just getting his feet wet. Anyway, he was getting certified for his position he had just been hired for at the College of Science and Geology at Superior State University, up in Sault Saint Marie. That's pretty close to you, right?"

"Yeah. It's practically in our backyard. It's only about forty-five miles from us."

"Good deal. I gave Matt a call, and he's available. He says there's not much going on in his department this time of year. I didn't give him too much info, other than there was an unknown artifact we would like his help in identifying. His forte is more in the geological arena, but he has the right equipment and does know a bit about the local flora and fauna, so to speak. So we can tell if this thing you have is geological or biological, for sure. Beyond that, the college's resources would be available to us. So, if your contact is willing, I'll get set up with Matt and book a flight."

"That sounds great. Hang on a sec. Let me see if that is good with the owner. Well, what do you think?"

Rick nodded his non-verbal okay.

"Looks like a plan, Bill. Just one thing. My contact won't let us touch it unless he's there the whole time. Any problem with that?"

"Shouldn't be an issue. He's just another researcher, as far as I'm concerned. I'll let you know the details on timing as soon as I can. Talk to you soon."

"Okay, Rick. As soon as I hear from Bill, I'll let you know. And, if I know Bill, it'll probably be in the next week or two. When he gets everything set for the tests, I'll come pick you up, and we'll go together. That way, if we get more snow, I can dig your road out again."

Mike knew Rick could change his mind at any time about letting them test his item, so he wanted to maintain as much control over the situation as he could. He also knew that Rick's snowplowing rig was broken, so reminding Rick he could plow his road for him gave him an extra edge to make sure Rick would stay engaged.

"Okay. I'll be waitin' for your call. Guess we're gonna find out just what this thing is, huh?"

"I hope so. It's a good thing you got a shot off at it so there'd be some hard evidence to look at. Without that, this would just all be some good campfire story. Still is, I guess."

And on that note, Mike left Rick's and headed home. Between getting up so early and Rick's leaded coffee, a good nap would be just the ticket. Good thing he didn't live too far away; he was feeling pretty worn.

7

ARRIVAL

It had only been a few days since Mike and Bill had spoken on the phone, but here he was, landing at Chippewa International Airport. For an airport with *international* in its name, it wasn't much of a destination for people from around the world. It was more for locals and Canadians that lived in the Canadian half of Sault Saint Marie. But, catering to Canadians made it international. There were no covered gangways or multiple gate locations. There was the tarmac and one gate, which was more like a big door. Only one airline flew out of there, and there were only two passenger flights a day on average. Mostly commercial, air taxi, and military flights operated out of the airport, and those flights were subject to the winter weather. The planes that flew in were turbo props. Any plane large enough to handle the harsher weather would need a longer runway. So, high winds, snow, or both often delayed flights. Fortunately, today was calm, and Bill Young landed without a hitch.

Mike and Rick were there to pick him up, and Bill would have an opportunity to examine the scale at his hotel before the serious tests the next day. As Rick had said, he wasn't going to let his find leave his sight.

"Welcome to the UP, Bill."

"Whew, what a flight. Long, but other than that, pretty good. You were right. This is probably the smallest international airport I've ever seen."

Until now, Bill didn't even know Rick's name. He only knew that the owner of the artifact would be accompanying them during the tests. Rick didn't want anyone. Truth be told, he hadn't wanted anyone knowing who he was ahead of time, because he wasn't sure he'd actually go through with the tests and didn't want anyone pestering him about it. Having Mike Perkins know was bad enough. It wasn't just the stigma of being a person who claims to have seen a monster. He could handle that. It was more because he lived a secluded life. He only had one or two people he called friends and rarely interacted with others outside that small circle. Even his family was just him and his sister. Both parents had passed, and there weren't any other siblings. Small circle, simple life, and the freedom to not care what others thought. He wanted to keep it that way, but now things were becoming a little more intertwined than he liked. And here was another person he didn't know entering his life to examine the one thing he had kept to himself for almost two years. These situations made him feel a little uncomfortable.

"Bill, I want you to meet Rick Towne. Rick is the one who owns the artifact."

Mike had called Bill shortly after his call at Rick's cabin to give him a heads up on Rick's reluctance. Mike wanted him to be aware Rick might change his mind, and to be prepared to cancel or alter his travel plans, so Bill understood to tread lightly and try not to spook him off.

"Great to meet you, Rick. I just want to thank you for letting us have a look at the item. I think it's important you be part of this. After all, you discovered it, and you should know exactly what you have as soon as we find out ourselves. From what I've seen of it, it's very unusual."

Important to find out what he has? Rick already knew what he had. A scale off a monster. Rick didn't really care about what kind of monster it was; he just wanted to know how to kill it in case he ever came across it again. And if doing these tests showed some kind of weakness in its armor, then test it they would.

"Nice to meet you, too."

Rick was not a big conversationalist. The fewer the words, the better—less chance of saying the wrong thing.

"The hotel's just down the road from the college, only about five minutes, but it's about an hour from here, and I'm guessing you're ready to get there. It is close to rush hour, so the roads will be busier than normal. We may have six or seven vehicles on the road with us instead of the usual, two or three."

"Judging by the size of the airport, I would've thought we'd be all backed up."

Mike and Bill were from more populated cities than Sault Ste. Marie. Even the outlying towns were much larger than the Soo. Plus, it was the beginning of winter, when traffic drops to almost non-existent on a lot of the roads.

The conversation on the drive to the hotel was benign. Bill talked about how things had changed in Idaho since the pandemic. States like California, Washington, and Oregon had strict pandemic rules, and many residents of those states got fed up and moved to states like Idaho, where mandates were pretty much non-existent. Housing prices, populations, and poor attitudes were all on the rise. Mike felt they got out just in time. He talked about house projects and plans, and Rick kept silent. The elephant in the room, the scale, wasn't even eluded to. But Rick knew that when they got to the hotel, the conversation would be all about his "trophy."

Bill started feeling a little uncomfortable with Rick being left out of the conversation, so he thought a little ice-breaker might be good.

"So, Rick, how long have you lived in the Upper Peninsula?"

Rick wasn't one to talk about himself, so his answers were always one or two words. It wasn't that he was an ass or anything. He just wasn't much for what he considered useless talk.

"About fifteen years."

"Really? I had the impression you were raised there or something. What brought you there?"

"Privacy."

"Well, according to what Mike's told me about Paradise, you certainly have plenty of that."

Bill could sense Rick's reluctance to talk. Maybe a change of subject would open him up.

"Looking at all these woods we're passing, I'm guessing the hunting's pretty good. Am I right?"

"It's better downstate. More farmland. Better food. Not so many wolves."

"There's a wolf problem up here? I guess I never thought about wolves living in Michigan. I always picture them in the Rockies or Alaska. You know, places like that."

"Well, these wolves ain't here naturally. The government introduced them a few years back. Since then, there ain't nearly as many deer or moose. Used to see moose all the damn time. Not no more. Wolves done hunted them out of most areas. Most of the moose in the UP are on Island Royale out in Lake Superior. No wolves there. Seems like every time the government gets involved, things go screwy."

Bill had touched on a nerve. Rick was *not* a fan of government intervention in *anything*. His thinking on the wolf issue was simple. Wolves got hunted out. Man replaced the wolf as the predator species that would keep the deer and other game animals under control. No need for wolves. They not only depopulated the wildlife, but also preyed on livestock, family pets, and, according to some, humans. There was no evidence of the latter, but people like Rick figured it was just a matter of time. But the one trait most hated about the wolves was that they seemed to occasionally kill for sport and not for food. Several instances of mass killings by wolves had been documented where none of the kills were eaten. No one really knows why the wolves did that. The best guess was adults in the pack teaching the junior members how to hunt and kill. In any case, the results were less wildlife. More importantly, the subject gave Bill and Rick something in common, something to build trust with.

"I know about wolf reintroduction programs. We have the same problem in Idaho. Idaho used to have a sizable wolf population before they were hunted out, and most Idahoans didn't miss them. But some good intentioned government wildlife folks—and I say that with some reservation—got it in their heads to reintroduce the wolves. They reasoned that with decreasing numbers of hunters from year to year, that the deer and elk populations would explode, and if they brought in wolves, they would keep the animals in check. By the time the deer and elk numbers reached their predicted numbers, they could have a viable wolf population all ready to step in.

"Problem was, they introduced gray wolves, not timber wolves. Gray wolves are a much larger and more aggressive species. Not only that, they multiplied like crazy and migrated out of the experimental area and formed multiple packs throughout North Idaho. Game animals have seen dramatic decreases in their numbers. I've seen this first hand. Our department was called in to look at several of these mass wolf kills. They wanted us to test the carcasses of some of the kills to try and determine if the wolves had rabies or some other malady that would cause them to kill so many elk and deer and not eat them.

"We found nothing to indicate that there was anything wrong with them. In one incident, eight elk were killed and left untouched. Elk and deer were one thing, but the moose population had been starting to make serious progress in re-establishing their numbers, and the wolves put an end to that. Idaho had a limited, by draw, moose hunting tag. But now, those tags are all but gone. If they had introduced timber wolves, the moose could've dealt with those. But these grays are so much larger and more aggressive, they really don't stand a chance. There is limited ability to hunt wolves, but the wolf lobby is strong and politicians being politicians... Well, you know how that's gonna end. You'd think an educated wildlife biologist or conservation officer would've realized that introducing an apex predator like the gray wolf into an environment where they could come in contact with humans and domestic livestock would be a bad idea. Anyway, just wanted you to know I totally understand your position on this."

Bill's words seemed to comfort Rick about him being involved, so he listened intently to everything Bill said, and it seemed to him that Bill might just be okay.

Mike listened, too. Like Bill, he had seen the wolf problem up close and had seen the game numbers decrease in his hunting areas. There were many times he'd hunted an area and come across wolf tracks. They were everywhere. Just about every county in North Idaho had wolf complaints. But Mike also knew what Bill was doing; he was building trust with Rick, and Mike could see a slight shift in Rick's body language that showed he was getting more comfortable with what they were getting ready to do.

The conversation progressed along those lines for the rest of the drive. The whole government-should-stay-out-of-all-things-unrelated-to-their-actual-duties mantra. All three men were pretty much in agreement on this subject. Bureaucracy always led to overreach, over-regulation, and over-taxation. The more levels involved, the less effective. The idea of a government of the people, by the people, and for the people had become a government of the lobbyists, by the lobbyists, for the lobbyists. But here, in this vehicle, were three individuals that were going to attempt to handle an issue without government assistance. Eliminate unnecessary measures and try to find answers and possibly solutions to a potential threat. Even the testing would be conducted without government intervention. After all, not one local government agency that had been contacted about this would confirm there was a problem and all were reluctant to get involved. This would be solved by people, not government. Rick was feeling more and more that he might just be among kindred spirits.

"Well, Rick, you wanna show Bill the item?"

After Bill checked in to his hotel, they all went to his room to view Rick's "trophy" and hear the story of how he got it. Rick had put the box containing the scale into his backpack for the trip to the Soo so it would be out of sight and less likely to attract attention.

Bill was having a hard time not showing how excited he was to see it for himself; it was all he'd been thinking about ever since Mike told him about it. What was it really? Where did it come from? What kind of animal did it come from? Could this be from a thought-to-be-extinct animal? So many questions. So many possibilities.

Mike was not of the same mindset as Bill. He just wanted to know if this creature was real, and how to defend his family against it if it was.

Rick took the box out of his backpack and placed it on the room's small dining table. Bill would have to wait just a little longer to examine the item in the box. Rick recounted the story of the deer hunt in the Timberlost that led up to the encounter with the Shoo.

As anxious as Bill was to look at the item, he was equally interested in the encounter itself. It might hint at what Rick and his hunting partner, Pete, actually saw.

As Rick came to the end of his story, he reached for the cigar box on the table, looking at it as if he might change his mind, before handing the box to Bill.

"After me and Pete shot this thing and it took off, this is what we found."

Bill opened the box with great care, making sure Rick noticed how he respected this moment. The first thing Bill noticed about the item was that it really did look like a scale of some kind, but much thicker, and it was heavier than he imagined. Leaving it in the box, he rubbed his fingers across its surface to get an idea of texture. It was smooth, but with small, round, evenly distributed humps across it. Then he gingerly took it out and held it up to the light. It was somewhat translucent. He put the item up to his nose and sniffed.

"Still has a distinct fishy smell. This is amazing. I have to say, this is definitely off of a living creature of some kind. But I've never seen or even heard of such a thing. I mean, if this is a scale, it's awful thick. Just with the naked eye, I can see that it's layered. It's not just a scale. It's several—maybe hundreds of scales fused into one. That would make this one hell of an armor-plated animal."

"Tell me about it. Me and Pete both unloaded our rifles on it, and all we managed to do was knock this off it. You can see a small chip out of it where one of our bullets hit it."

"Yes, I see that. Not much of a chip for being so close. I have to admit, I mainly made this trip out of curiosity and respect for Mike's opinion. I never really thought this would be anything other than a hoax or misidentification of something else. But I think you have an unknown creature living and lurking in the waters of Lake Superior."

Mike had been pretty quiet during this time, listening to Rick's story, again, and trying to see if it changed at all. It didn't.

"Well, I wouldn't say this thing is totally unknown. Apparently, lots of people have seen it, and even officials with the Brimley police department eluded to it. It's called the Mishipeshu by local Natives. It's supposed to be some sort of lake protector. But some of the locals just call it the Shoo. And I've got to tell you, the more I looked into this thing, the more it looked like there was something out there. Even before I heard about Rick's story. If you really dig into this, it's kinda spooky. There are lots of people that go missing every year in the UP, and most of those are during the winter, the very time this thing is supposed to be prowling around. If you plot the areas where these people disappeared, most of them are on or near the lake and the rivers that feed into it. It really looks like we have an apex predator that has gotten a taste for human flesh. Now we need to know how to deal with it."

"You know, there is a large Native population in the UP that wouldn't support any efforts to kill this thing. One of the reasons I didn't want any attention thrown on me was because of that. I don't need a bunch of Natives parading up and down my property, claiming I harmed their great lake protector. They take these things kinda seriously. You got to keep in mind, the Shu is part of their spirit culture, their core beliefs. They think this thing only goes after you if you're violating or disrespecting the lake or something. If it comes at you, you deserved it, is how they feel. Remember, even me and Pete were basically trespassing on that property where we came across it. Maybe there's some truth to the stories. I don't know. But I'll tell you one thing. I ain't never gonna break the rules like that again. Just in case."

Mike hadn't considered that there might be ramifications from the Native cultures if they killed the Shoo. His only concern was protecting his family.

"Well, if it comes down to protecting me and mine or pissing off some Natives, I guess I'm pissing off some Natives. Hopefully, I'll never have to deal with it, and it'll just be something we talk about around a fire with some beers."

Deep down, Mike had a feeling it would be more than that. While doing his research into all the missing person reports, he had noticed a pattern. Initially, the largest percentage of those who went missing were in more remote areas, where it was easy to conclude that they had succumbed to some sort of accident like falling through the ice, or maybe they were injured and died of exposure and were scavenged by all the hungry creatures of the forest, never to be seen again. But, over the last couple of years, the reports showed that fewer cases were in those remote areas and were increasingly coming from more populated areas. Even unexplained disappearances from town, or, as with Stan Bromley, some went missing when they were supposed to be at home. Mike thought maybe this thing had discovered it was easier to hunt among the humans, and not waste energy covering vast amounts of remote terrain only to have to drag its kill over those distances to its deepwater lair. Again, that took a lot of energy. After all, if Bromley was a victim of the Shoo, all it had to do was climb out of the lake, kill Bromley, and drop right back into the lake. This creature might be losing its cautious nature around humans, becoming more and more aggressive in its pursuit of prey. If Mike was right, chances were becoming more favorable for an encounter, and he needed to be prepared.

"I know one thing about this, uh—I'm going to call it what it looks like—scale. It definitely looks like some kind of scale. But nothing like I've ever seen. There are several types of scales in the animal world, each serving a particular purpose. But this scale looks like it's some kind of hybrid. It has a layered pattern and seems to change from a typical fish-like scale and becomes more rigid, like the armor of scaled mammals like armadillos. But there also seems to be rubbery or cushioned connective material. Seeing that the damage from being shot is limited to the upper scale layer, and not the other two layers, I would say those two layers acted as a bullet stopper. The spongy center absorbs the shock and flattens out the bullet, then the armor layer stops it cold. Looks like the best bullet proof vest ever."

Bill's intellectual excitement was showing through. In his hands, he held an anomaly. Something never seen before by human eyes. A part of a creature few people had ever even heard if, let alone have a piece of. It shouldn't exist, yet here was physical evidence that it might just be a real living, breathing animal. His mind raced with the possibilities. Was this a brand new species, or had it been around for ages, hiding in the depths of Lake Superior? What were the ramifications if they were to prove its existence? What would it do to the scientific community or his career? Yes, the thought of how this discovery might affect him personally had crossed his mind. This could put him in the crazy cryptozoology camp, or in with an elite league of scientists. Either way, he was in.

Here they were, three men with three different reasons for being here. One who wanted to prove he wasn't crazy. One who needed to know how to kill or repel it, if it was real. And one who wanted to prove it was real, for scientific purposes. All had come together under the umbrella of discovery to work as a unit toward varying ends. Their missions could all be accomplished by the next day's endeavor.

Day one, the meet and greet, was over. Day two would begin at 8:00 in the morning at Superior State's biology lab with Professor Matt Wallace. It would prove to be an historic, and problematic, day.

8

THE BIG DAY

No one got much sleep that night. Too many thoughts raced through each man's head, all of them on different tracts. But one theme was common in each of their thought trains. What if...? The possibilities were almost endless. Mike couldn't help but think of one of his police academy instructors saying, "I hate what-if questions. You can what-if something to death." Those words had stuck in Mike's head almost as firmly as one of his academy classmate's response: "Well, what if it's a good question?" Needless to say, that cadet didn't last long. Funny how long-lost memories rush to the forefront at a moment's notice.

Bill was waiting in the lobby when Mike and Rick arrived to pick him up. He didn't want to show it, but it was difficult to contain his excitement and eagerness to get to the university. Saying he'd gotten up would be inaccurate; he'd been out of bed since 4:30 in the morning—his thoughts had kept him from sleeping, too. He decided the best use of his time would be to go online and do as much research on the Mishipeshu as he could. Any information he might find could help determine its origins and, possibly, help guide the team in their testing of Rick's scale. There wasn't much. Most of the information he found was based on tribal lore or secondhand accounts. There didn't seem to be a consensus on its traits. All agreed that it was some kind of water panther or water lynx, but there was much disagreement on whether it was a protector or a destroyer. It probably depended on one's point of view. If someone was prone to think the lake and surrounding areas were to be left alone or undeveloped, then it might be considered a protector. If someone was developing the lakeshore and rivers and fell victim to it, it would probably be thought of as evil. Perspective.

One thing Bill did find interesting was the mention of a possible underwater lake *under* Lake Superior. It was called Lake Inferior. It was supposedly discovered by a French explorer in the 1600s who dubbed it Lake of Hell. Every account of Lake Inferior was a mix of legend and fact. It made for a confusing issue, but Bill thought, *What if the underwater lake is real?* It might explain how the creature could stay hidden for vast periods of time. For now, he would keep that thought to himself and focus on the facts first. There was already one myth to solve; two might send the research out on a tangent they didn't need to address at this point.

"Well, are you guys ready to possibly make history?"

Mike and Rick could tell Bill was eager to get started, so Mike decided to string him along for a bit.

"Sure, but Rick and I haven't had breakfast yet. I thought we could get something to eat first. I saw a nice little place just on the other side of town when we came in. Lots of cars outside, so it must be a good place to eat."

Rick had already eaten. He had been ready to go since 5:30 in the morning. Always was. He was an early-to-bed-early-to-rise kind of guy. So when Mike suggested they go eat, he was a little confused. It took him a minute to put it together that Mike was messing with his friend.

"Breakfast? Oh. Yeah. Uh, sounds great. I could eat."

Rick's attempt to keep Bill's anticipation picqued was a little awkward. But, as Rick was not prone to long, drawn out, conversations, Bill didn't catch on.

"Breakfast? I thought you guys would've eaten already. I ate first thing. I've already called over to Matt to let him know we would be there by eight or so. It's already seven-thirty. I don't want to get off on the wrong foot on this thing. Maybe just grab something from the breakfast buffet here in the lobby. You know, get it to go."

"I don't know, Bill. I was kinda looking forward to some eggs Benedict, and maybe some scones. Or maybe some of that French toast with the strawberries on top. A real stick-to-your-ribs kinda breakfast."

Bill stared at Mike with one of those blank what-the-hell-are-you-talkin'-about? stares. That's when Mike couldn't keep from laughing. Bill knew then that he was being played.

"Holy shit, you guys. You really had me goin'. Is it that easy to see I'm chompin' at the bit to get over to LSSU's labs and poke around on this thing?"

"Yes. Yes, it is."

Mike's lighthearted tone even had the ever-stoic Rick smiling. Truth was that neither Mike nor Rick got much sleep over thinking about today. So many questions. So many possibilities.

"Well, let's get this show on the road and see where it takes us."

With Bill's prodding, they headed out of the hotel lobby and made their way to the LSSU campus and the School of Biological Sciences.

Lake Superior State University is a modest campus to look at. Its campus spans only 115 acres. Compared to the thousand-plus acres many other universities have to house their centers of learning, LSSU is tiny. Serving as Fort Brady from 1894 until 1944, it was established as a university in 1946 to serve the needs of returning World War II veterans. Originally, LSSU was attached to the Michigan Technological College and, eventually, became its own entity in 1987, when it received university status. There are no grand halls of learning, no marble statues erected to honor the achievements of past attendees, and no football team. The buildings have the look of an old federal-style military base. They do have a pretty good division-two basketball team and some fun traditions, like the annual snowman burning in March, which is done to mark the end of winter, and the snowmobile race in February on campus, which draws a huge crowd every year.

What LSSU lacks in glorious adornments, it more than makes up for in academics. It's mostly known as a selective university specializing in fishing and fishery management, as well as other biological sciences. Being so close to Lake Superior and the St. Mary's River is the perfect setting for these studies. The biology labs have some of the country's best equipment for virtually any type of testing one should need, including FTIR spectrometers, Q-PCR thermocyclers, and several others. The spectrometers identify chemical bonds within a molecule by studying how the infrared spectrum is absorbed in a sample. This could be a sample in solid, liquid, or gas form. But the thermocycler can analyze DNA , as well as detect viruses, bacteria, and rare targets. Other technology at LSSU can detect contaminants, trace elements that may be present, and what properties or chemical strands may be in a sample. Coupled with the forensic science lab, LSSU's equipment can determine the age of a sample, where it may have come from, its chemical and elemental makeup, and its biological identity through its DNA—if there is a sample to compare it to.

After checking in with administration and obtaining their visitors passes, the three made their way across campus to Crawford Hall and up to the third floor, where the biology and other science labs were housed. Crawford Hall is one of the largest buildings on campus, and a large addition was added to accommodate the ever-growing need for environmental and biological sciences.

Matt Wallace was waiting for them when they got out of the elevator. Matt wasn't what Mike had pictured. He imagined Matt as a skinny, nerdy type with glasses too big for his face and wrinkled clothes. Matt was the opposite. He looked more like a Hollywood star than a college professor. Matt was six-foot-three, well built, and his clothes were impeccable. He did wear glasses, but they suited his features just right.

"Bill! Great to see you again. Welcome to my world."

"Good to see you too, Matt. Thanks for lettin' us come in for this on such short notice."

"No problem. Winter's setting in, and things get a little slow then, so the timing couldn't be better."

"This is Mike Perkins, and this gentleman here is Rick Towne. Rick's the one who owns the artifact."

"Wow! It's a pleasure to meet you. Let's step into my office where we'll have a little more privacy. I haven't said anything to anybody about what your visit is about, and I don't need anyone listening in on the details. If what you have is truly what you think, it's *big*."

Not the reaction any of the three men expected. Each one had thought, to different degrees, that Matt would show mild curiosity or a detached scientific interest in the item. But he seemed genuinely excited.

"I have to tell you guys, I've heard stories about the Mishipeshu, or water panther, ever since I've been here. You see, we do a lot of work with the Department of Inland Fisheries, the Department of Natural Resources, as well as Native fisheries. One of our missions in this department is to help maximize fish harvests, help keep a healthy fish population, both native and stocked species, and identify any threats, such as invasive species and predators. We have had many—I'm talking over a hundred— requests for help in identifying what may be damaging the Native gill nets that are used for whitefish, and those are only allowed to be used by indigenous fishermen, and even a few inquiries from the government fisheries who have lost complete harvests used for stocking some of the smaller lakes and streams. We've looked at the usual suspects. Bears, large cats, raccoons—you know, the typical culprits. But none of those could be responsible for the vast amount of fish lost, or the damage to the nets. After all, the nets are set well offshore and in pretty deep water. I don't know of any one of those going out there and diving that deep. The one suggestion, and it only comes from some of the elder indigenous fisherman—the ones who've been around a while—is, they say it's the Mishipeshu. Funny thing is, based on what they've told us, and what I've found in my research, it's the only thing that fits, but it doesn't really exist. Or, at least, that's what I thought. I didn't want anyone else overhearing our conversations just yet, because if what you have proves its existence, it may change the nature of our relationships with the Native fisheries, and it may not all be good. Many of them are deeply rooted in their culture, and this could hinder or completely ruin all the progress we've made with them. Now, tell me all about how you came to have it."

Matt listened intently as Rick recounted his encounter with the Shoo; he even took notes. This was the first time Rick didn't feel awkward talking about it. Here was a college professor, a man of learning, asking *him* to tell him about something he didn't know about or even believed could be real. The fear Rick had felt about being ridiculed by just such a person, was completely removed from his mind as he saw the deeply interested look on Matt's face as he told the story. There were no snickers, no condescending tones, and no indication he wasn't being taken seriously. When Rick had finished, and only then, did Matt ask to see the artifact. Rick proudly presented his box containing it.

Matt carefully opened the box and just visually examined it for several minutes before asking Rick if he could pick it up. He understood how sensitive Rick might be over his find and didn't want to upset him. There were quite a few more, invasive, tests to come. Better to ease him into things. After getting Rick's okay, Matt putt on some protective gloves before touching it. He gently picked it up and held it in his palm to get a feel for its weight.

"It's heavy for its size."

Matt thoroughly inspected it, rolling it over in his hands, examining it from every angle and paying close attention to its texture and structure.

"Well, I can tell you this. This is the real deal. I'm seeing an internal structure that is difficult, if not impossible, to fake. Looking at it with the electron microscope will give us a better idea of its structure, but this is amazing."

Something Matt said had Mike wondering. Just what time of year were these inquiries about damaged nets and loss of fish harvests reported?

"Before we head over to the microscope, I'm curious. You said you've had reports about damaged fishing nets and even loss of fish from hatcheries. Do you remember if there was a specific time of year, or is it a year-round issue?"

"Interesting you should ask that. I know exactly what time of year the inquiries have come in. Late fall and early winter. The reports of damaged nets have historically been in the early fall, right before the ice can lock the nets in place. You see, fishing is a major source of revenue for the Native fishermen, and winters are long up here. So they tend to push the season, if you will. They will wait until the ice is starting to roll in before giving up on their cash crop. One of our theories about the damaged nets was that it might've been caused by the ice. But the ice that is usually present at that time of year is small. Any damage caused by that ice would be minimal, not the total destruction of nets we've seen. Something big did the damage.

"The fisheries are a different story. Those reports have been well after the ice has established itself along the shores. Usually about November or early December. The fisheries need to have a viable crop of fish ready for stocking by spring break-up, so there are a lot of fish being raised at that time of year, but they are small —too small for most larger predators to mess with. Unless it's used to feeding underwater, like a whale might. You know, swim with its mouth open to scoop as many as it can. Why did you ask that question?"

"Well, I've been looking into some pretty strange and unexplainable missing person reports, including the person who originally owned the home we purchased. Most of the reports, I'd say about seventy-five percent, occurred in winter. Rick's encounter was in the winter. Some have seen something they can't explain, or come across tracks in the snow that don't look like any known animal tracks, or have lost livestock, all during the winter months. And now, you're looking into reports of damages and loss of fish, also during the colder months. I'm just wondering if the pattern is holding true, and it seems to be."

Matt hadn't considered that there may be a loss-of-human-life component to the stories. He was a little embarrassed he hadn't considered that there might be more than damaged nets and loss of fish. It put things in a different light for him.

"I haven't really heard about that until now. I mean, the Natives sometimes say the Mishipeshu might be protecting its territory and to be careful, but they've never directly said it could kill you.

Have any bodies ever been found in any of these missing person reports?"

"Not that I've been able to determine. Listen, Matt. I'm about eighty percent convinced we're dealing with something that's never been seen by modern man—at least the ones who haven't gone missing. With the exception of Rick, here, and very few others I've found. And those people have been deemed a little out there, if you get my drift. I know how important this may end up being. That said, my concern is my family and those around me, not the scientific significance of such a discovery. I need to know, if it comes down to it, can I protect my family from it? Can it be killed? Don't get me wrong, I've lived with apex predators around my home for most of my life. We learn how to avoid them and, if necessary, how to defend ourselves from them. But we didn't go looking for trouble. As far as I'm concerned, I'm not going looking for this thing, either. But if it comes looking for me, rest assured, I'm all in for taking it out. So, as we go forward, I would like any answers you can provide on how to defend ourselves from it, up to and including killing it. Although, that would not be my desired outcome."

As a biologist and an environmental scientist, Mike's words were somewhat grating to his ears. After all, his job had always been to save a species, not kill it. But, he also knew Mike was right; after all, humans are a species as well.

"Point taken. Let's get down to it, and I'll do what I can, if anything, to help expose any weaknesses it may have. Looks like, if this truly is some kind of outer covering, we'd have to figure out how to get around it. I understand your concerns, but it would be a shame if we discovered an unknown species just to turn around and destroy it. As a species, we do way too much of that already."

Mike was well aware of the conundrum. On one hand, there was the historic aspect of such a discovery. Monumental, would be more accurate. But the possible danger to Mike's family and his new community was just as important to him. He never anticipated ending up in the middle of such a significant and difficult situation. This whole thing started out as a mystery, and had turned into a full-fledged quest. Not exactly how Mike envisioned spending his retirement; although, he had to admit, it felt good use his investigative skills again. Once a cop, always a cop.

"I think we all agree that understanding and preserving what we may discover here is paramount. But we can't let that stand in the way of preserving human life. Let's hope what we discover will help us do both."

Bill was trying to avoid tension. After all, they were just getting started, and there were already opposing views on the subject.

"But, aren't we getting a little ahead of ourselves? I mean, we don't even know if we can identify or even come close to any kind of definitive solution yet. Let's let the process of discovery take us where it will—let the facts guide us, not opinions."

Again, Bill was stepping in to keep the investigation on track. He'd been in the political arena for over thirty years; he knew his way around the block. He wouldn't have kept his position with the state for that long without being able to play the game and keep his cool. People in those appointed positions came and went on the whims of the elected, and Bill loved his job, so he had learned the art of manipulation. Not to achieve some nefarious end, but to keep his position as chief forensic investigator for the State of Idaho. So, too, he would attempt to direct the flow of this potentially sensitive subject.

"You're right, Bill. Let's let the test results speak for themselves. Let's head down the hall and have a closer look at this thing."

The four men made their way into the lab. It was a candy store of technology. The expansive room was full of almost every type of testing tech available, and there were several, such as the electron microscopes, that had multiple stations where several students could do their work without waiting. It was a very regimented process to acquire time on the equipment—virtual sign-up schedules, time limits, and what was being tested, as items like hazardous materials or narcotics required a professor be present. The local police used LSSU's labs on a regular basis. Small towns don't have big budgets, so being able to utilize such equipment was a godsend. Fortunately for the mission at hand, there was no one scheduled for any of the equipment today. The campus was pretty empty, as students were away for Thanksgiving and prepping for finals. They had full run of the facility.

"All right, let's see what this thing looks like under the scope. We should get a real good look at the structure. This microscope is 4K. Very detailed."

Rick handed Matt the scale, and he placed it on the specimen holder of the electron microscope. No one said a word. The only sound was the low hum from the cooling units that keep some of the testing equipment from overheating.

"Wow! I want you all to take a look at this. I'm going to bring it up on the monitor

overhead"

With a push of a button, the image Matt was looking at flooded the sixty-inch screen above them. It was a crystal-clear, very detailed look at what certainly was a scale.

"Do you see this right here? This is an elasmoid scale. Very unusual. It's like the kind found on the arapaima fish in the Amazon. These types of scales are like bulletproof vests; they have a mineralized outer shell bound by a very thick layer of collagen to a softer inner shell. This allows the outer layer to deform without breaking. Basically, it's the world's best body armor. What makes this extremely odd is the size of the scale and the thickness of the collagen."

"Now, how in the hell could you know that this is like the scales of a... ara-whatever fish? I've never heard of such a thing."

Mike thought Matt was pulling their collective legs and was making it up.

"Well, if you look over on that wall over there. You'll see a picture of a arapaima with descriptive drawings pointing out its unique biological features. For instance, it's an air-breather that can stay submerged for up to twenty minutes, it can stay out of water for up to twenty-four hours, it sucks in its food like a vacuum, and its scales can absorb piranha bites up to one-point-seven million pounds per square inch. That's one tough fish. It also happens to be my in-your-face example to my students to not come to conclusions before understanding the subject. You see, arapaima seem to be goofy, easy-to-eat prey for other fish. But, they are among the toughest fish in the world. They have to be to live in the environment they do. Piranhas, caymans, giant otters, anacondas, and even bull sharks all prey upon the hapless-looking arapaima. And, apparently, our mystery has the same type of scales as our Amazonian friend, so, if I was to assume anything about the Mishipeshu, it would be this—it's probably every bit as tough as the arapaima, if not more so. After all, it's living in one of the most difficult bodies of water to survive in. And that's not even going into the land predators that may be looking to make a meal of it."

"Kinda weird how you just happen to have an example of a fish with the same type of scale hanging on your laboratory wall. I mean, what are the odds? You would think you'd have some illustrations of native fish on the walls. But a fish from the Amazon hanging front and center? *And* it has the same scale structure? I find the coincidence interesting, to say the least. I mean, how many different types of scales are there anyway?"

"Well, there are four basic types of scales, each with several variations. But *this* is the type of scale the military is studying so they can make ballistic armor. It's the perfect design. The problem is weight, and getting the proper bond between layers. Turns out, Mother Nature does a much better job than humans. As for the coincidence? Well, yes. It's a funny coincidence. When I was a kid, I loved everything about the Amazon. Its size, the vast numbers of species that inhabit the area, and the prehistoric nature of the environment. I would imagine chugging up the Amazon in my *African Queen*-style boat and coming across dinosaurs and giant cayman and huge anacondas. I've had that drawing of the arapaima since I was fourteen. It seems as though I was put here in this very situation to work on this very mystery. I guess science can't explain those types of coincidences."

The four men sat quietly as each pondered the strangeness of the situation, all while studying the image on the screen.

"Well, what else can you gather from this scale, Matt?"

"I can tell you this. Whatever this came from is big. Very big. If we compare the size of the arapaima scale to our mystery creature's scale, I would say the creature would be somewhere between fifteen and twenty feet long. The arapaima can get up to ten feet long and four hundred pounds. Being that you said this thing had legs, I'd guess it to be around eight or ten feet tall. Does that sound about right, Rick?"

"Pretty close, best I could tell."

"Shall we see if there's any viable DNA in this thing? If there is, we might better understand this creature. We have the latest in sequencing equipment. We've been able to cut the sequencing down from two to three weeks to just a few hours. This equipment was developed with the help of Stanford University's genome department, and it has dramatically improved the process. The trick is finding a viable sample to test. After all, this has been handled quit bit, and there's going to be human contamination.

So, I suggest we try to get a sample from between the layers. There would be less chance of cross-contamination, from there."

Matt deftly probed the inner layer of the scale with a syringe containing sterile water. Once he found a site where a good sample could be collected, he depressed the plunger on the syringe and allowed the water to drip into a Petri dish. From there, he could use cotton swabs to collect the sample to be tested. To maximize the probability of collecting a good sample, Matt used several swabs. Once collected, he placed the sample swabs into the PCR, or polymerase chain reaction machine, for sequencing. Using the PCR machine allowed for testing of multiple samples at once.

"And now, we wait. Should see some results in about six or seven hours. In the meantime, I would like to test this with our OES. This will allow us to see what elements may be present without damaging the sample. It might help us determine exactly what part of the lake it calls home."

"What the hell is an OES?"

Mike and Bill were at least aware of some of the technology used in different forensic sciences. After all, Bill had used some of them himself, and Mike had been present during some of Bill's testing. But Rick was more or less a backwoods kind of guy. Not much for all this technical stuff. But even he had to admit, it was pretty cool watching the machines operate.

"Well, the simplest way to explain it is this. The machine fires an electrical charge stream into the sample—kinda like a laser, but without the destruction of the sample. Some small areas do get vaporized, but not enough to really damage it. The electrical charge creates a plasma discharge, and the color or colors that the plasma creates tell us what may be in the sample. It's normally used in metallurgic applications but can be used for items such as your scale. Hopefully, it sheds some light on what elements are present either on or within the scale. It could help with locating its main territory. If we can, maybe we can be proactive in locating it, instead of reactive."

"Now that sounds like a plan. Maybe there will be some way of capturing or deterring it from hunting the shores of Paradise and Chippewa County. We might be saving lives here."

Mike was feeling a little better about facing winter. Even though there were no answers yet, it was looking like they may have the technology to unlock a mystery that went back hundreds, if not thousands, of years. More importantly, they might find something that would help keep his family safe. All because a local, a Yooper, stood his ground against the beast and was able to recover the scale. Even though he was somewhere he shouldn't have been. But, without that small act of criminality, they would not have the ability to perform these tests. Sometimes, doing something wrong leads to something good.

Matt placed the scale into the OES and pressed the start button. Rick watched in awe as the machine whirred to life and what looked like a small, straight lightning bolt stabbed into the scale. In milliseconds, the plasma discharges filled the chamber with a myriad of colors, but one color struck Matt as very curious.

"Ahh. See that yellow-green color there? That indicates there is barite present. Now *that's* interesting. You see, barite, especially barite around the Great Lakes, is only found very deep. It's normally found in the depths of the ocean but can be found in some of the deeper parts of Lake Superior. It's a remnant of a time long before man, when the Earth was evolving, forming oceans and mountains and valleys. It was a tumultuous time, indeed. What life was here, was basic amoebas and other single-celled life. But, in geologic time, it wouldn't be long before this planet was teaming with all manner of more complicated organisms. Over time, these life forms adapted, evolved, and multiplied. Those species that couldn't adapt or evolve to survive the changing planet were doomed to a short life span and eventually extinction. All the while, the Earth was changing. The tectonic plates were moving, continents were shifting, and ecosystems were born and destroyed. The creatures that were here had to evolve or perish. Cold-blooded animals wouldn't survive a sudden freeze. No animal would survive if food sources were lost. Carnivores would, more than likely, survive these changes better than the herbivores due to the simple fact that, if plants died, there would be plenty of corpses for the carnivores to feast on. But even they were subject to the changing environment. Evolve or, in turn, die as well.

"It was during the end of the Cretaceous period, a time called the Maastrichtian period, when the comet struck somewhere around the Yucatán Peninsula, wiping out almost all life that existed at the time. This is estimated to be around sixty million years ago. The only life that survived were birds and some amphibians, like salamanders, frogs, and turtles. At least, that's what science understands about that time.

"Now, fast forward to about ten thousand years ago, the ending of the last ice age. That's when the glacial melting formed the Great Lakes. It is believed that there weren't many large species to survive the comet and the subsequent ice ages, but the discovery of a very large predator that lives in Lake Superior could rewrite all of that. And this barite being present in the scale is very interesting. It's not that it's rare; it's that, in Lake Superior, high quantities are only found in very deep water.

"You see that plasma reading there? That's a very strong reading. It suggests that this scale has been in the deepest areas of the lake, say, around a thousand feet deep or so. But there's something else here. You see that magenta color there? That's iron. But not just any iron. The color tells me that there's something else in there. It's definitely an indication of iron, but I've never seen this particular depth of color in any of the iron samples I've seen. We'll need to look a little harder at this,if we want to find out what it is."

All Rick could think was that Matt was showing off. Blah, blah, blah, science, blah, blah, blah. He had no idea that iron, as with all minerals, had a signature of sorts. Knowing its exact makeup could determine where it came from. But to Rick, iron is iron and it rusts—so what? He could also tell that Mike and Bill seemed to understand at least something about what Matt was saying, and that made him feel uncomfortable.

These thoughts of being inadequate stemmed from a lifetime of judgmental attitudes from those who thought themselves better than him. Even some of his teachers had assumed he was not as intelligent as the other children. Oh, they didn't intentionally treat him differently, but the subconscious mind can be a powerful thing. It's like an internal voice whispering into the ear, "He's not as worthy of your efforts as the others," and so on. Fortunately, those types of teachers were few, but negative input could be more powerful than positive feedback to someone prone to having an inferiority complex. Those types of personalities tended to only believe the negative and ignore the positive. Everyone knew someone like this: They are told it's a beautiful day, and they come back with, "Yeah, but it might rain later."

What Rick didn't understand was that he had abilities a lot of others didn't have a clue about. Of course, he knew how to hunt and how to care for the meat once harvested. But he could also rebuild an engine or transmission, or completely rebuild an entire vehicle. He had no formal training, just a knack. He built his own garage without plans, including electrical and plumbing. And there wasn't any type of heavy equipment he couldn't operate, and operate at a high level of proficiency.

When one thinks about it, when the shit hits the fan, which type of individual is more valuable? One who knows how to operate high-tech equipment and understand its results? After all, if everything goes south, there won't be enough power to run those pieces of equipment. Or, would someone who can keep things running, or even build just about anything that may be needed to get through any challenge, be more of an asset?

As for the results of the testing so far, he felt relief. Not that he was worried the tests wouldn't prove his scale as the real deal, but that scientifically minded people, the very intellectual type people who would look down upon him, were the ones proving him right. They were validating his story through the very science he found impractical. In his mind, everything a person needed to know was out there, out there in the real world. After all, humans have been figuring things out and learning how to accomplish things for centuries without all these fancy machines. All he could think was, *What's the big deal about what kind of iron it may be?*

But Rick was wrong about one thing. Mike didn't have a clue about the differences in iron either. He just had a better poker face. The type of control an experienced police officer gains through years of hearing lies, tall stories, and misleading information, and being able to sift through the bullshit to find the truth. Don't let them see you sweat. That was the one secret his training officer had drilled into him from the start.

He would tell Mike, "Once they see you lose confidence or get nervous, they will pounce all over you. Take advantage of you. Maybe even kill you. It's funny how those who live in the criminal world develop that sixth sense, and you'll need to develop it, too."

In other words, Mike would have to master the bluff. Fake it till you make it. In the over two decades honing his skills, Mike got real good at controlling his facial expressions, body language, and tone of voice. It had become so ingrained in his psyche that it just came naturally. It was the one thing Sarah hated. She could never tell what he was thinking when he was in cop mode.

"We need to break this iron reading down to see if we can determine exactly where it might've picked it up. All iron ore is made up of different elements. Each has its own signature of sorts. Once we determine its makeup, we should be able to pinpoint where this thing picked it up. The trick is isolating the iron from the scale. Once we do that, we'll head over to the XRF. That baby will tell us everything we need to know about that iron."

"Geez, Matt. How many initialed machines are we gonna use, anyway?"

Rick tried to make his question humorous, but it was hard for him to disguise that all this technology made him uncomfortable; he'd sounded a little irritated. Not his intention, but the others picked up on it.

"I'm sorry, Rick. I work around these things every day, and the students are all pretty familiar with them and their workings. I forget these are not a part of most people's everyday lives. I'm just so excited to be able to test this, I get a little ahead of myself. Hopefully, this test gives us what we need to lockdown a territory.

"The XRF uses a fluorescent beam to create a reaction with whatever might be in the sample. Different elements glow in different colors. I'm thinking this test will be the last, at least until we get the DNA results. But, even then, I believe we should have enough info to research this for months, if not years. You know, Rick, if it turns out that this is truly the Mishipeshu, it will change everything we understand about our prehistoric past. Having that scale could prove very fruitful to you. Between museums, scientists, and academia, it will surely be in high demand. I would make sure you insure it and put it away someplace a little more secure than your cigar box. The black market for this type of thing can make people resort to whatever means necessary to acquire it. Happens all the time with dinosaur fossils. A known animal, the T-Rex, can bring five or six million dollars. Imagine having the *only* relic tied to brand new ancient species. That scale could be worth tens of millions of dollars."

Up to now, Rick had only thought of his souvenir as proof to back up his story. A sort of in-your-face to all those who might poke fun at him. Now, he was both excited and worried. Excited that he may have hit the proverbial jackpot with his find. But worried about making sure it stayed in his possession. He could think of six or seven people he'd shown it to over the last couple of years. Who knew how many others those people told. One thing was for sure—as soon as they were done at the university, he was going to get a safe deposit box to keep it in.

Matt returned to the electron microscope in an effort to locate where the iron sample may be located in the scale. It took about twenty minutes, but he finally found what looked to be a testable sample lodged inside one of the layers. Extracting the sample from such a small space without damaging it was difficult, but the lab had just about every tool needed. Matt placed the scale into an ultrasonic cleaner. These devices create high frequency sonic waves that pulse through a solution to remove material from submerged samples. After another ten minutes, they had their iron sample for the test. It wasn't much—just a few minute grains.

"Holy crap! All that just to get that little, tiny dot of a sample. You sure you got enough?"

"Oh, it'll be plenty for what we're looking for. These machines are so sensitive now that this small sample is more than enough."

Rick was having a hard time wrapping his head around all the large, high-tech equipment being used to test such small things. He could barely even see the iron sample Matt placed in the vial.

"Okay. Let's see what we've got."

Matt started the XRF and waited for the light show. It only took a few seconds to reveal the composition of the iron sample.

"This can't be right. I've never seen an iron ore sample with this composition. I'll be right back. I have to check something."

Matt quickly got up and went to a computer station in the corner of the lab. The men could hear him mumbling to himself as he rapidly entered information into the computer and read the results. The three could tell Matt was completely confused as to what he was finding. After about fifteen minutes on the computer, Matt came back and double-checked the test results.

"Well, gentlemen, we have a conundrum. You see, Michigan has a well-established iron mining history, mostly centered around Marquette. I was expecting to see magnetite and maybe some sulphur in the sample. That would indicate our creature spends time in that area. However, what we have here is completely different. It has nickel and cobalt in its makeup. There's only one iron in the world that has nickel and cobalt, and that's telluric iron, or native iron. Telluric iron is actually iron. The iron we find everywhere else is actually iron ore, not iron. Telluric iron is what our Earth's core is made of, but on the surface, it's only found in Greenland. The primary theory as to how telluric iron got to Greenland is that a comet brought it here sometime before the continents as we know them now were formed. Greenland would've been connected to what would become the Great Lakes Region at that time. Which means, somewhere in Lake Superior, there's a deposit of telluric iron. Somewhere yet to be surveyed, which seems impossible, as this area has been extensively studied. Wherever it is, it's not going to be easy to find."

Mike's thoughts drifted to what his research had revealed about an undiscovered lake *under* Lake Superior, Lake Inferior. Should he even mention it? After all, if this lake was real, wouldn't Matt already know about it? On the other hand, if he didn't bring it up, and it turned out to be important, he would never forgive himself.

"You know, I read something about some lake under Lake Superior. Some French explorer supposedly discovered it. Could that iron be there? Someplace that's well out of the norm? Could there be something to that?"

Matt leaned back in his chair while staring blankly at the monitor. He seemed to be wrestling with some thoughts of his own for what felt like an awkward eternity before slowly spinning around in his chair.

"Funny you should mention Lake Inferior. Not many people have even heard about it, let alone believe it's real. But I'll tell you something. Some of our research in the deepest part of the lake, around Munising, has shown some interesting anomalies. For instance, a definite, audible burp has been heard on our deep-water listening devices. We listen for fish sounds to determine migrations and whether the numbers of fish is stable, increasing, or decreasing. You see, it's about thirteen hundred feet deep there. It's impossible to put divers at those depths, so we rely on our equipment to monitor fish populations and overall health of a species. There are several species that not only live at that depth, but thrive.

"Anyway, this burp is kind of like when you pour water out of a jug. You know, that glug-glug-glug sound? Well, that's what it reminds me of. But it's not that fast. The glugs happen at a fairly regular rate of about one every fifteen minutes. It has baffled us, as well as other scientists who've heard it, for years. It's almost inconceivable that there could be another lake under Lake Superior. But, there are lakes under other bodies of water all over the world. Most of them are called brine pools, due to their high salt content, and they are not very hospitable places to be. If there is a Lake Inferior, and I'm inclined to think there is, it could explain that sound.

"As for your question about the iron, Mike. Could be. Millions of years ago, what is now known as Lake Superior was pretty well lined up with Greenland. Both are part of the North American tectonic plate. So it's conceivable that telluric iron was part of that. If there is a Lake Inferior, and if telluric iron is found there, it would explain how this creature has stayed hidden so long. It could be living in around the shores of Lake Inferior unseen. And, if what you're telling me is true, that it's only coming around after the lake freezes, it would mean it would have to have enough food to survive from winter to winter. And *that* would explain your theory about all those missing people, Mike. Still, it doesn't explain how one creature could account for every sighting or incident since recorded history. It would have to be able to reproduce somehow and, if it follows the typical pattern, there would be several of these, if not more."

The group spent the next hour and a half discussing all the angles, all the possibilities, and the ramifications of such a find. But they only came up with more questions. How could this creature have evolved to survive the severe cold of the ice ages when virtually every other living thing of its size died off due to lack of food or an inability to handle the cold? Does it hibernate? Is it an omnivore, or strictly a carnivore? Does it hunt other species, such as deer, moose, or even bears? After all, the deer and moose populations have decreased over the years. Most put the reason for this decrease as wolf predation, but could it also be due to the Mishipeshu's terrestrial hunts? Would it scavenge if necessary? That last question could prove vital if they were to try and capture it. They would need bait, and putting a live animal out for possible slaughter was not very appealing to them, nor would it be viewed by the public as humane. Optics. It drove just about every decision in every corner of the country these days. Bad optics could taint any results, no matter how positive. Lots of questions; very few answers. Maybe the DNA sequencing would provide some answers, but those results were a couple more hours away. Rick always relied on his common sense approach to everything; simple solutions always seemed to work best.

"Well, if it comes down to it, we know it hunts humans. If we need bait, we should be the bait, or, at least one of us, and the others could spring the trap. That way, we don't include anyone else in the mix. The fewer people know what we're doing, the better."

"You may be right, Rick. But let's not get ahead of ourselves. We don't even know if trying to capture it is in the plans. Right now, we just need to know what we're dealing with and whether we keep it from preying on humans. We'll deal with the rest if we need to."

Mike was right. No need to overthink the situation. This whole thing had gotten bigger than he wanted it to. All he was concerned about was, first, determining whether or not the Mishipeshu was real and, second, if he could kill it if it came around his cabin again. Capturing it? Not even a consideration for him. That would mean getting agencies involved. Government agencies. And once the government got involved in *anything*, it becomes more of a pain in the ass. One thing Mike hated was government intrusion. Why on earth would anyone want to have a bunch of lawyers who decided to seek office so they could pad their resume and get rich telling them how to do things from hundreds of miles away that they have absolutely no understanding of. Boots on the ground. Local boots that know the area, the people, and the problems that may come up. After all, when speed of action may be necessary to adjust to unknowns, a big, cumbersome, over-bearing regulation machine was the last thing they needed.

"Well, let's get some coffee while we wait for the DNA sequencer to finish up. Should be another thirty minutes or so."

Rick took the scale and placed it in its box for safekeeping.

Even though the university was relatively empty, he wasn't going to take any chances that word of what they were doing wouldn't tempt someone into taking it. While on the way to the cafeteria, Mike looked out the windows that lined the hallway that led from the lab to the elevators. It was snowing. Winter was coming, and coming fast. He felt a sudden nervousness about the upcoming winter season. All he could think about was it would soon be hunting season for the Mishipeshu, and they didn't have any solid plans to stop it if it came back. Mike had put together around a hundred rounds of the dragon's breath shotgun shells, roughly a fifty-fifty split between his twelve-gauge and twenty-gauge shells for Sarah. One of his stops while they were in town would be at Bob's Gun Shop to buy Sarah her twenty-gauge shotgun. He hoped that between the two of them, they could fend off any attack with the heat and flames of the dragon's breath shells. He knew the shotguns wouldn't do any damage to it, given the structure of its armor, so he would also load some special "hot loads" for his Browning 7-millimeter magnum rifle, which he nicknamed Big Bertha due to its massive, destructive power. He had purchased Big Bertha for a moose hunt in Alaska, where he wanted a larger caliber than his .243 deer rifle. He had used it once for a deer hunt, but it created too much tissue damage. As a hunter that hunted for meat and not trophies, loss of that much meat seemed like a waste to him. The .243 was more suited to deer. He had considered selling Big Bertha but decided to hold on to her just in case. And, now, it seemed as if his "shoulder cannon" might be needed. After all, if there was ever a round that could penetrate the Mishipeshu's armor, the 7-millimeter was it. He would make some full metal jacketed rounds to keep the round from deforming. Penetration was the key, not knockdown power, and the FMJ rounds were less prone to deformation. There was a lot to do, and time was ticking down.

"So, Matt, what do you think we'll find out from the DNA? Do you have any theories on what we're dealing with?"

Mike was trying to ignore the snow and play down his growing concerns by asking Matt about his thoughts. He knew Matt would have some long, deeply detailed ideas, and Mike welcomed the mental distraction.

"Well, it's hard to say. It's been long thought that the dinosaurs couldn't survive the cold of the ice ages, that their food and climate were dramatically affected by the comet that is believed to have struck around the end of the Cretaceous period. This would have caused a type of nuclear winter when the debris from the impact blocked out the sun, and they simply either froze or starved, leaving plenty for the meat-eaters to feed on, as long as they didn't succumb to the cold.

"But recent studies have shown that many dinosaurs actually thrived in the cold, but food sources, not so much. The most likely candidate for our mystery beast would be some type of theropod, like a T-Rex or velociraptor, that evolved or mutated into an amphibious type of predator. If, as our evidence seems to point to, one of these theropods found the hidden lake under Superior, probably before Lake Superior was formed, it could've been the perfect place to develop into its current form. And, once Lake Superior formed over top, it would be protected from future cataclysmic events. It would make sense that after ages of surviving at such depths where it's very cold, that it would develop an aversion for warmer temps.

"Think of it this way. Yoopers live in a much cooler environment than those who live downstate. When it's fifty degrees in the UP, they think it's time for shorts, while those, downstate think it's still cold. When Yoopers go downstate in the summer, it takes them a few days to acclimate to the heat. There can be as much as a twenty-degree swing in temps between the UP and those below the bridge.

"Same for our lake creature, only more dramaticly. Temps in the deepest parts of the lake never make it above the low thirties, while the surface temp of the lake can be mid- to upper-sixties, and air temperature in the seventies. It might feel like hell on Earth for a cold-climate dweller. Its ability to adapt to such cold temperatures, let alone the pressures at those depths, may have allowed it to survive, but that very ability has it trapped for a large part of the year. Who knows, with climate change, it may eventually develop a tolerance to warmer temperatures, and that could prove devastating. Species typically reproduce at lower rates when food is limited but proliferate when food is plentiful. Imagine a whole herd of these creatures roaming the shorelines year-round. The word carnage comes to mind. So, gentlemen, there's a lot more hinging on our tests than a simple case of identification and classification. As I said, this could be an historical find that rewrites the history books. At the very least, it will upset the scientific community."

Mike was thinking, *Oh, great. No pressure.* This whole damn thing had gone from him just trying to take care of his home and family from an unknown threat to a possible, major scientific discovery. Not exactly the quiet retirement he was imagining. He was thinking that he and Sarah had only been in Paradise for a few months, but Sarah had two sisters with husbands that had cabins in Paradise too. He wondered if they had ever had an encounter or even heard of the Mishipeshu. With all the stories and missing people, he couldn't imagine they hadn't caught wind of something. But, then again, most people go through life with blinders on, barely even noticing things that happen around them every day. But a story like the Mishipeshu should at least spark some interest.

One thing was certain: if this thing turned out to be real, and it certainly looked like it was, Mike and Sarah wouldn't be the only family threatened by it. Sarah's two sisters and their families came to mind. He hadn't said anything to Sarah's other family members about what he had found out or what he was doing. He didn't want to get into any discussions with them until he knew for sure that there was a legitimate threat.

Sarah's sister, Cathy, was a realist and highly intelligent. She had been a nurse and eventually the administrator for a large medical facility in the Alma area. Her husband, Jared, was a farmer and a pragmatic man. Neither would accept that there was some sort of prehistoric creature lurking and hunting in Paradise without some serious proof.

The same was true for Sarah's other sister and her husband. Leslie was also grounded in the scientific arena; although she wasn't a nurse, she was around medical professionals every day and was more prone to a black-and-white understanding of an issue, as opposed to the unknown, imaginary realm. Her husband, Pete, owned his own construction business and was a farmer as well. He was a bit adventurous but not prone to fanciful stories. He was also known to poke fun at those who made missteps or believed in unproven things. Once, he and Jared went on a five-day fishing trip in Canada. The road to the camp was about sixty miles of muddy, wet tire ruts. When they got to camp, Jared noticed his suitcase was missing, and they had to go back to look for it. It had fallen off the top of the truck because of a faulty latch. Pete blamed Jared for not tying it tight enough. That went on even after they returned home. He was relentless, but it was all in fun.

Even so, Mike didn't want to be the target of that type of mockery. He would wait until he had some hard facts before he spoke with those family members.

Sarah had two other sisters living downstate. Lucy and her

husband, Max, and Donna and her husband, Burt. They came up to Paradise a few times a year, but rarely, if ever, in winter. Lucy hated crossing the Mackinac Bridge, even in perfect weather, but Donna and Burt liked to travel and got up to Paradise as often as they could. They had both recently retired, but Burt still conducted some training classes for some universities across the country. He was an engineer-type, grounded in facts and what he could prove.

Even though Mike was more of a wisdom-through-experience person, and Burt was definitely more intellectual in his thinking process, they got along better than Mike did with the other family members. This was probably due to having similar personalities and shared interests. They both liked to hunt; although Burt and Donna didn't eat venison, they didn't let the meat go to waste. Burt would give his harvest to those in the community that needed it. Mike was always impressed by Burt's sense of right and wrong and how he and Donna lived by the golden rule of do unto others as you would have done unto you. This was also ingrained in Mike's makeup. It's what inspired him to become a police officer. That line of thinking and his drive to protect others were what drove Mike now.

He once had a supervisor tell him, "Do the right thing because it's the right thing to do." That had stayed with him—as had another, but for a different reason. One of his first cases while assigned to the detective office involved a business owner charged with fraud. Once all the evidence had been collected and the owner arrested, the businessman turned to Mike and said, "There's right, there's wrong, and there's business." Mike couldn't help but remember it—it went completely against his core beliefs. In his mind, there was only right and wrong, and what he and the others were trying to do was the right thing.

If they could definitively prove the Mishipeshu's existence, then Mike would have what he needed to inform Sarah's family about the danger without being ridiculed. Having hard facts to back him up was the only way he would even mention it to them. All this time, Mike hadn't given them any indication as to what he was doing, and neither had Sarah. Although Sarah's family was loving and supportive, they wouldn't understand all the concern over an unproven rumor.

The four men spent over an hour on their coffee break. It turned into a sharing of backgrounds. Of course, Matt was more in tune with Bill's story as the two shared the same passion for discovery. But, after all was said and done, Rick's story impressed everyone the most impressed—a self-taught man in mechanics, construction, and running heavy equipment. Matt couldn't help but feel jealous, for lack of a better term. Matt couldn't hit a nail with a hammer, no matter how hard he tried. Sure, he knew what buttons to push on his equipment, and understood the results, but he had always wanted to become more self-reliant when it came to life out of the lab. But Rick's education in these matters came from necessity, not desire, and Matt never wanted for much. His family was quite wealthy and provided Matt with everything he needed throughout his life. The phrase "Necessity is the mother of invention" never played a part in his life.

But Rick's journey started early in his life. His parents never made much money, surviving by the sweat of their brows. His father cut lumber on his personal sawmill and sold firewood. On occasion, he would tinker with someone's vehicle for some cash, or take the odd construction job. It was enough to pay the bills, and hunting helped fill the freezer, and Rick's dad was an excellent hunter.

His mother sold baked goods to mom-and-pop stores. There wasn't much profit in it, but it usually covered her costs with a little left over. She would put every extra penny in a coffee tin in her kitchen cabinet to be used in emergencies. But it almost always went to someone else in need in the area. Although Rick's parents were well respected and liked by those who knew them, Rick didn't warrant the same respect. As a young boy, he had trouble learning in school. He was dyslexic, but in the small school system he attended, there wasn't much help or resources for a student with dyslexia. So he struggled, and that made him appear stupid to the other kids, and that would end in name-calling or, in many cases, a fight. Rick barely graduated from high school, but what he lacked in formal education, he more than made up for in practical learning.

He had paid very close attention to everything his dad did, which proved advantageous in his future. When Rick's dad passed away, Rick was only seventeen, and that forced him to step up to help take care of his mom. He started working as a mechanic in a local shop, earning a good income. Once he graduated from high school, he worked at the shop full-time, and when he was twenty-five, the shop's owner retired and worked out a pay-as-you-go plan for Rick to buy the business.

It was around this time that the off-trail riders and snowmo-bilers flooded into Paradise. Word had gotten out about the great trails and small-town hospitality. So Rick became good at repairing and even customizing off-road vehicles and snowmo-biles. This was very lucrative for Rick as people with his skills were limited in the Paradise area. This earned him enough money to pay off his mom's house and build his own home. The lessons he learned from his parents about taking care of those in need weren't wasted on him. Many times, someone would come into his shop with an issue with their vehicle or tractor or some small engine and not have money for the repairs. Rick would work out trades for services, or even fix it for free.

Once, Rick repaired a riding mower for a teenager in town

who cut people's lawns, including several who couldn't cut their own grass due disability or age. The teen wouldn't charge for those lawns; he didn't feel it was right, and Rick knew this. He also knew the boy didn't make enough money to even pay him for the $200 in parts, so Rick just did the repair without charging him. A few days later, when Rick got home, there was a styrofoam cooler filled with Walleye on his front porch and a thank-you note from the boy. That's how it was in Paradise. No good deed went unnoticed or appreciated. It was funny how someone like Matt, who seemingly has everything—success, money, prestige—could be jealous of what Rick had; of how a man of few words, raised by common people with little means, could have more than what money and prestige could buy. He had respect.

Granted, it was a hard-earned respect, but isn't that usually the case. It's funny how no matter one's station or standing in life, there's always something else to yearn for. Poor people want money, rich people want simplicity, sick people want health, famous people want anonymity, outsiders want fame, the young wish to be older, and the elderly long for their youth. The grass-is-greener adage serves not to focus one's attention on one's strengths, but on one's idea of success or happiness. Of course, if they ever reach that greener grass, there will be another patch of green to envy. It's a never-ending cycle of dissatisfaction with their own self-worth. But, in Rick's case, there were no such envious aspirations. He was a man who knew his place in the world, understood how to work within his talents, and didn't concern himself with unimportant longings. At least, until this moment, he had had a good grasp on life. Now, *that* was something to be envious of.

"What'd you say we head back to the lab and see if we have any results yet?"

They were all anxious to get back and see if there were any

answers from the DNA sequencer, especially Matt. It was hard for him not to think about the significance of being able to definitively identify what species the scale belonged to. But, he also realized that the chance of the sequencer coming up with a match was slim. After all, there weren't that many prehistoric DNA references in the database. The problem was simple: too much time had elapsed since the prehistoric era. Although there had been DNA extracted from sources such as insects, amber, and some species whose remains were frozen in tundra areas, most of the matter that would contain DNA would be contaminated or degraded so badly that viable DNA would be nearly impossible to extract. In fact, the only possible dinosaur DNA that has been found within a fossil is in China, and came from a peacock-size bird called the Caudipteryx, an animal that roamed the Earth around 125 million years ago. Not exactly a *Jurassic Park* aha moment. On the plus side, if there was no DNA match, but the test showed an actual, living creature, Matt would have the luxury of naming it, with the help of his research associates, of course.

When they got back to the lab, the sequencer had printed out results from the sample: *Excluded*.

"What the hell does that mean, excluded?"

Rick was confused. He had thought it would come back as some known animal that might have mutated into something else, or something that had at least a piece of some known animal in its makeup. To him, unknown meant they had gone through all this for nothing. A complete waste of time.

"Well, it means there is nothing in the records. Nothing. That means that whatever this scale came from is a completely undiscovered species. But, it *is* a species none the less, or we wouldn't have a sequence, which is what this data shows. Excluded does not mean non-existent. It means it's viable DNA with no known match in the vast system of verified DNA records. That's almost five thousand modern-day species, and about two hundred recently extinct species. That is significant because, if it's not a modern-day species or a recently extinct species, it's older than the last known dinosaurs, and, my fellow researchers, we get to name our find."

"With all due respect, Matt, I believe it already has a name. Mishipeshu."

Mike was a little put off by Matt's comment. After all, Mike had been researching the Mishipeshu for months without any input from the scientific community, and, it seemed, that Matt was hijacking his efforts.

"Don't get me wrong, Mike. Of course, its common name is Mishipeshu, but we get to assign a scientific name to it, one that will be accepted and recognized by the scientific community. And I think we need to do it today, before anyone else gets ahold of this information and names it themselves. I think the name we give it should be a combination that represents us and the species' characteristics. If you look over here, this column gives us some suggested areas to research further in order to help identify our friend. The suggestions include amphibians and vertebrata. In the vertebrata, it specifically suggests the Pisces class. We're talking fish here. More accurately, ancient fish. A class of fish that no longer exists. Acanthodians. It's believed that acanthodians are where sharks originate from. Kind of makes sense, huh? They had spiny, bone-like protrusions along their body, much like the drawings of the Mishipeshu. It could very well be what evolved out of isolation. There would be nothing else like it in the world. The closest thing we have in a modern-day species would be the lake sturgeon, and Lake Superior has sturgeon. Looking at these results, there are some possible links, but not quite a match, and among those hits, there's sturgeon. I think we've got our genetic line for our little friend."

"C'mon, Matt, how do we go from sturgeon—granted, a large, boney fish—to a giant, man-hunting amphibious monster? I don't understand how that happens."

Mike was getting impatient with all the scientific hoopla. He felt Matt was just trying to show everyone how smart he was, when all Mike just wanted to know if it could be killed and how. He didn't care about formally naming it or how the scientific community would view their discovery. After all, it boiled down to two people in the room. Mike and Rick. Rick shot it, and Mike's property had apparently been the scene of one of its killings. As for Bill and Matt, well, they were outsiders looking in. Oh, Mike was appreciative for their help, but he really didn't care about all the fluff, as he called it.

Fluff was just the extra stuff that made seeing the basic problem a little harder to define. In investigations, fluff got in the way. As Sergeant Friday used to say in *Dragnet*, "Just the facts, ma'am." People always seemed to add fluff to any story. It's like, "I was walking in the park, enjoying the flowers and all the birds singing. It was a beautiful day. I even forgot about how bad my morning was. Until I heard gunshots and saw that poor man get shot. It was horrible." An investigator would ignore everything up to the point where the witness stated they heard gunshots. The investigator would want to know what time they heard the gunshots, which direction they came from, the number of shots they heard, whether or not they saw the shooter, what the shooter was wearing... That kind of stuff. Not all the flowers, birds, and bad-morning stuff. It slows the investigation down. And that's how Mike was starting to feel about how this investigation was going. They'd been at it for almost five hours, and he hadn't learned much more than what he already knew, other than all the history and science crap.

"I appreciate the significance of such a discovery, but my main concern is simple. What's our best chance at warding off or killin' this thing, so I don't have to sleep with one eye open the rest of my life? I don't want to be known as the killer of an ancient species, and probably the only one of its kind. But I also don't want to be read about in some missing person report, or worse, the obituary page. And, another thing. This thing is pretty damn big. Rick's seen it, and by his account, it's huge. So why aren't there more sightings, pictures, stories—*anything*? Not even anything caught on any of the game cameras hunters have scattered all over Chippewa County? So, now we know it's real, so how the hell does it move around without being seen?"

Matt had gotten caught up in the excitement of discovery and had totally lost sight of the reason the others were here in the first place. He would have to try and straddle the fence between saving the species and helping Mike and the others deter or, if necessary, eliminate the threat.

"You're right, Mike. I forgot the original mission of this study. Once I saw we were dealing with an actual living, breathing creature lost to history, I just saw the prestige, not the human toll. There has to be a balance, though. If we can find a way to salvage this thing, while at the same time stopping its winter killing spree, I would call that a win-win, right? As far as how it can go from a boney fish to the current manifestation of the Mishipeshu—it's not unheard of. There are some species of reptile that can mutate from male to female or vice-versa when the survival of the species necessitates it. And this doesn't happen over hundreds of years. It occurs within, say, months.

"So, let's assume for a minute that the Lake Inferior story is true. That would mean that—assuming our friend entered that lake from some opening, an opening that would almost certainly need to be there to keep that lake supplied with the water needed to keep it from drying up—the entry point is probably very small, or else Lake Superior would have a discernible whirlpool or some other noticeable feature pointing to the access point. So far, that point has not been located, so, most likely, it would've been a one-in-million chance that any animal would've found that way in. Being isolated like that, it would have to evolve into what it needed to be to survive, or else it would go the way of the other dinosaurs no longer with us. Without competition, it had no other outside pressure to reach its current manifestation. And, we're not talking hundreds of years. It most likely occurred over thousands, maybe tens of thousands, of years—a short time frame, as far as Earth's history is concerned. As for why there aren't more sightings... Well, there aren't a whole lot of people hanging around the beaches and shorelines of Lake Superior in the winter. Plus, it's most likely a nocturnal hunter. I think it's using the ice as its access to land. When the shelf ice piles up along the shores, it can get pretty high—fifteen or twenty feet high in some cases. That would provide great cover for it to cruise close to shore without being seen. It could move behind the shelf ice using its senses to sniff out prey, then, when ready, it could slip under the ice and find a hole of some kind to exit the water. It would be nearly invisible then."

Of course, Matt was right. Protecting a human life shouldn't require the destruction of another. It was time to look at the possibility of deterrence, and not elimination. As far as killing it went, it was pretty clear that a more military type firearm would be needed to penetrate the Shoo's armor. And, Matt's theory about the ice made sense; if true, predicting where it might exit would be very difficult.

Rick had a different take. After all, he was the only one in this group who had actually seen the Shoo up close. He was not at all concerned about preservation.

"I really don't care about all this science stuff. Name it, don't name it—I don't really care. If you had seen this thing like I did, you wouldn't be all fired up about getting cozy with it. It kills people. Period. We need to get rid of it so it can't kill anymore. Now, is there anything you've found in all this technology that can help us do that or not?"

"I understand your point, Rick. This creature is definitely a danger to any human that wanders into its path. However, as a scientist, I must look at this as a conservation effort, not an extermination, but that doesn't lessen the impact of such a creature on the environment. It's quite the conundrum for me. So, let me say this in response to your question. The tests we've performed here today will not determine a definitive means to kill it. We can only speculate. But, given its similarity to the arapaima in the structure of its scales, we can assume it has other similar characteristics, such as a softer, less-protected underbelly. As the arapaima hunts along the bottoms of the river, its greatest threats are from above, so its armor is dedicated to attacks from above, not from below. I'm pretty sure the Mishipeshu has the same type of structure, so, other than hitting it with some serious firepower that would render its scales ineffective, going for the underbelly might offer the best chance to kill it with standard hunting rifles. At least, that's my best guess. But if deterring it is an option, based on its normal environment being cold and dark, I would think heat and bright light might keep it at bay, allowing it to possibly be trapped, which would be my preferred method of dealing with it.

"So, my fellow cryptozoologists, I say we attack this from a two-pronged front. You and Mike should approach this from an elimination standpoint, while Bill and I, if you're available and willing, will work on deterring it and a capture plan. If this is acceptable to all, I say we come up with our scientific name for this and go from there."

With all four in agreement on the plan, they set out to give the

Mishipeshu a new scientific name. The only input from Rick was that it had to have Yooper somewhere in the name. After all, it only traveled and hunted in the Upper Peninsula, and, being that Yoopers were the ones having to deal with it, it should have a designation that recognized that fact. A couple of names that didn't make the short list were Yoopersaurus and Yooper-shoo-aqua-panthera, or Yooper-water-panther. They finally settled on Panthera-aqua-gigas-yooper. Or, Yooper water panther, with gigas being a reference to the arapaima gigas, the Amazonian fish with scales similar to the Mishipeshu. It also made sense as the Shoo is more commonly known to the Native tribes as the water panther.

Now to register the name with the International Code of Zoological Nomenclature and make it official. This was Matt's assignment, as he was familiar with the process. All four men would be credited with the discovery, with a special consideration given to Rick as the only one to collect a sample of the species. The rest of the day was spent working on strategies to capture, ward off, or, if necessary, kill it.

To Matt and Bill, it seemed like such a waste to go through all the effort of discovering then classifying a new species just to kill it. It was like putting an animal on the endangered species list and not doing everything they could to save it. This would drive the two of them to develop viable alternatives to conserve, not kill. Mike and Rick also understood the importance of saving the Shoo, but they were more concerned about protecting their families, friends, and community. After all, Mike and Rick lived in the Shoo's hunting grounds, while Matt and Bill would never really be in a position to face it. Matt rarely ventured far from the city, and Bill lived in Idaho, not exactly in the thick of it. It would be a Herculean effort for Bill and Matt to come up with a workable plan to save it, while Mike and Rick only had to come up with the right weaponry to stop it. A much simpler, but still difficult, task.

They would need to be able to make a kill shot on its underbelly to make sure of a clean kill; not an easy thing to do, as, according to Rick, it never offered its underbelly, even after he had shot it. The Shoo moved low to the ground, much like the arapaima probably did while hunting the river bottoms, its heavy, armor-like scales protecting it from predators that may try to make a meal out of it by attacking it from above. This would be futile, as its scales could keep all but the most powerful predators from penetrating into its flesh. And so it is with the Shoo, as Rick found out when he shot it. They would either need to get it to rise up, exposing its belly, or they would have to get below it and hope to get a shot off before being discovered. Not a very good plan.

"What if we used some kind of land mine setup? You know, it walks over it, and *bam!* Problem solved."

Rick had always been fascinated with things that go boom. Not in a nefarious way; he just liked seeing thing blow up. As a kid, he would fill spent rifle casings with black powder, stuff a dynamite fuse down the neck, crimp the top, and wrap the fuse connection with waterproof tape. They made quite the explosion, so Rick would cut the fuses extra long to give himself plenty of time to get out of the way. When those things went off, sometimes shrapnel from the brass casings would fly out. Pretty dangerous, but what a blast, literally. He stopped making those when he started reloading his own ammunition. Brass casings were just too expensive to use in that way. But there were other options, and if they were to make explosives, they would need to be much bigger than a rifle casing, and lighting a fuse was not an option. Too many variables.

"Rocket fuses."

"What the hell are you talking about? Where the hell are we gonna get rocket fuses?"

Rick was confused about what Mike was talking about.

"Not real rockets, model rockets. You know, the ones you shoot up, and they parachute back down. Those fuses are remotely set off with a battery or some type of electronic connection. They can be set off from a distance and almost instantly. All we would need to do is get the thing to walk over them. *That's* the challenge. I think we should figure out a way to attract or push it into the kill zone, so to speak."

Mike remembered his childhood fascination with model rocketry. He and his friends would launch rockets just about every week during his pre- and early teens. They even found ways to creatively destroy the rockets that would inevitably become damaged. They rigged rockets to blow up midair or even catch fire during flight. They initially launched rockets using lit fuses, but they sometimes fell out before the fire from the fuse could set off the rocket, so they went to the specialty fuses designed for use in model rocketry. They consisted of a thin wire coated in a helical called pyrogen. When an electric current passes through the pyrogen, it reacts to the current by burning, much like a lit fuse, and that burning ignites the rocket engine, which is primarily made up of black powder. It could be a fairly simple process to expand the use of model rocket fuses to set off a much larger explosive charge. It was the perfect plan for Rick to work on. Once Mike explained his idea, he could see the wheels turning in Rick's brain.

"Plus, I've reverse engineered the dragon's breath shotgun round. It's kinda like turning your shotgun into a small flamethrower. I figured that since this thing lived in the dark, cold waters of Lake Superior, it probably doesn't like bright lights or heat. Maybe we could use that, too."

While Mike and Rick seemed to have at least a rough plan to kill the Mishipeshu, Bill and Matt were looking into trapping it. To capture it, they would need to attract it so it would become caught in the trap. They didn't have anything in mind that would attract it, or even a trap of some kind that could hold it without injuring it. Needless to say, they were behind from the beginning. Seems it was easier to come up with ways to kill something than to save it. But Matt had some ideas that involved modifying systems used by commercial fisherman to catch fish.

The nets had to be able to hold tons of fish without breaking, a characteristic that would be needed to hold the Shoo long enough to get a tranquilizer in it. And, what type of tranquilizer would they need to use? The wrong type or dose could kill it, which contradicted their intended goal. In any case, their time was limited. Bill only had two days left before he needed to get back to Idaho. They decided that, if they couldn't come up with a viable plan before those two days were up, Bill would work on researching tranquilizers for their mission, while Matt would focus on the bait and trap setup. Time was not on their side, as winter was knocking on the door of the Upper Peninsula, and it wouldn't be long before the Mishipeshu would be able to hunt.

9

BOMBS AWAY

Only a week had passed since going to the LSSU lab and learning that Rick indeed had an sample of what was now known as the Yooper water panther, and Rick was already in production mode for his remotely detonated landmine idea. He had called Mike to come out and see his work so far.

Boom!

"Holy shit, that was a big explosion."

"That ain't nothin'. That was just a taste of what I'm plannin'. It's just to test out your rocket fuse idea. It works pretty good so far."

"I would say so. Let's just hope the ATF doesn't get wind of what we're doin'. They don't like homemade bombs, you know."

"Well, what they don't know can't hurt us. I wanna do a test to see how far away we can get before the electrical charge dissipates too much to spark the fuse. Those fuses ain't got a lot of powder on them, so I feel we could be several hundred feet away. So far, I've run the line about a hundred feet with no problem, but even that's gonna be way closer than we wanna be."

"Yeah, the farther away, the better, I'm thinking."

"Especially after I add some surprises into the mix. I'm thinkin' we put some nails or screws inside the bomb, you know, for shrapnel. The more damage, the better."

Rick had made the sample bombs to test the ignition system. They were simple explosive devices, commonly known as pipe bombs. Simple devices, but assembling them could be tricky. The body of the pipe bomb was made from threaded plumbing pipe, the galvanized ones. The tricky part was when the pipe cap gets screwed onto the pipe. If any explosive medium were to get on the threads of the pipe, the act of screwing on the cap could create a spark or enough heat to set off the bomb prematurely, severely injuring or killing the bomb maker. In Rick's bombs, he used black powder, a stable yet low-yield type of powder. But once confined inside the pipe, even low-yield powders can produce a tremendous explosion. It's not the powder that causes the damage, but the shrapnel from the pipe fracturing.

While Mike and Rick were perfecting their explosives, Matt and Bill were working on a system to capture the Shoo. Bill had returned to his office in Coeur d'Alene, Idaho, and was working on a capture system idea similar to how they used to capture killer whales, but those systems relied on a series of concentric nets that confined the orcas in an ever-shrinking space where they could be corralled. Trappers sometimes used small explosives called seal bombs to push the orcas towards the traps. But they figured netting the Shoo was out of the question. A system that used nets would have to be extremely large, and the risk of drowning the Shoo was high. After all, the Shoo was not a fish, but more of an amphibian. It would need to come to the surface at some time to breathe; netting was not going to work. So, Matt used his connections in the fishing industry to help him design a modified trapping system much like the types used to live-capture animals like raccoons or skunks, but it would need to be much larger and stronger to withstand the Shoo's massive body. The shallow water along the shores and rivers where it hunted would offer several good locations to set up these traps, but the ice would make trapping the Shoo difficult. The other problem would be to know when and in which areas to set them. They had limited resources for their project, so they would only be able to construct a couple of the pens. Hopefully, they would be big enough and strong enough to hold it.

"The big problem here is that there really isn't any way to do a test run on these things. It's going to be trial by fire."

Bill and Matt kept in touch almost daily through video calls. That way, they could share any information in real time.

"I'm trying to get some time off to come back out there to help you, Matt, but we're short-staffed, and I've used most of my vacation time already this year. Do you have anyone else that can assist you on those days I can't be there?"

"I have a couple of graduate students I've lined up to help me. They will get some extra considerations when exam time comes."

"That's good news. Have you talked with Mike or Rick? Have you heard how they're doing on their end?"

"I've spoken with Mike a couple of times. It looks like they're working on some type of explosive device to stop it. If it works, it'll make a big mess of the creature. I'm hoping we get our shot first, but winter's closing in fast. We don't have much time to fine-tune our system. I'm not even sure what to bait our traps with, or even if using bait is going to work. I mean, it's got to be big enough to get the thing interested. I'm talking about a cow or something along those lines."

"Maybe talk to the Fish and Game guys up there. They might have some large roadkill that might work, but I wouldn't mention anything about our little project. We don't need a bunch of people getting involved. Maybe tell them you need it for some research on predatory fish species or something."

"Good idea, Bill. I've got a contact there I've worked with before. I'm sure he'll be able to get us what we need. Now, with that, when do you think you'll be back out? The ice is already rolling in, and it won't be long before it starts forming the shelf ice, maybe a couple of weeks. Once the shelf ice is in place, the bay starts freezing pretty quickly. I'm thinking we probably only have three weeks or so before the water's frozen between the shelf ice and the shore. If our theory is correct, that's when the Shoo will start to hunt the shores."

Matt was right. Hunting season for the Shoo was fast approaching. There wasn't much time to do any fine-tuning to either of the team's efforts. Matt hoped to at least practice deploying the traps. His best guess as to where was based on his knowledge of predatory fish habits; setting up close to river mouths or streams that fed into Whitefish Bay would be his plan. Those areas had easy access into landlocked areas and provided the paths of least resistance in getting back out to the bay. Plus, the shelf ice formed right up to and sometimes over those points of entry and exit. It would also be easier for the team to get the traps into position. The next week would be filled with practice, practice, practice.

"I'm trying to get back out sometime in the next two weeks. I've worked out a deal with the state to let me use some of my sick time. I can stay about three weeks. I know it's not much time, but let's hope it's enough."

Mike and Rick's plan, however, was progressing well. They had worked out just how much distance they could have between the improvised mines and the Shoo, about 500 feet. A thousand feet was the hope, but 500 would give them enough time to react and, hopefully, keep it from going any farther. Now all they had to do was make enough bombs to put a protective barrier around Mike and Sarah's cabin, while leaving a few out to use like hand grenades. Those would have to be set off by lighting a fuse then throwing—not ideal, but they didn't have time to experiment with impact detonators. Those weren't readily available for sale to the public, for obvious reasons, so they would have to be homemade, and they could be tricky. Many a would-be bomb-maker had met his demise by trying to create that type of detonator.

While the two teams were perfecting their respective plans, the ice was on the move. The first waves of snowball-size ice balls had formed along the shoreline. They float in in ribbons of ice, driven ever closer to shore by the waves. This is when predators like coyotes, foxes, and wolves start patrolling the shorelines by using the ice as their highway. This is also when the Mishipeshu starts its hunting season. Right now, the ice was just starting to catch on the sandbars. It wouldn't be long before the ice volcanoes formed all along the shores of Lake Superior.

10

THE AWAKENING

No one really understands for sure how an animal knows there's a change in seasons coming. Is it an innate sense of timing? Is there something in the smells, the changing light conditions, or a feeling in the air that tells an animal it's time to hibernate, to wake up, to move out of its den? Most feel that the simple changes in temperature and the shortening or lengthening daylight hours tell them to find shelter or to rouse to action. But, in the case of the Mishipeshu, these changes go unnoticed. From its summertime den deep below the surface of Lake Superior, sheltered from the sunlight above, within the enclosed walls of Lake Inferior, the Mishipeshu wouldn't be able to sense the change in light, nor would it feel any temperature variations in such a deep and protected lair. The water is always cold, almost freezing. The only connection to the open waters of Lake Superior high above is a small opening in the ceiling of the littoral, or sea cave, where it spends nearly eight months a year confined by cold, damp, dark walls.

The only illumination comes from bioluminescent plankton,

holdovers from when the Great Lakes were formed. Not normally found in fresh water, these plankton light up when agitated or when they multiply through budding or fission. This low-level light helps keep the Mishipeshu from being a blind cave-dwelling creature and thus allows it to hunt the fertile grounds above. But the Mishipeshu must still hunt at night and during low light conditions such as snowy, cloudy days without direct sunlight. Otherwise, its eyes could be temporarily blinded, as it lacks the pupil control that dims bright light. Instead, when confronted by any sudden introduction of bright light, its pupils completely close, effectively blinding it. The pupils will not reopen or adjust back and forth like most mammals; they will stay closed until it can get back to the water, where they can safely reopen. For this reason, the Mishipeshu's sense of smell is extremely sensitive. As it makes its way along the shoreline and onto land, it secretes a type of slime from scent glands at the base of its tail. The scent is faint, almost undetectable, but when the Mishipeshu needs to follow it back across an unfamiliar land, it produces an image in its brain that is like a line on a map that it can follow. This has helped it escape detection as it doesn't take much light to cause this reaction in its eyes. A distant headlight or the light from a small flashlight can cause this. As an act of self-preservation, when this happens, its immediate response is to turn back into the water. If anyone actually got a glimpse of it at those distances, they would likely see the movement and not the creature itself. It would be dismissed as a bear or moose running through the woods. This has kept the creature in the realm of cryptozoology and not a proven, biological creature. But even cryptids can be found to be real. New species are discovered fairly regularly, and science fiction becomes science fact.

As the Mishipeshu moves through its cavernous lair, a trigger of sorts alerts it to the change in seasons. The very plankton that provide it with the limited light within its walls slows its reproduction rate, causing a reduction in the creation of the light it emits. This change occurs in a normal pattern brought on by minute changes in water temperature and food sources. As water filters into the cavern from above, nutrients that are plentiful during the warmer months decrease as the waters above cool. This forces the plankton into a somewhat dormant state that will last until the nutrients from the lake increase again with warmer temperatures and longer days. This is how it knows when to leave the confines of the cavern and start its annual hunt for the food that will sustain it through the months of seclusion. During this period of change, shipping on Lake Superior is also changing. Sudden ice flows can damage and even sink the large cargo ships that travel the shipping lanes on the lake, so there will soon be a cessation of ship traffic on the lake, further protecting the Mishipeshu from detection. Soon, it will make its way up the well-worn pathway that leads to the opening above, and it will make longer and longer probing trips through the floating ice balls and along the shores of Whitefish Bay. Always keeping hidden from the shore by staying far enough out until veiled by night. It will stay off the land until the ice builds into the ice mountains on the sand bars, and the ice was already starting to stick on the shallower sand bars that ran close to the mouth of the Tahquamenon River.

Known simply as the river mouth, it is normally a busy boat launch area, but the ice shuts that down. The normally full camp grounds along the river empty out, providing more and more cover for the Mishipeshu to travel under. A relatively shallow river for most of its length, only sixty feet deep at its deepest, it will freeze over thick enough for snowmobiles to traverse much of its surface, not a recommended path to travel as thin spots have swallowed many a sled. But to the adrenaline junkies of the snowmobile world, the thrill ride is hard to resist. The Mishipeshu knows where these thin spots are likely to be and will lie in wait on the bottom for those unlucky enough to fall through. A snowmobiler will break through the ice and sink due to the heavy snow gear they wear, and the Mishipeshu will grab and drag the unsuspecting victim down and then swim under the ice to the bay, having never been spotted by any other sled jockeys that may be traveling with its victim. Another missing person report, never to be solved.

These are the early hunting grounds. Later in winter, those thin spots eventually freeze solid, and the Mishipeshu moves to more land-based hunting. But, for now, it's all about probing, scouting, and waiting for the ice pile-up before building its frozen fortresses to stage its attacks from. Winters are always a little different in the UP. Sometimes snow and ice pile up by late October; other times, not until early December. This unpredictability can force the Mishipeshu to hunt in more exposed areas, leaving it vulnerable to detection. So the during the early hunts, it is critical for it to harvest enough food to sustain it in case of a late winter. But one thing's for certain—it always comes, and it wouldn't be long, now.

11

ANOTHER IDEA

Matt Wallace wondered how they would know when and where to place the traps, and what to do if they actually caught their target. What if the traps didn't hold it? What if the tranquilizer didn't work fast enough, or at all? Too many what-ifs. In science, there are always what-ifs; it's what helps scientists work out theories and solutions. But you could what-if something to death. One thing Matt knew was, if they did got a chance to catch the Shoo, they would need an a secondary plan if it escaped. And Matt had just the thing.

"What you got there, Matt?"

Bill and Matt were on there now weekly video call going over updates and changes to their plan.

"This, my friend, is a geo tracker. We use them all the time to track certain migratory species to see just where they travel and any other habits they might have. They are picked up on special tracking satellites that are specifically dedicated to conservation efforts around the world. Hell, they use this system to track Great White sharks all over the world, and I want to try and get one on our little project creature, if we can. If we are fortunate enough to actually trap it, we will shoot it with a tranquilizer, but it may still escape before it takes effect. This little baby would attach itself to it as it enters the trap, it's automatically deployed once the trap door closes. That way, if it does escape, we can see exactly where it goes, no matter how far or deep. It might just give us an idea of how to deal with it."

"Excellent idea, Matt. I don't know why we didn't think of something like that from the beginning. As a matter of fact, tagging and tracking might just be the way to go. That way, we'd have an opportunity to study its habits, maybe find out where it spends the warmer months. All the while, we would know its exact location, so we could keep the authorities notified to keep it from harming folks."

"Yeah, I thought of that too. Only problem with that approach is that, if someone was to go missing from an area we knew it to be frequenting, and we didn't do everything to stop it, we could be open to some pretty large lawsuits. I'm not sure the University would look at that very kindly. I'm thinking we need to go with trying to catch it as our number one priority, with this as a backup plan. That should help if the worst case scenario should occur."

"You're probably right there, Matt. People are so sue happy these days. They don't take into account other factors that may be relevant. They just want that big-money settlement. Sometimes, I think some people don't even care about the loss as much as the money these days. It's a sad commentary. Anyway, how's it looking out there? I see the temps have come down to freezing and below. Is the ice forming yet?"

"It's starting to. I've done some preliminary scouting for placing our traps, and I think one should go close the Tahqua-menon river mouth area. Ice seems to build there pretty early, and it's shallow enough for us to work fairly safely. According to the missing person reports from that area, several people have gone missing from there over the years. Mostly in late November and early December. And all but two were snowmobilers running the river before it was frozen enough to hold their sleds. The other two were kayakers who were thought to be fishing an open area of ice upriver a bit about three years ago. Only found the kayaks, and one had some strange scratches on it, but authorities attributed those to the current dragging it under the ice. I looked at the photos of the kayaks, and the scratches seemed a little too symmetrical to me to be from the ice. But I could be wrong. When are you thinking of coming out? I wouldn't wait too long. It gets tough to fly in and out of our little airport with some of the weather we get up here."

"I know. I was thinking about that. I'll get online and see if I can get a flight out sometime in the next week. I really want to be there before the ice gets set up. I pulled some strings and plan on being there a month, maybe five weeks. I hope that's going to be enough, because that's all I was able to negotiate."

While Matt and Bill were working on finalizing their plans, Mike and Rick were planning too. Only their plan didn't rely on attracting the Shoo; it was all about deterring or killing it—if it happened to show up. Although Mike was primarily concerned about his family, he was also worried about someone crossing its path somewhere down any number of the county's remote areas. Covering all those locations would be impossibly difficult anyway. So the plan was to focus on where they knew it had attacked before and try to be ready if it did.

Mike and Rick finished placing their homemade bombs, ten in all. "That should do it. I think we have your shoreline covered." They had buried the bombs in shallow holes every fifteen feet across the lake side of the cabin. All the wiring for the fuses were buried, with all the wires culminating on an rudimentary electric switchboard mounted to a small wooden box. A car battery was placed inside the box; one wire attached to the positive terminal, one to the ground. All the other wires were mounted so Mike—or Sarah, if Mike was unavailable—only had to take the wires attached to the battery and touch them to the desired bomb wires and *boom!*

It would be that quick. No waiting for a lit fuse to run to the bomb. That had too many risks. Wet or broken fuses could mean missing their chance to end the Shoo's hunting spree. Always the out-of-the-box thinker, Rick suggested they run the fuse lines through plastic conduit to further protect them from getting severed before the signal could reach the bomb. None of fuse lines were spliced. Each was a single line of fuse, with the only connections at the bomb and terminal. They had done every test imaginable to make sure their system would work. It was as good as could be, and reliable. The only failures during testing were when a fuse disconnected from the bomb. This was solved by using heat-shrink connectors to link the bomb to the fuse line. Simple but effective, these connectors are basically vinyl tube where the end of one wire goes in one side, and the other end of the other wire goes into the opposite end. The wires are forced together at the junction, and then heat is applied to shrink the vinyl around both wires. This type of connection is waterproof and difficult, if not impossible, to pull apart. The part that was actually connected to the bomb was soldered to the terminal for addition security against separating. It was virtually foolproof.

"Sarah! Come on over here and let me show you how this thing works."

Sarah was not happy about needing to know how to blow the bombs. She had gone along with Mike on the homemade dragon's breath shotgun rounds, not thinking she would need them. She just figured Mike would handle it and that would be that. But

Mike needed her to understand and be comfortable with every aspect of their defense system, even though he knew she wasn't in any way prone to violence. With Sarah, there always has to be another way. But with this threat, she understood there would be no reasoning with a hungry carnivore, so she paid close attention to what Mike and Rick told her.

"It's simple, Sarah. Each one of these wires mounted to this board is connected to a bomb. Each bomb is fifteen feet away from the bombs next to it. They start over by our property line at the beach, and end over on the other side of our property, by the property stake. There's a small blue flag where each bomb is, so it'll be easy to see if our creature is in position. I'll paint the snow in those areas so we can see them when the flags get covered. Hopefully, you won't need to do this, but just in case, you'll know how. We're going to keep our shotguns loaded and close by all winter if need be. The flames from the dragon's breath rounds should keep it from getting too close. We might even be able to push it closer to one of those bombs."

Sarah was listening, but not really. Talk about sewing, gardening, or cooking, and she was laser focused. But when it came to anything technical and unrelated to those three subjects, and her brain just kind of fogged over. Mike knew this but hoped enough of his instructions got through to her, just in case she had to activate a bomb or two. In any case, they were as prepared as they could be for a legendary, unknown, and mysterious creature that only the local Natives and a few other locals really believed in.

"Hey, Rick. What're you doing about all this?"

Sarah hadn't really talked with Rick about all the Mishipeshu stuff. She'd barely even spoken to him since Mike met him. They usually met at Rick's house or some other location, and he was only at their cabin today to make sure the bombs were wired properly.

"Not a whole hell of a lot, to tell you the truth. This thing seems to be mostly where there's water. There ain't no water around my place, at least not close enough to worry about. But I am going to be huntin' it when I can. It's been in my huntin' area before, so I'll keep an eye out for it there. I have some of these bang pipes I can use when I'm in the woods, so if I see it, I'm going to kill it."

Sarah was a little surprised at Rick's nonchalance, like he was just going out to run errands. But that was just how Rick was; he saw everything as just something that needed to be done. A chore or task, nothing more. He figured that getting all worked up or emotional about things just leads to mistakes or poor results. The Shoo was just another job that needed doing. But Rick wasn't being completely honest. He wasn't just going to "keep an eye out for it." He was going to actively hunt the Mishipeshu. It would be his primary focus for the winter. After all, he had seen it and survived the encounter, and he knew what he would be up against if he found it. Either he would kill it, or it would kill him; that was the measure of his resolve. All or nothing, push the envelope, do or die... Whatever the cliche, Rick lived by it, a true Yooper through and through.

"Well, you be careful going after this thing. You might be looking at it as a hunting trip, but this thing's out there for survival, and apparently it's pretty good at it, because it's been around an awfully long time. I doubt you're the first person to try and get rid of it. Besides, how do you know there's only one of these creatures? There might be a whole pack of them for all you know."

Sarah hadn't completely bought the stories of the Mishipeshu until this very moment. It was the look on Rick's face of utter determination that finally convinced her. From what Mike had told her about Rick and his lifestyle, she knew him as a serious person, not prone to going off the rails or expending energy going after foolish ideas. During the few times she had actually spoken with him, he barely smiled or gave any indication that he didn't mean every single thing he said. In other words, Rick was a serious man. The determination she saw in his eyes when he said, "When I see it, I'm going to kill it", brought the reality of the situation into full focus. They had a monster on their hands, and they might actually have to face it.

"Mike, go over how to set these bombs off again. I just want to be sure I do it right."

Sarah paid close attention. All the while, she kept one eye on the water and the ever growing ice. She could see larger pieces of ice rolling in the waves and moving towards shore. Big pieces— some the size of small cars. She could see those larger ones getting stuck on the sandbars that paralleled their property, and it gave her a sick feeling in the pit of her stomach. Winter was upon them.

12

TRACKS

It had been almost two weeks since Mike and Rick placed their bombs, just in time, too. Almost overnight, the ice had set in all along the shoreline of Whitefish Bay, and the ice mountains had established all along the furthest sandbar from the Perkins' cabin, and a secondary line had formed along the second, middle, sandbar. The bay was frozen over as far as they could see, leaving only a thin section of open water about 600 yards wide towards the middle of the bay. Looking at a photo of the bay, it could be mistaken for the North Pole or Antarctica. Mike and Sarah had seen a couple of wolves out on the ice, as well as a coyote and a fox. The hunters were venturing onto the ice in hopes of finding leftover fish carcasses the otters didn't eat. Food is difficult to find for these predators this time of year, and anything edible made a fine meal.

Bill had flown in just two days earlier to meet with Matt, and the two were heading over to Mike and Sarah's to go over their plans and see what Mike and Rick had worked out. On their way, Matt would stop at the mouth of the Tahquamenon River, simply known as the river mouth, to show Bill where he was planning on setting one of the traps. It was just another three miles to the Perkins' cabin from there.

"You see how the river splits just on the west side of the bridge? I think we should put one trap right there. That way, if it comes this way, it will have to pass by the trap no matter which fork it takes. I've got some deer carcasses a friend at Fish and Game confiscated from poachers. Hopefully, it will be enough to lure it in. Even if we don't catch it, the trap has a geo tracker that deploys when the bait is tugged. The same mechanism trips the door and locks it down. A red bar springs up once the system is set off. It's made to break through up to two inches of ice, so we'll be able to see if the trap's been tripped even from shore. And if the geo tracker is deployed, I'll get an alert on my phone, so we should be all set once we get the traps set."

"Great set up, Matt. Any idea where to put the other trap?"

"Well, that's a tougher decision. There are just so many places that this thing could go. So, I figured we'd set it where the highest number of people were reported missing. The Maple Barrens. It's pretty wild in there. Anyone who lives in there is off-grid, and there isn't any cell service. The Shelldrake River cuts right down the middle. It's a narrow and shallow river, popular among snow-mobilers due to the rugged terrain. About five percent of all of the missing person reports come from somewhere close to the Shell-drake. It's thick in there, hard to traverse even with sleds. As a matter of fact, the only vehicle big enough to safely transport our trap is a snow cat, but its size limits it to staying on the trail, so we're going to have to get the trap in position manually. There's three of them in Paradise as part of the Night Riders trail grooming group.

"I got ahold of the supervisor, John Maxwell. He said he would help us out as long as it didn't interfere with grooming operations.

We'll be on their schedule for getting the trap out there. But once they drop off the trap, they're back to work. There will be no ride out, so one of us will have to follow on a snowmobile. I've scouted a couple promising locations on Google Earth. They're spots that can easily be reached close to the trails, but far enough away from them not to attract attention. I only worry about those sled heads that use the frozen river as their trail. The river isn't that deep anywhere along its path, so it freezes pretty solid. This trap will have to be set on land. Otherwise, the ice will encase it, and it won't work."

The traps Matt had built for the job weighed almost 600 pounds, so maneuvering them into position, especially in snow and ice, would be difficult. Not to mention whether or not it would catch their target. Matt had chartered a large fishing boat to set the trap at the river mouth; that one would be easy to set—just drop it in place. But the Shelldrake trap would be another story. Because of the trail grooming sled attached to the snowcat, it wouldn't be able to place the trap exactly where they wanted it. John would get as close as possible, but then he and Bill would have to move it by hand into its final position. No easy task. They would have to figure out the best way to get it in position without damaging the trap or getting hurt. They were heading over to the Perkins cabin to go over everything the with Mike and Rick. Matt and Bill were hopping, with Rick's skills, they would come up with a viable solution.

As they drove down Route 123 towards Whitefish Point, they couldn't help but notice the ice accumulation along the shore. In some places, the ice had piled up over six feet high, where the sandbars reduced the depth of the water to under three feet, but the river mouth was still mostly water and a thin layer of ice leading out into the bay. But the ice was getting thicker by the day in the protected sections of the river, including the fork where they hoped to place one of the traps.

Seeing this scene for the first time gave Bill a true sense of foreboding. The icy cold temperatures, the barren landscape of shades of gray and white, and the lack of traffic on the road helped him understand why it was easy for people to just disappear. It was an eerily empty sight. There was plenty of evidence of human activity, though. Well-worn snowmobile trails paralleled the road, and recent crossings from one side of the road to the other as the trail zig-zagged from the lake side to the heavily forested west side had left telltale snow debris across the road. Looking at the trail of snow that crossed the road that the sleds had left, it was easy to see that theirs was the first vehicle to cross over those tracks, as there were no tire tracks cutting across them. Bill couldn't help but wonder if the Mishipeshu had already been hunting in this area, and it made him uneasy.

As they approached Paradise, the scene changed dramatically. There were over 200 snowmobiles scattered throughout the small town, and the hotels and rental cabins were full. The restaurants were filled and, at eleven in the morning, the bars were doing their fair share of business as well. Alcohol and snowmobiles in rugged, desolate, hard-to-reach areas. What could go wrong? Not to mention there might just be something lurking nearby, waiting for the opportunity to grab an unsuspecting victim and add them to the list of missing people.

In fact, there had already been a victim, but not in the Paradise area. A few days ago, near the Keweenaw Peninsula, a young woman by the name of Carol Thacker was snowshoeing alone along the frozen shores near Copper Harbor, a popular destination at the tip of the Keweenaw. According to the police report, Miss Thacker fell through a thin spot in the ice and never surfaced. The strange thing was, all the surrounding ice was at least five inches thick, more than enough to support a person. One of the investigating officers said it almost looked as if something had somehow thinned out the ice from underneath in about an eight-foot diameter. Large enough to make it difficult for someone to climb out, especially with snow-shoes on, but small enough to refreeze quickly. Thin spots in the ice were not. However, this thin spot was in an area that had been frozen for weeks, and it was unusual for that large a spot to form after the ice had been established and without some kind of outside force to cause it, such as creek water feeding into the lake or runoff from melting snow. Neither factor was present. It was just an anom-alous spot in the ice. Divers searched the immediate area but only recovered a single snowshoe. The straps were broken, as if they had been subjected to tremendous force, but other than that, nothing.

This event had not made the news in the town of Paradise. And, even if it had, it probably wouldn't have gotten a whole lot of attention from the adventure seekers gathering to enjoy all that winter in the UP could offer. If the details of this story were true, Bill and Matt might have thought the Mishipeshu was intelligent enough to set traps of its own. This would indicate a level of intel-ligence they hadn't considered, and this one piece of the puzzle could cost them, if they weren't careful.

The moment Carol Thacker broke through the ice, her fate was sealed. It had been lying in wait for this instant. As soon as her feet struck the water, it was on her, grabbing her by her feet and dragging her out to deeper water. She didn't even have time to scream; the only sound was a loud crack as the ice broke and the splash as her body hit the water, which nobody heard. As she fell, she tried to scream, but it had pulled her under too fast, and she was the only person who could hear her gurgled scream as the Mishipeshu pulled her down. The water was cold, so cold, and the force of it as she was taken farther and farther down and out broke her neck. She didn't die right away, so her paralyzed body fluttered in the water like a leaf in a stiff breeze. She could see the light from above grow dimmer and dimmer until there was no light at all. It's said that in emergency situations, the rule of threes applies. One can live for three minutes without breathable air or in icy water, three hours in extreme heat or cold, and survive three days without drinkable water. Carol didn't last two. An eternity. There had been other victims of the Mishipeshu this year, but some of the locations of their demises had not been discovered yet, and might never be. Mother Nature erased many of the scenes with snow and wind, or the Earth simply swallowed up the evidence in the swamps and bogs of the UP, never to be found, and there would be more... many more.

"Holy crap! Look at all the snowmobilers. It's like, there's hardly a soul in sight, and then—*pow!* Here they are. Amazing. I wonder if any of these folks will come into contact with our little friend. It might be a good idea to hang out at one of the bars later and see if any of them mention seeing anything unusual. Could give us a starting point."

"That's not a bad idea, Bill. Let's run it by Mike and Rick and see if they want to join us. We could split up and cover more of the bar."

Pulling into the Perkins' tree-lined, freshly cleared driveway, Bill thought it looked like the idyllic lakefront cabin with its gray and white paint and tasteful country-style flair. The recent snowfall made it look like a Christmas card. It was hard to think of this scene as a possible place where someone's life was taken by an unknown or mythical creature. Surreal.

"You made it. Welcome to our little slice of Paradise."

Mike and Sarah met them at the door, but Rick stayed in the living room staring out at the lake. He was searching the ever-increasing ice for any sign of the Shoo. He knew it probably was too early for it to be making an appearance, but he couldn't stop thinking about it. The ice had piled up pretty good along this part of the bay, and he could see larger chunks of ice bobbing up and down on the water for as far as he could see. By morning, there would be much more built up along the sandbars, and the water between them would start to freeze solidly enough for snowmobiles to traverse. With the ice quickly becoming firmly established, it could soon be hunting season for the Shoo. Unbeknownst to the team, it was already hunting season farther north where winter comes earlier and harder.

This has always been the pattern for the Mishipeshu. Start as soon as the ice sets up, wherever it may be. Historically, that area has been the Keweenaw Peninsula and the shores of northeast Ontario. Winter starts much earlier in that part of its world, and winter snow accumulations can reach over 300 inches in the Keweenaw, as opposed to around 200 inches around Paradise. Over the ages, the Shoo has learned not to stay in one area too long, moving steadily southward as winter seizes more and more of the hunting grounds. That way, its exposure to being discovered is minimized. It's not that it actually knows this, but history has taught it and its bloodline that too much contact with too many humans means more difficult hunting. Humans are not its only prey, but their size and shape make people easier to transport back to its lair, and the lack of awareness most humans have of their surroundings makes them easier to hunt. As long as it sticks to lone humans or those who make serious missteps, it doesn't stand much chance of discovery. It knows that staying in one place too long, no matter how successful the hunting, brings too much attention to its presence, so it moves with the season, drifting ever southward as winter progresses and then back north as warmer weather returns. It always finishes its hunts in the UP where they began, the Keweenaw. From there, it may hunt along the shores of

Ontario before finally, making its way back to its den in Lake Inferior. But, for now, hunting season was open.

"Nice place you have, here. Great view of the lake."

Matt and Bill were looking out at the quickly changing lake
scape, as the waves crashed into the ever-heightening ice mountain range that was building all along their shoreline. But not one
of them were enjoying the view; they were scanning the ice for
tracks or signs of the Mishipeshu. They stood there in silence for
what seemed like an eternity, mesmerized by the icy water
spewing from the mouths of the ice volcanoes along the range. It
was hypnotizing.

"How about a drink? I think we could all use an adult beverage
right about now."

Sarah's observation was spot on. They were each on edge from
thoughts of what may happen over the next few months. Matt and
Bill were concerned about getting their traps set and whether they
would hold it. While Mike and Rick were hoping that if they had
an encounter they could fend it off and, hopefully, kill it. Sarah
was just plain stressed out over the whole thing. She just wanted it
to go away, never to return.

"That sounds like a good idea, hon. What's everyone want?
Wine? Beer? Something with a little more kick? I've got a pretty
stocked bar, so what's your pleasure?"

That broke the trance. Everyone seemed to loosen up after
that. Rick showed Matt and Bill his bomb setup. Mike gave them a
show with his dragon's breath shotgun shells, and Matt and Bill
covered the workings of the trap and geo tracker. They all felt
good; they were prepared if the Shoo actually showed.

While most of the group was taking a primarily defensive
stance, Rick was the only one planning an aggressive pursuit of
the creature, but he kept that to himself. He didn't want anyone
messing up his hunt.

"Well, everything seems to be in place. I hope we haven't forgotten or overlooked anything."

Mike's voice had a tone of uncertainty to it. He couldn't help thinking there was something more they could do to prepare, but there wasn't. Nothing they thought of could really prepare them for an encounter with it. There wasn't any precedent for what they were doing. There were only vague historical references and the odd story of sightings or strange disappearances. Nothing concrete to base any plan on. Matt's scientific input was the only foundation for any of their plans, except for Rick's personal observation, so it was all a best guess as to how to proceed.

"So, Bill and I had an idea. With all the snowmobilers in town, maybe we should head out the bars and see if any of them have seen anything strange out there. You know, eavesdrop on their conversations. We might be able to find out if it's here yet and where it might be. We've got our traps coming in two days, and we know for sure we're putting one at the river mouth—the boat's bringing it in in the morning, so that one's set. But we're still not a hundred percent sure of our second location. We're thinking somewhere along the Shelldrake. There's been some missing person reports in there over the years. But if we could get a better handle on it, like a sighting or something, we could fine-tune it a bit."

"Well, that sounds like a good idea. There's only a couple bars in town, so maybe we should split up and cover more ground. If you do hear anything that sounds like our target, try to get some specifics like trail number or some other landmark. Just don't give anything away about our little project. We don't need a bunch of extra hands in the mix. If we're able to get any specifics, maybe Rick will be able help us locate the area. I'm still not all that familiar with the trails and such. The cabin's been kickin' my ass."

"Well, I just have two things to say about that plan. First, you better eat something before you head out drinking. I've got some chili in the pot ready to go. And second, you're not leaving me here all by myself. It'd be my luck that that damn thing would show up while you guys are gone, and I'm not going to be here if it does."

Sarah was dead serious. From this day forward, she would not allow herself to be left alone at the cabin. When the men were out, she'd head down to Julie's house or go to Newberry or the Soo until they got back.

"Okay, baby, we'll just make it a date night."

Mike hadn't really included Sarah in much of the planning or discussion, just an overview. The only in-depth details about the plans were about what to do at the cabin. It wasn't that he didn't think she was important or had anything to add; he knew how she could get herself all worked into a ball of nerves if she got too much information on a bad subject. She's always been that way, so Mike got used to limiting her involvement in delicate or difficult situations. Sarah understood this and would be the first to admit how she handled stress. She usually appreciated that Mike tried to protect her, and this problem was no exception. She didn't want to participate in the capture or killing of the Mishipeshu, but she didn't want to be completely left out of the conversation. She just didn't want too many details.

After they had eaten, they gathered in the family room to discuss how to handle themselves if they heard anything about the Mishipeshu. Being that Mike was the only one who had a practical, working knowledge of how to interview someone, he would be trying to help the others understand the ins and outs of the process. He would keep it simple—just the basics. There were just too many subtle things an interviewer used to acquire information to pass on in just a few minutes. Things like body language, tone of voice, eye contact, and the art of listening not just to what someone said but to how they said it, took months or even years to perfect and become second nature. Mike would focus on the listening part of interviewing. Most people do not know how to listen; they usually focus on what they have to say and only half hear what others are saying in response. That's the basis for having misunderstandings. One key thing to remember in any conversation is to not be too quick to speak. Silence can be a very effective way to gain information. People hate silence during a conversation, so they tend to blurt out things just to fill the void. Those utterances can provide a lot of information. Mainly because what is said is what is at the forefront of a person's thoughts and less prone to the person censoring themselves. It's where "think before you speak" comes from.

Eye contact is hard for most people; they tend to look anywhere but in someone's eyes. It makes people feel vulnerable and uncomfortable, so they avoid it. But eye contact is key for two reasons. It lets those you're talking with know you're paying attention to what they have to say, that what they say is important. But, for those with something to hide or a subject that may be uncomfortable for them to discuss, it can make them feel extremely self-conscious, and that's when they will shift their body position or glance away. It's almost as if they are trying to hide, but more often than not, it causes them to divulge information they otherwise may not want to. In a police interrogation, it will let the interrogator know if the subject is lying or hiding something. This gives the officer an edge. In normal conversations, it serves the same purpose, except it also gives the interrogator the opportunity to use the "Keep your mouth shut" technique.

It's usually only five or ten seconds before the silence does its trick, and the interviewee opens their mouth first and gives up valuable information. This is where Mike focused his training, on eye contact and keep quiet. Don't be too eager to speak. If anyone has seen something strange, they may blab about it to all their friends but not want it known outside their circle. With human nature what it is, even those who don't want to talk about it will be overcome with the need for attention or to feel like they've experienced something unique or interesting that not everyone will. Everyone, to one degree or another, wants to feel special, and this type of sighting is definitely special.

Mike did some role-play exercises to help them recognize those techniques, and everyone got to play both sides of a conversation. There was a lot of uncomfortable laughing as they each realized their shortcomings in conversational situations and their lack of basics like eye contact. But, after a little over an hour, they all had a better understanding of how to influence a conversation. This was harder for Rick than for the others, as he was used to being alone or with just a few close friends who thought as he did. But even Rick showed great improvement. Being aware of a communication issue means being able to work on that issue to become a more rounded conversationalist. With their newly acquired skills, they all set out to hit the bars. Mike, Sarah, and Rick went to the Goat Locker, the bar attached to the Wheelhouse Restaurant. Matt and Bill headed over to the Magnussen. It was a popular spot for groups of snowmobilers to congregate. It wouldn't be long before both teams were engaged in lively conversations.

"Hey, Jim. Looks like business is hopping."

Mike always made it a point to say hello to Jim Harrison, the owner of the Wheelhouse and Goat Locker. He never let on that he knew his Shoo story; Sarah had told him he wasn't really comfortable talking about his encounter. But tonight would be different. Jim talked with everyone that came into his establishment, and he might let them know if he'd heard anything. Besides, by now, Jim probably assumed he knew the story. Small town and all.

"Hey, Mike, Sarah. I see you're hanging out with some of our local riffraff."

"Yeah, good to see ya' too, Jim."

Rick and Jim knew each other well and always took jabs at each other, but they were good friends.

Mike knew Sarah had already heard Jim tell his story about the Mishipeshu, so he thought it best if she approached him about what they were up to; after all, if anyone could overhear a conversation in the building to do with the Shoo, it would be Jim. He wandered the area and say hello to all the guests, chatting them up and making sure his patrons were enjoying themselves. He would sit at the bar all night and observe the ever-changing flow of people. The restaurant and bar were separated by a short hallway, and the two areas weren't particularly large, only about 600 square feet each, so overhearing conversations wouldn't be difficult. Plus, Sarah had a disarming way about her that put people at ease. Mike hoped it would help open things up if there was anything to learn.

Sarah asked Jim for a word. Jim, being the friendly type, had no problem with giving her some time. He was a little confused when she asked to speak in his office, but she covered that by telling him there would be less chance of interruptions and that she only wanted a few minutes. Jim agreed, and the two went upstairs.

Jim's wife, Rhonda, was in there working on the books.

"Oh, good. You're here, too."

Sarah didn't want to give the impression that Rhonda should be excluded from what she had to say. Besides, Rhonda made the rounds with the customers as well; she may have heard something too.

"I'm sorry to bring this up. I know you guys aren't really

comfortable talking about your, uh, encounter a while back. But I think I should fill you guys in on what's been happening."

Jim's expression went from happy to stern. No, he did not like talking about it. Rhonda, however, was less defensive. In her thinking, it was just something they saw, nothing more.

"Sarah, I appreciate your situation with the whole Bromley thing, but I'm—"

Rhonda stopped him. "Jim, let's hear her out. She already knows the story, so let her say what she has to say."

"I know this is awkward. I'm a little nervous to talk about it too. But there's been some developments in the situation. Well, after Bromley's son came to visit us, Mike was concerned enough to do some digging into the subject. Seems there might just be some real proof of this creature's existence and it frequenting the Paradise area every year. Mike met a scientist over at LSSU, and they found some pretty disturbing facts about it. So much so that they're planning on trying to capture it. They even had some special traps built and will be putting them out in a couple days."

"So, what does all this have to do with me? We haven't seen that thing since that day, and I don't care if I *ever* see it again."

"I understand. I'm not asking you to do anything with the trapping operation. The problem is this. They only have two traps, and they're big and heavy, not easy to relocate if placed in the wrong area. We thought, since so many snowmobilers come in here to relax and share their stories about their adventures on the trails, you might have caught wind of something, let's say, unusual. Mike and Rick are hanging out downstairs on the chance they might hear something. It might give them a placement for one of the traps. One is going down at the river mouth, for sure. It's the second one they're not completely sure of. All we're asking is that if you hear something, if you could let us know, that would be a big help. What do you think?"

"Well, I think I could do that. Some of these folks get a little crazy and sled in some pretty rugged areas. Places where most sled heads don't go. But I got to tell ya', I think it's pretty risky going after this thing. What we saw was big and fast, and I don't think trapping it is a good idea. Those things better be T-Rex proof. That's how badass this thing was."

"I'm with you on that. Mike's friend from Idaho and a professor at LSSU are doing the trap thing. There's some kind of tracking thing that's supposed to stick to it somehow if it sets off the trap, just in case the trap won't hold it. Mike and Rick are more or less just keeping an eye out for it."

"All right, I'll keep my ears open, but, remember, you can't put any of this on me if it goes south. You tell that husband of yours to be careful if he's planning on stomping around out in those woods. They're swampy and full of hidden sinks and lots of things to get tripped up on, especially when covered in snow. That damn snow blows around in there and makes everything look smooth and flat when it ain't. I can't tell you how many times I've had to go help pull out some sled that hit one of those sinks or a hidden log, and I gotta tell ya', I don't like divin' out in that dark, sludgy crap. Especially when it's fuckin' freezin'."

"I will, Jim. But I got to ask you. What's a sink?"

"It's kinda like a sink hole, but smaller, about the size of small car. It's where some tree came down and rotted out. All that's left is a big hole where the root ball used to be. It gets filled in with that wet, gooey mud and crap. You step in one of those, and it'll swallow your ass right up. If it's deep enough, we'll never find your ass."

Sarah thanked Jim and Rhonda for their help and headed back downstairs to the bar. She was thankful for their willingness to help and happy Mike wasn't going to be involved with trapping the Shoo. She'd had no idea about all the hidden dangers in the woods. As she reached the bottom of the stairs, she saw Mike and Rick at a table close to a another table with six people in snowmobile gear. They were all talking together, at least on a surface level. Mike motioned to Sarah to join them, and he introduced her. There was nothing important being discussed. Mike and Rick were just blending in and trying to become part of the crowd so as not to attract a lot of attention. Blend in. Be seen but not noticed. Be engaged but not obvious. These were the techniques Mike had used in undercover operations to help him fit in. It was a proven technique, and it was already working, as they were welcomed into the circle of friends at the table next to them. Of course, it didn't hurt that those at that table had been drinking for a while, so their inhibitions were down. Way down.

"Why didn't you tell her about the group at table seven? They were discussing exactly what she was talking about."

Rhonda had kept silent during Sarah and Jim's talk. She was waiting for her husband to bring up what was said by the four at that table, but Jim had kept silent about it.

"I want to talk to Rick first. See where his head is on this. I don't want to have this whole damn thing turn into some kind of circus. That could be bad for business. Besides, I could tell she was a little stunned to hear about the risks of trudging around in those woods. Imagine how she would feel if she heard that some sled heads had come across some unusual tracks just outside of town. No sense in worrying her any more than she already is."

Rhonda understood. She and Jim didn't live on the water like Mike and Sarah did, and they were quite a bit away from where this thing seemed to travel, but she still got a sick feeling when Jim told her about what the snowmobilers had seen. Head-on-a-swivel time had come to Paradise.

Jesse Carr was a frequent visitor to Paradise during the winter. He and his friends were from the Detroit area, and they rented one of the many VBROs scattered all over Chippewa County. The six of them would head up to Paradise at least three or four times a season to enjoy the vast trail system open to snowmobiles, and to play cards, drink too much, eat too much, and sleep too little. Basically, they were here to relive their bachelor years without the woman-chasing and to feel young again. Each was over sixty, overweight, and had a type-A personality. Obnoxious. But, when attempting to gain someone's trust, certain things must be tolerated, so Mike and Rick ignored their boisterous conversation and immature jokes to blend in. But when Sarah got to the tables, the conversation became a little less colorful. Amazing how a wife's ongoing training of their husband kicks in automatically, even when they're nowhere in sight.

"This is my wife, Sarah. These guys are sleddin' hard on the trails, and so far, no problems out there. We have Jesse, Pete, Randy, Craig, John, and Walter. Did I get all the names right?"

"You sure did. That's pretty good. I can't hardly remember all their names myself half the time."

Jesse seemed to be the unofficial leader of the group. He was the loudest, anyway. Downstate, he was the general manager at Big Rigs and Tractors, Inc., a heavy machinery company, and being loud came with the job. Randy, John, and Walter worked there with Jesse, while Pete and Craig were co-owners of PC Excavating. They frequently used Big Rigs in their business, and that's how they all became friends. They had been coming to Paradise for over ten years.

"Well, I wouldn't say there weren't *any* problems. We had to pull old Craig here outta some muddy-ass hole when his sled broke through. No damage except for Craig's pride, and the fact that the rest of his ride was a tad damp. We have a tradition in the Bog Busters—that's what we call ourselves. If you have to get pulled out of a mess, the first two rounds are on you. So, here's to Craig for getting this party started."

They all laughed hard at Jesse's recalling of the incident. Fact was, they were lucky. They called themselves the Bog Busters because they would go off-trail every time they came across an open snow-covered area to do some shredding. Those open areas were usually frozen ponds or marshy expanses riddled with submerged logs, sinks, and wire grass. Any one of those could cause a serious accident—in a hard-to-reach location with little or no cell service. Not very smart, and completely illegal, but with the vast number of these types of areas, coupled with a lack of resources, these acts went largely unchecked. Most snowmobilers obeyed the rules, but quite a few didn't care, or felt the rules were more of a suggestion.

"Those are called sinks. It's the hole that's left when a large tree comes down, root ball and all. The tree will sink into the mud or rot away, but the hole gets filled in with mud, water, and all kind of debris. Some of them will eat your sled, so be careful out there".

Mike and Rick just stared at Sarah while she told them about sinks. Sarah didn't usually talk much when first meeting strangers, let alone offer a warning. Even Mike didn't know what a sink was, and Rick was just as impressed, but Sarah saw it as a way to share her newfound knowledge while fitting in with the group. And, even though they all knew what the Bog Busters had admitted to was illegal, they stayed away from that conversation. Confronting them would be counterproductive to their goal. So the conversation between the two tables stayed courteous and lively, a good combination considering the amount of alcohol flowing. All Mike could think was, how in the hell would they be able to ride their snowmobiles all the way back to their rented cabin without falling off?

Jim came downstairs and walked over to the tables in his usual friendly manner, joining the conversation and asking if everything was good. The usual manager checking the satisfaction of the food and so on. Then he leaned in towards Rick and asked if he would go look at something with him, and the two headed outside.

"What's goin' on, Jim? Everything okay?"

"I hope so. I just talked with Mike's wife, Sarah, and she tells me you guys are planning on tryin' to trap this... whatever it is. Just what the hell have you gotten yourself into? I mean, you *shot* this damn thing and didn't even put a dent in it. Do you really think you can contain it?"

"To be honest, no I don't. But that's not what I have in mind, anyway. Trying to trap it was Matt Wallace's idea. He's some professor over at LSSU. When he suggested it, I thought it was the dumbest thing I've ever heard, but you know those college types, always tryin' to save the whales. The only good idea that came from it was the geo tracking thing. Personally, I think the Shoo will destroy the trap they've come up with, but it has some kind of system for attaching a tracker to it. That could actually give us an edge. At least we'd be able to know where it is. My plan is to try and kill the damn thing, and I've got a plan for that."

"Jesus, Rick. Are you nuts? Kill it? You tried that once already. How'd that work out for ya'?"

"Yeah, I know. But I didn't have the right gear that day. I think I've got it figured out now."

"Really? How in the hell can you figure out *anything* about a creature we know *nothing* about? You're gonna get yourself killed, and probably no one will even know it. I got a call from a buddy up in Copper Harbor five days ago. He said a lady went missing on Saturday. She was snowshoeing alone and cut across a frozen part of the lake and fell through the ice. Gone. No sign of her. They only found one of her snowshoes, straps all torn—and part of the shoe was missing. You want to know what's weird about that?

Every other damn part of that section of lake was four or five inches thick, but where she went through was only a couple inches. He told me there wasn't any reason for that. The ice has never been that inconsistent, *ever*. People go out on that ice all the time, no issues. I think it's that thing. I think it's been watching and figured out how to make a trap of its own. If I'm right, that means it's thinking. Learning. Hell, maybe even evolving. But one things for sure, it's no dumb animal. And another thing—it's fuckin' *fast*. I heard some sledders at one of my tables talkin' about crossing some strange tracks over near the Two Hearted. They were over twelve inches long and claw-like, kinda like a cat track. If it's our creature, that's almost three hundred miles in just five days. Sixty miles a day, brother. Sixty fuckin' miles a damn day."

"No way it traveled that far in five days. No way. They must've been moose tracks or somethin'."

"Well, maybe. But they were lookin' at some pictures they took of 'em, and they didn't look like moose tracks to me."

"If it is the Shoo, maybe there's more than one. That could be a problem. The Two Hearted, huh? I better get ahold of Matt to let him know. He was thinking about setting one of his traps somewhere along the Shelldrake. Less chance of bein' seen,there. But the Two Hearted would be an easier setup. Plus, they ain't that far apart, but that's gettin' kinda close to my place."

"You guys better watch your backs, or we'll be fillin' out one of those reports on you."

"I hear ya'. You think you could get them to show us those pics? After all, I've seen them prints up close and personal. I could tell if they were the Shoo or not."

"I'll see what I can do, but they seemed a little skittish, if you know what I'm sayin'."

"Thanks, Jim. We'll keep it on the down low, if that helps. Meanwhile, I've got to call Matt and let him know."

Rick went back over to let Mike and Sarah know what Jim had said, then he went back outside to call Matt and Bill. Meanwhile, Jim approached the table that had the pictures of the prints. He made up some story about Rick being a trapper who had come up on some strange tracks too and wanting to see if they were the same ones. After a little persuading in the form of a round on the house, they agreed.

"This is Rick, the trapper I was tellin' you guys about. He says he's come across some strange tracks too and wants to see if what you got pictures of are the same kinda tracks."

Rick and Jim thought making up a story about Rick being a trapper would give him some credibility. The plan was to identify the tracks as some known animal or tracks that may have been altered due to wind or erosion. That way, they might be able to head off anyone getting nosy and possibly disrupting their plans or, worse, ending up on the Mishipeshu's dinner menu.

As Rick studied the pictures, he saw they were indeed the same type as the tracks he had seen last year. There were only five or six tracks in the pictures. They started at the edge of a narrow but deep creek, crossed the snowmobile trail, and vanished on the other side as they entered a marshy bog.

As big as it is, its weight pushes its body deep into the mud, but the evidence of its presence is quickly erased as water and debris fill it in. Only an extremely capable tracker would be able to discern a pathway. All the untrained eye would notice was mud, water-filled holes, and swamp.

"What do you think? Pretty weird, huh?"

The conversation about the pictures, around the table covered the spectrum of possible creatures. Bigfoot, the lizard man, chupacabra, and even space aliens. Most of those suggestions were made as jokes. Not one person at the table was seriously considering any them. Most of them figured it was probably bear or moose tracks altered by wind or sleds zipping by, maybe even someone's idea of a joke. Rick saw it as an opportunity to deflect attention from the subject.

"Not really. I know *exactly* what these tracks are. Beaver. A big one. I'd like to know where this ole boy is so I can lay a trap for him. I'll bet this guy's close to a hundred pounds."

"Beaver? No way. Look at the size of those tracks. No way that's a beaver."

Kevin Rollins, the one with the pictures, wasn't buying it. Fortunately, the ground had been frozen for weeks, so the weight of the Mishipeshu wasn't able to imprint very deeply, and Rick would use that. Normally, Rick would call him an idiot or some other derogatory name; he wasn't one to mince words. But this time, he decided to give Mike's conversational training a go. He thought a few seconds on how to respond without upsetting his "source."

"I can understand your reluctance to believe these are beaver tracks. They're *huge*. But, if these tracks were made by something larger, say, a bear or moose, they would be much deeper, wouldn't they? These swampy areas are lousy with beavers. They're everywhere. I trap them because they get into people's yards and eat their trees, decks, power poles, fence posts—you name it, they'll chew it. Here, let me show you some beaver tracks from one of my sets."

After his encounter last year, Rick had taken some pictures of his own of the tracks left by the Shoo. They were a little distorted, but they would, hopefully, serve Rick's purpose.

"You see these tracks? I followed them all the way to a beaver dam. I was able to trap it a few days later. The biggest beaver I ever got, and the tracks you got pictures of look a little bigger. What can I say—beavers have big feet."

Kevin and his buddies studied Rick's pictures and compared them to the ones on Kevin's phone.

"Damn! I thought we had us some kind of monster tracks here. Nothin' but a damn beaver. I'll tell you where these were as long as you send me a pic of it if you get it. How's that?"

Of course, Rick agreed. He had no intention of sending him the pictures of what really made those tracks, if he were to "get it." But this would give him the location so he could possibly pattern the Shoo's movement, and that might just help him set his own trap for the creature. He was impressed Mike's training had actually worked.

"Thanks, Jim. I really appreciate you helping us out."

"No problem, but you guys be super careful out there. I don't want to get any calls to go ice divin' lookin' for your sorry asses."

"Will do. Hey, how 'bout one of your special concoctions before we head out. I'll bet these two transplants ain't never tasted nothin' like one of your special mixes."

While Jim mixed up the drinks, Rick shared what he found out about the tracks and their location.

"I say we finish these and go find the others. I've got a map on my wall at the cabin we can study to see if we can figure this thing out."

"Holy moly! All I can say is *wow*."

Sarah was gasping for air from the alcohol content in Jim's special concoction. Three different types of alcohol, juice, and a splash of Fresca. Jim called it the Widow Maker, and for good reason.

"Yep. The Widow Maker. You drink too many of these, and you're either gonna die from alcohol poisoning, or your wife'll kill ya'."

Jim always explained why his drinks were named the way they

were with a chuckle. He derived great pleasure from his twisted sense of humor. Like the Liquorator—four types of liquor—rum, gin, vodka, tequila—a lemon-lime soda, grenadine for that blood color, two cherries for the terminator eyes, and—Bam!—the Liquorator. Jim told anyone who ordered it, "One of these, and it's *hasta la vista*, baby."

"Okay, you're drivin', Sarah."

As an ex-police officer, Mike wasn't going to risk driving on icy, snow-covered roads with his head swimming like it was. He was not about to give the Widow Maker a chance to live up to its name. It was one of the things Sarah always respected about Mike; even when they were dating, he wasn't too proud to give her the car keys.

The trio headed over to the Magnusen to pick up Matt and Bill and then go over to Rick's cabin to work out their plans for placing the traps. Of course, Rick was also going to be making his own plans based on the information they gathered. His plan was to actively hunt the Shoo without interfering with the trapping operations. Maybe hunting it would drive it to the trap. Even though he didn't trust the traps to hold it, he believed in the tracking aspect of it. If they could track it, they might be able to ambush and eliminate it. Science be damned, he just wanted it gone from his town, his hunting grounds, and his world. He had heard too many suspicious disappearance stories and wanted it *gone*. Besides, science could have the corpse.

"What's up guys? Any luck?"

Bill and Matt had barely finished their drinks before being called to meet in the parking lot. They hadn't even talked with anyone.

"We struck pay dirt."

Rick suggested they continue their conversation at his cabin. Less chance of someone overhearing.

"Well, welcome to my home. There ain't no housekeeper, so forgive the mess."

Normally, Rick wouldn't care about a few things not cleaned up or scattered around, but Sarah was here, and he felt he needed to apologize for anything out of place.

"I got the map of Chippewa County hangin' on my shop wall over here. I use it to plan my hunts every year. I put a clear sheet of plexiglass over it so I can use a dry erase marker to show where I see stuff or where I think I might put a stand. Stuff like that. Things change, so I erase what didn't work or if I want to move my stand."

"Wow. That's a pretty big map."

Matt was impressed. No tech needed. No electricity except lights, no high-end 3D images. Just an old school setup that worked just fine. Simple and clean, the Yooper way.

"Yeah, I don't like squinting, and I like to be able to see the whole picture without having to unfold a map or turn a page. Makes it easier to see patterns, game corridors, and signs like scrapes and rubs. I mark every successful hunt in permanent marker so I don't accidentally erase it. I can see trends from year to year that way. If you look towards the right of Paradise, you'll see where I had my encounter with the Shoo. It was pretty much right next to the Tahquamenon River, so you're probably on the right track thinking it's using the waterways to get around. Plus, all the stories I've heard about where it's been seen or where someone was when they disappeared—all of them are around or on the water."

"Now, Rick, where did those snowmobilers see the tracks?"

"Right in here, close to the Two Hearted River. The river ain't that deep. Maybe five feet at its deepest, but it does empty into Lake Superior. But, man, is it thick in there. It could be using the river to access the snowmobile trails that run through there. Pretty swampy, too. A big animal could easily hide in there. But I doubt it's hunting in the river. Wouldn't make sense. It would stick out like a sore thumb. The tracks crossed the trail somewhere in this area."

Rick took his marker and circled the area.

"Let's not forget what Jim told us about that lady going through the ice, up in Copper Harbor. I know it's not on this map, but about where would it be in reference to this area?"

Rick took a piece of paper, wrote *Copper Harbor* on it, and pinned it to the wall as a reference to its rough location.

"Right about here. It's way out on the point of the Keweenaw. About three hundred miles north. If you were to drive the speed limit, sixty-five, it's about six hours. Jim said there was a lady that disappeared after fallin' through the ice five days ago. I doubt this thing swims that fast, but who knows? I was wonderin' if maybe there's more than one of these things. That could explain the speed."

Matt wasn't so sure the Mishipeshu couldn't cover that distance in five days.

"I wouldn't rule that out. Great whites can swim fifty miles per hour, and makos can do sixty, so covering that distance in that amount of time is plausible. If our theory is correct, that it's not eating these victims as it takes them, that it's storing them as food for the warmer months, it would have to be fast to go back and forth from its den to the hunting grounds and be able to gather enough to sustain it. It's probably feeding on fish as it goes to keep up its strength, and I'm betting a free meal in our traps might just be tempting enough to bring it in.

"I've got one of my grad students bringing our research boat with the trap we're setting at the river mouth. It's got a small crane mounted on it that we use to pull nets in. He will be there tomorrow afternoon. The other trap's coming with my Fish and

Game contact, John Frizzel. He's got access to a flatbed truck, and he'll be bringing our bait too. I'm meeting him in the morning, but we do have one challenge with the second trap. We need to get it off the flatbed and into the sled the snowcat's going to pull. Any ideas?"

"I've got a small backhoe. I'm sure I can use the scoop to unload it."

They studied the map and marked where the snowmobilers saw the tracks. They thought that the Shoo was moving south towards Paradise, and that it most likely would stay in that area for at least the next few weeks. They determined that placing their last trap somewhere along the Two Hearted River might offer them a better chance of success. Instead of being close to the southern edge of what they believed to be its hunting grounds, it would be more central. This could allow them to capture it as it headed north at the end of its season, or maybe as it returned from taking victims to its lair. The latter was not ideal, but they had to face the reality that they might not be able to stop it from killing again, or that they would even be able to capture it. Hell, the possibility that they wouldn't even come close to it was pretty high.

Matt and Bill were excited about the scientific opportunity, but they were reluctantly realistic in their thinking. Mike and Rick, however, were more certain they would have an encounter. Rick was counting on it. While he was showing everyone the map and helping them plan their trap placement, he was using the movements and evidence to plan his own ambush spot. He knew those bogs and river bottoms better than most; he'd been hunting those woods and utilizing the trails, especially the hidden game trails and topography, since he was a kid. It was his backyard, and he wasn't about to let some scientist geek beat him to the punch. To him, it was personal; the creature had bested him because he had let his guard down. He allowed the stories to become just that, a story to be told and nothing else.

Up until now, it had only been just a campfire story, something that stayed in the back of his mind, way back. There were only rumors and vague sightings that had no evidence. There had been no photographs, videos, or pictures of footprints. There hadn't even been any proof that any of the people who went missing were victims of anything other than their own misfortune. But the long-time residents in the area and elders of the local Native tribes knew better. They knew the true risk that winter always brought to their little part of the world. And Rick almost learned the truth the hard way; he had almost become a victim himself. He would not let that happen again. He would be as ready as he could to face it, as ready as anyone. He wondered, would it be enough?

13

THE TRAP IS SET

"Here he comes. I don't think we could've waited any longer to do this. The ice has almost closed off this part of the river."

Bill and Matt stood at the boat launch at the river mouth parking lot. They were fortunate the winds were calm and the waves out on Whitefish Bay were almost nonexistent, an unusual thing for this time of year. Smooth sailing. Bill thought the boat looked like a WWII landing craft, and he wasn't far off. The university's research vessel was a twenty-eight foot jet boat with the front drop ramp of a landing craft. Being a jet boat instead of a traditional motored boat allowed it to get into shallower water. Motored boats had a disadvantage in these areas because the props could easily become damaged on the rocks that were submerged everywhere. It had a crane welded to the back of the wheelhouse that could swing 180 degrees to either side of the boat. Perfect for offloading fish traps. There was also a rig at the front of the wheelhouse for rolling in netting, and the ramp was to aide in loading the netting while the boat was docked.

As the boat made its way slowly towards the boat ramp, Bill noticed the traps strapped down on the deck, one on the stern, one on the bow. The stern trap was the one they would place at the fork in the river, as the crane could lower it in position. The one on the bow would be offloaded by Rick using his backhoe. The traps were much larger than he had pictured in his head, and he wondered how they were going to get the one being set at the Two Hearted in place.

Rick had brought his backhoe with a flatbed trailer towed behind his rusted 2001 Chevrolet Silverado pickup. Most of the older vehicles in the UP had at least,some rust on them from all the salts used to de-ice the roads, but Rick's truck was all but eaten up by rust. The quarter panels were almost completely gone, and all the doors had large holes in them, but the engine still ran strong. This was Rick's task truck, the one that did all the dirty work; it didn't need to be pretty.

"Holy crap, Rick. Looks like that truck has seen better days."

Bill was amazed it held together at all.

"Don't let her fool ya. She's a beast. She can tow just about anything anywhere and out of almost any jam, and we've done it all. That's why she looks like she does. I got some steel back at the shop I'm gonna cut and replace all the rusted stuff with—just been a little busy lately."

"I better get that backhoe offloaded and get it in position. Have your guy get as far up the ramp as he can. I don't want my equipment to slide into the river. There's a lot of ice on the ramp."

At the wheel of the boat was Tom Wilson, a twenty-five year old grad student that had been piloting the research vessel for four years now. He knew just about all the waterways and hazards around the shores of Whitefish Bay, but he had never had to deal with the ice before. The river mouth was starting to freeze over, with just a small sliver of open water in the middle. Being that the river's water was warmer and moving, it froze over last. But just past the boat ramp, on the other side of the bridge where Highway 123 crossed the Tahquamenon, ice had closed the open section of water. Fortunately, it was only about a quarter of an inch thick. Moving slowly, the jet boat could break through that. But once the river froze solid over the trap, the only way to reach it would be by snowmobile or on foot. If the Shoo were to be caught, and if the trap was able to hold it, they would need to use battery-powered jack hammers to break the ice and several snowmobiles to pull it free. Not the best scenario, but there was no other way.

"That's it. Perfect. Hold 'er there."

The team tied the research boat firmly to the pylons that lined the boat ramp, keeping it secure, while Rick attached chains to the trap and the bucket on the backhoe. Once attached, Rick deftly maneuvered the bucket and backhoe until he had the trap sitting in the parking lot.

"Piece of cake. Now, where's your game warden guy? I'd like to get this thing in the water as quick as we can. There's a winter blast coming in later, and this ice is gonna get too thick to deal with."

"I got a text from him about an hour ago. He was leaving his office in the Soo, so he should be here any minute."

While they waited for Warden Paul Atkins, the team familiarized themselves with the trap and the geo tracking deployment system. It was a fairly simple trap, similar to the common animal traps used to catch raccoons, skunks, and strays, only much bigger. There was a pressure plate that would activate the trap's door. A heavy spring attached to the plate would activate the door when the Shoo stepped on it, causing the door to quickly drop down and lock in place. The tracking system was simple too. When the door swung down into place, it triggered a small charge that launched the tracking device, which would automatically attach itself to the underbelly of the Shoo, where there was a better chance of the mounting system penetrating the hide. Once deployed, the device would start providing real time positioning, which could be accessed by an app that NOAA, the National Oceanic and Atmospheric Association, designed to help track fish migrations, among other things.

"Pretty fancy rig, Mr. Wallace. Think it'll work?"

Mike was impressed by the design and quality of the trap. Especially considering the short time it was built in.

"Oh, I think it'll do the job. I mean, the trap system will work, and the tracking system will deploy. The questions is, will it hold the animal it was designed for? We have a lot of information about it, but until we have a specimen, we really don't know enough."

About that time, Matt's Fish and Game contact pulled into the parking lot and backed up close to the boat ramp.

"Is this where you need me? I figured what I have for you is goin' in these contraptions."

"That's perfect, Paul. I really appreciate you helping us out on this one. Let me introduce you to everyone. This is Paul Atkins, from Michigan Fish and Game."

After Matt had done all the introductions, he got busy baiting the traps. Paul had brought two large whitetail bucks that had been killed by poachers a couple of weeks earlier. The antlers helped them load them into the traps a little easier—better handholds.

"Holy shit, Matt! What the hell are you trying to catch with these things, alligators or something?"

"I wish it was only alligators. Remember me telling you there was something very large in the lake we were going after? Well, let me fill you in on the whole story."

Matt proceeded to retell Rick's encounter, Mike's research results, and the scientific tests they performed, which all pointed to a very large apex predator hunting the lake and its rivers. Paul listened with a shocked look on his face. When Matt finished, he expected Paul to poke a little fun at him. Instead, Paul was quiet for a minute, then he told the group his own little unexplained story.

"You know, I've worked these shores and wetlands for almost fifteen years now, and I've seen some pretty strange things. Things I couldn't explain. So I kept my mouth shut. But, not too long ago, maybe two or three years, I was patrolling the Shelldrake out by the Maple Flats in late fall. We had some snow, and the river had a thin layer of ice on it, but being that my canoe is aluminum and has a reinforced bow, it wasn't any problem bustin' through it. We'd had some reports of poaching, and I was trying to sneak in with my canoe with an electric motor—you know, quiet. It was almost dark—just enough light where I could see the river just fine, but dark enough where I could slip into the shadows and not be spotted.

"I'd been canoeing up river about thirty minutes when a saw what I thought was a big bear, only it was way too big to be any bear around here. It was approaching the river about fifty yards up from me, and it looked like it had something, or someone, in its mouth. It was dragging it towards the river and it was *fast*. The reason I thought it might've been a person in its mouth was because I swore I could see a flash of orange, like a beanie or maybe a glove or something. I didn't have much time to look at it, because it headed straight into the water and disappeared. It barely made a splash as it went under.

"I pulled over to the edge and watched as the surface of the water undulated like something large was swimming below. Bears don't do *that*. I went to the spot it went in, and all I found were some weird tracks, kind of cat-like but huge. I've never seen anything like that since. Spooked me a little.

"Anyway, turns out some cross-country snowshoer went missing somewhere near that same spot. His friends said he always wore an orange beanie while on the trail. Just in case he stumbled across some hunters or got injured, the orange beanie would stand out, make it easier to see him in the woods. All I could think about was that I thought I saw a flash of orange, but there wasn't any other evidence it was the missing person. I told my sergeant what I saw and we went back to the spot to look around. It had been a couple of days since my encounter, so there wasn't much to see. Just some muddled up impressions in the mud, nothing we could make out, so the sergeant said it was probably just a very large beaver, and that the light conditions were just playing tricks on my eyes, making me see things bigger than they actually were. He said that was the only animal that could swim under water like that and to forget about it. He said there's no such thing as a man-eating beaver out there, and not to tell people what I saw, so I haven't up until now.

"Thing is, I know it wasn't a giant beaver. I saw where its back was in relation to a certain branch on a tree. That branch was six or seven feet high. There isn't a beaver in the world that tall. My sergeant just said it probably wasn't that tall, that I just thought it was because I was low in the water and the bank was higher—optical illusion or something. Bullshit. I've been in these woods way too long to be fooled like that. Anyway, they never found that snowshoer. I always thought that was weird, someone just vanishing like that. No trace or nothing. So you're tellin' me that I might've seen this thing that night?"

"It's possible. Apparently, this thing's been frequenting these waters for a very long time, and it's managed to stay relatively hidden. From what we've found, most sightings are like yours—quick, bad light, and in remote areas. But it's difficult for something as big as the Mishipeshu to stay hidden forever. Sooner or later, the odds will catch up to it, and its secrets will be revealed. We feel that time is now. Looking back on how the four of us got to this point, I'd say the odds have collided."

"Did you say the Mishipeshu? Holy shit! I was out on the ice years ago, and some Native guy came up and said the Mishipeshu stole his fish. I just thought he was drunk or crazy or on some kind of drug. He was certain it was this thing. I gave him a lift back to town, and the whole time, he was going on about how the Mishipeshu was going to get him—blah, blah, blah. Looks like he might've been right. That's the only time I've heard of it until just now."

Matt was anxious to get the traps set up, but he knew Paul needed to be brought up to speed, so he gave him the short version of the story, and when he finished, he made sure Paul wouldn't let anyone know what they were doing. Unsuspecting people might get hurt if they approached the traps at the wrong time.

"Yeah, I'm not telling anyone about this. They'd put me on some desk job or something. Let me know if you find anything, or, if this thing actually catches it, you'll need a Fish and Game officer to sign off that it's a legal catch. Otherwise, the state will lay a hefty fine on your ass, and they can confiscate it. As a matter of fact, I'll try to patrol a little closer to the area for a while. I'd like to get a closer look at it if you catch it."

"I never even considered needing a permit or anything. I just figured it wasn't necessary since we're looking for an, as of now, non-existent creature. What would we even say we were trying to catch, otters? Beavers? As far as I know, there aren't any cryptozo-ology permits."

"Doesn't matter to the state. As far as they're concerned, every living creature, known or not, is subject to their protection—or their exploitation, if you ask me. Imagine the bureaucratic hoops you'll have to jump through to study it if it's not a legal catch. I'll take care of that one. You just make sure no other legal entity sees it before I do, okay? I'll just say I'm part of a joint venture between LSSU and Fish and Game to identify invasive species that may be in the watershed. It's already an established program because of the lamprey problem. I'll get the paperwork all taken care of so it's neat and tidy. I'm going to backdate the forms a few days just to give us some breathing room, but I'll need you, Matt, to sign them as a representative of the university. That'll give it the look of an official program permit."

Paul knew how the state could be if there was a money angle to it. He'd been part of the system long enough to understand how bureaucracy worked—or didn't, depending on one's point of view. And, if they were to discover a new species, he wanted to be in on the discovery. After all, it couldn't hurt his career to be part of such a find, and he was hoping to pad his retirement with some prestigious position a little farther up the food chain. Oh, Paul was a good man, and he really wanted to help out, but there weren't too many paths to the higher paying positions within Fish and Game unless you knew someone or made a name for yourself. Catching an newly discovered species would definitely do just that.

Rick loaded the deer carcasses into both traps, and Matt and Ben secured them, making sure the mechanisms were firmly fastened. Once the traps were baited, Matt activated the tracking device and synched it with his cellphone. Then it was time to place the first trap. Tom maneuvered the boat through the thin ice and positioned it so the trap could be lowered by the hydraulic lift. Once set, they marked it on their GPS system, a formality required for any trapping done by the university. They didn't want to misplace any equipment in case those in charge of the gear were to no longer be associated with the university either by death or termination. The trap was gently lowered into place so as not to trigger the trap. A small portion of the trap's gate was exposed above the water, so they tried to conceal it as best they could with some debris that had gathered along the banks.

It was wet, cold, and muddy, and Matt, Tom, and Paul were glad to be done with the task. Mike, Rick, and Bill loaded the second trap onto Rick's flatbed trailer and then watched the others set the trap from the boat ramp. They thought they would just be in the way of the operation when, in fact, they really didn't want to get wet. Turns out they made a good decision, as the boat crew was pretty wet and muddy by the time they were done. Good thing the boat's wheelhouse was enclosed and heated, or Ben would have had a miserable trip back to Sault Ste. Marie.

"You guys look like you just finished a mud wrestling contest."

"Go ahead and laugh it up. You guys are going to have to help with the next trap, and we won't have a crane to help move it into place. Hope you have some good mud boots."

After they got off the boat, and all the gear was stowed, Tom wasted no time heading back to the Soo before the weather changed. Weather around the Great Lakes, especially Lake Superior, was subject to change on a dime, and the university's boat would be no match for Superior's waves.

"You know, fellas, I'm lookin' at this ginormous trap sittin' on that trailer, and I'm thinking it may draw some unwanted attention headin' down the road. We got anything we could cover it with? You know, a tarp or somethin'?"

Rick was right. The trap was a hard not to miss, and they didn't need any curious people following them or asking questions. They would need to cover or disguise it somehow.

"I've got a big twenty-by-thirty tarp we can use. I'll run home real quick and grab it. It'll only take about ten minutes, but you might want to keep any sledders away. They come through here a lot."

While Mike headed home to get his tarp and some rope, the rest of them set up a makeshift blockade to keep unwanted eyes from getting too close. Paul's Fish and Game truck was placed at the entrance to the parking lot so it was blocked to traffic. He made it look like he was setting up a game check station, but he didn't put up any signs for hunters to stop. That way, most people wouldn't even give it a second look, and the trailer was far enough from the road that the trees around the parking lot shielded it from view. Mike returned, and they quickly went about covering the trap.

"That wasn't too bad. Thanks for picking up on that, Rick. Now, let's get this thing up to the Two Hearted and get it set. It'll be dark soon, and it's pretty damn cold. Going to need some anti-freeze after all this."

"I have just the stuff, if you guys want to stop by my shack on the way out. It's pretty close."

Rick had the stuff, all right. He had a fresh batch of apple pie moonshine all bottled up and ready.

It looked like some type of a rag-tag carnival parade as they headed through Paradise and west towards the Two Hearted River. A rusted-up, miss-match colored Chevy truck pulling a long, goose-neck trailer with a backhoe and something funny-shaped under a giant blue tarp flapping in the wind was followed by a Michigan Fish and Game truck, a Subaru Outback wagon, and, bringing up the rear, Mike's black GMC pickup. They moved as one unit, keeping a uniform space between each vehicle so as not to allow any other vehicle to join their little convoy.

The plan was for Rick to lead the way to Two Hearted, as he was the most familiar with the area. Paul would position his truck so he could block anyone who might come down behind them. Although it was unlikely that another vehicle would drive into that snow-covered dirt switchback road, snowmobilers ran that road all day. Their goal was to set the trap without anyone seeing them do it and get out of there before attracting any attention. Rick had scouted the area earlier in the week and had found a good location fairly close to the road. It was about half a mile down the road, in an area that had a small hill about eight feet high that ran the length of the road for about 200 yards. On the other side of that hill, it sloped down to a branch of the Two Hearted that was about six feet deep. The hill would provide a visual obstacle for the trap. The hill was covered with scrub pines, so the snowmobilers wouldn't try to run their sleds up it. From there, it would be easy to slide the trap down to the water. The only thing to do after setting the trap would be to try and erase their tracks left in the snow, and Rick knew just how to take care of that.

"Why the hell did you bring a leaf blower out here, Rick? I don't think we're going to be cleaning leaves out of the woods."

"That's my little trick I came up with years ago for clearing snow. If the snow's not packed down or too wet, it blows pretty easy. The wind around here blows the snow all over the damn place, so I can use the blower to erase our tracks. After I'm done, no one will know we were up here."

Mike was amazed at its simplicity, and that he had never thought about using a leaf blower to move snow himself. Genius. These Yoopers, he thought, always thinking out of the box.

"Well, Mr. Wizard, do you have a trick to get the trap up this hill? I don't think we're gonna drag it up there."

"Funny you should ask."

Rick gave Mike a sly grin as he reached into a storage box mounted to his trailer.

"Work smarter, not harder."

Rick pulled out a gas-powered winch from the box.

"This little baby will make quick work of moving that thing. I'll attach it to that tree at the top there, and it'll pull that thing up here like it weren't nothin'. This baby is rated for four thousand pounds. That trap ain't nowhere near that."

Again, Mike was impressed at not only the ingenuity Rick had, but that he seemed to be prepared for whatever came at him. Most people who spent their lives living in the seclusion of the Upper Peninsula developed a self-reliant mindset, but few had gotten to Rick's level. If he didn't have the tool for a situation, he made it. If he didn't have the materials to make the tool for the job, he came up with another way to do it. But the one thing he wouldn't do was give up just because he didn't have the perfect tool.

"Okay, let's get this show on the road."

Rick gave everyone instructions on what they needed to do. While he used the backhoe to lift the trap off the trailer, Mike and Matt held guide lines to keep the trap from spinning in the air. Bill and Paul were to operate as traffic control if anyone came down the road. Once the trap was swung over to the top of the hill, Rick lowered it so most of its weight was heading downhill towards the creek. Once the trap was settled in that position, Mike and Matt would move to steady it at the top until all five men could work to move the trap down to the water. For safety, the trap would be moved using gravity and its weight to slide down to the creek while all five men controlled its decent with ropes. Before the trap could be moved, it had to be baited with the other deer carcass Paul brought. Once baited, the trap was lowered into position and secured to a large oak tree with a heavy-duty chain and lock.

The tracking device was activated and placed in position, and the five made their way back up the hill to their vehicles. Rick used his blower to erase their tracks, and the operation was done. They were able to accomplish the task without being seen by snowmobilers or even normal traffic, which was almost nonexistent this time of year.

"Well, that went smoother than I thought it would. Gotta love gravity assists."

"You got that right, Bill. That was slicker than snot. Thanks for your help on this, Paul. It really made a difference to this mission's probability of success."

"I'm glad to do it. I just hope this works like we want."

"Why don't we head on over to my place for a little antifreeze. I don't mind the cold, but I don't like being wet too."

They were all wet and muddy from placing the traps, and they were starting to feel it. The adrenaline running through them had kept their minds off the cold until now. Indulging in a little of Rick's moonshine sounded like just what was needed.

"I'd love to join you guys, but I really should get the permit paperwork filed for this, just in case we get a quick capture on this thing. Let me get a rain check on that though, if you don't mind."

"Sure thing, Paul. You know where I live."

Paul did know where Rick lived. They had crossed paths before. Rick was an ethical hunter, fisherman, and trapper, but sometimes he pushed the boundaries of the law. Even though he had never been caught doing anything that would be considered a violation of the game laws, his methods were sometimes questioned, and Paul had had to check on his activities more than once. Fortunately, their past encounters had been friendly or at least cordial, and Paul did respect Rick's abilities as an outdoorsman. Not many who participate in those types of activities were as successful at it as Rick, and Paul hoped that streak would continue in this particular endeavor.

After Paul left, the rest headed to Rick's cabin for some of his apple pie antifreeze and some conversation on what they might expect over the next few days, possibly weeks. It's amazing the thoughts that swim about in the moonshine glow. They talked about fishing and the best bait for whitefish, tracking invasive species, and the merits of homemade booze and homegrown remedies. There were police war stories from Mike, some funny, some not so funny. They traded jokes and jabs and laughed until their sides hurt. Then it got quiet.

Each man drifted into his own thoughts about what they were attempting. Was it a waste of time? Were they all crazy for believing there was a monster, alive and well, prowling the wilds and not-so-wilds of Paradise? Of course, their evidence of its existence was pretty solid, so the question of *if* it was real was pretty well answered. The real question was, were they up to the task? No one had ever read about, heard about, or knew of any story where the Shoo was killed or even severely wounded. But, then again, there weren't many stories about the Shoo. Most of what they knew came from hearsay or tales from local Natives. The only reliable eyewitness accounts came from Rick about his encounter while hunting, and Jim from the Wheelhouse, and the only thing that came from those stories was it was fast and almost bulletproof. Not much help.

Rick was the only one who knew for sure what they were up against; the others could only guess, and he had a plan of his own. He figured the traps and the tracking system would keep the others busy and out of his way. His plan was to hunt it down and kill it; it was just that simple to him, and his hunt would begin tomorrow. As for the others, tomorrow was going to be a rough one. None of them were used to drinking that much moonshine, and they were going to pay for tonight's festivities.

"*Whew.* I better call Sarah to come get me. I'm not seeing double. I'm seeing double the double."

Mike wasn't the only one feeling the effects of Rick's concoction. They were all having issues with their coordination, everyone except Rick. Rick was conditioned to drinking moonshine, his favorite adult beverage. He saw the others had been duped by the sweet apple pie flavor and had downed their drinks too fast; while he sipped, they gulped.

Moonshine creeps up on a person like a predator stalking its victim. At first, a comforting warm feeling engulfs the body, fooling the drinker into a sense of calm, almost zen-like state, where mind and body are in harmony. This only lasts a few minutes, and then comes the first inkling that too much of the ambrosia had been consumed. The mind and mouth become disconnected, like someone flipped a switch, and the first slurred words slip out. If this was a beer-drinking session, most people would think it was time to stop here, but moonshine doesn't let the brain make that connection. Instead, it tells the drinker it's time for another one. Most people don't know the signs because they have rarely, if ever, tasted good moonshine before.

Once bitten by the shine, there is no escape. The euphoria that started as a simple slurred word is eventually replaced by full-blown drunkenness. Balance is taken away, the inhibitions brought on by societal norms are erased, eyesight is ruined, and even one's own self-imposed boundaries are broken down. Most stories that start with something like "Do you remember that time when you went skinny dipping in the frozen pool?" are only because moonshine was involved. Usually, the answer is "No, I don't." Soon after this stage of moonshine influence will be the infamous pass-out, followed the next day by the worst hangover one can experience. Some have multiple days of a hangover.

At this moment, the three inexperienced shiners were at the threshold of all inhibition being erased, and Rick was having a hard time controlling his laughter at the sight of three grown men, men of stature in their own worlds, falling apart like pledges during rush week at some college.

"You think I could crash here, Rick? I don't think I can make it back to the Soo."

With that, Matt passed out right there at Rick's table. Bill just stared at Matt lying there with drool oozing out onto the table for several minutes with a blank, far-off look on his face. Yep, Bill was overtaken by the "moonshine gaze," the moment the alcohol short-circuits the brain for a few moments, leaving its victim dumbstruck with nothing but a blank expression.

Of course, Rick wasn't immune. It was also called giggle juice, which was how it hit Rick. He couldn't stop laughing at these grown men succumbing to his bootleg brew. Mike had gone outside to call Sarah to come get him, but he also needed some of that cold, fresh air to try and snap him out of his fog and was unaware of Matt and Bill's conditions. When he came back to the table and saw Matt passed out and Bill looking frozen in place, he joined Rick in his laughing fit.

"Sheez! Looks like some people can't handle their apple pie."

Mike was barely standing, but he was standing, at least for now. The room spun and he felt off-balance, so he grabbed a seat before he toppled onto the floor. He was still laughing while hanging onto the chair so he wouldn't fall over. The two were just sitting there, tears rolling down their faces from laughing so hard. It was a much-needed release from the stress of what they were preparing for. There wouldn't be much time for recovery, as their adversary was closing in on their little piece of Paradise.

14

CONTACT

The sunrise was magnificent over the frozen lake. The colors morphed from a deep red to a brilliant yellow as it rose in the eastern sky. The ice glistened and changed colors with the sunrise. It was a barren but beautiful landscape. The tracks of a lone coyote meandered southward as it hunted along the frozen shoreline. It was a magnificent scene; even the wind was still. Anyone with the privilege of witnessing this would be filled with awe, unless the bright sunlight shining through the window pierced the room of a severely hungover Mike Perkins.

"Oh, geez! Why are the damn blinds open?"

The bright sunlight and wondrous beauty of the morning was not appreciated by Mike. It was more like a laser beam shooting into his pickled brain, and the pounding in his head was amplified by the relentless light. His ears were ringing, his eyesight was still fuzzy, and the bed seemed to be moving. He felt as though he was going to be sick. Sarah was not sympathetic to his plight. She was all cozied up to the fire in her comfortable fleece pajamas with one of her favorite movies playing when she got the call from Mike to come and take him home. But it wasn't just Mike she gathered up; Matt and Bill hitched a ride as well. They were going to stay at Rick's, but he didn't really have place for them to sleep, unless sleeping in a chair at the table counted. Mike and Sarah had an extra room and two fold-out sofas, so they elected to stay there. Getting three drunk men into her vehicle and getting the beds ready for them was not in her plans for the evening. Suffice it to say that she was a little put out by them. The suffering she was seeing in her husband and knowing the other two were worse gave her a little satisfaction over being inconvenienced. She was heading out to do some grocery shopping, so the three men would be on their own for breakfast.

"Sorry, honey. But you know I hate a dark house. Besides, it's nearly nine in the morning. You're always up before six. I didn't think you'd mind."

Sarah had an evil little grin on her face as she turned and left the room.

"You may want to check on your guests. They were in much worse shape than you last night, and that's saying something."

Guests? Mike had completely forgotten that Matt and Bill had stayed with them. That meant that the one bathroom would be in high demand, so Mike made a beeline for it before everyone else woke up. He felt he might be in there awhile.

"I'm heading to the Soo. Coffee's on, and I made some biscuits. Thought you might need something to soak up what's left of whatever you were drinking. Make sure you don't leave me any messes. See you later this afternoon. Love you."

With that, Sarah was out the door. Mike briefly thought about going back to bed, but he knew it wouldn't be long before the others would start to wake up, and he needed to try to shake off the cobwebs of apple pie moonshine, so he decided to hit the shower instead. Matt and Bill had it a little easier than Mike, as they were on the darker side of the house where the sun couldn't punish them for their overindulgence, but they couldn't escape the grasp of the moonshine hangover. They wouldn't stir for another two hours, so Mike had plenty of time to clear his head. After the shower, a little coffee, some drops to clear the red eyes, and some toast to settle the stomach, Mike would rejoin the world of the living.

"Good afternoon, Matt. Feeling a little like a truck ran over you?"

It was only 10:30 in the morning, but Mike had been up for almost an hour and a half, so he thought he'd give Matt and Bill a little razzing. He would do his best to not let them know that he too was feeling a bit run over.

"Yeah, I think it was an apple truck. Holy crap. I wonder what the alcohol content was on the shine."

"Well, suffice it to say it's more than what you can get at the liquor store."

"Is Bill up yet?"

"Nope. I don't think he's moved since he passed out. I think it's time he gets up though, don't you?"

"Yeah, we wouldn't want him sleeping the whole day away now, would we? Just let me get some coffee in me first."

Mike had an idea about how to wake Bill out of his death sleep, and it would be effective, to say the least.

"You know what I'm thinking, Matt? I'm thinking if we don't get Bill to wake up soon, it might be tomorrow before he gets up. I just happen to have a couple of air horns in the old fishing supplies—you know, for an emergency. This may qualify."

"You sure about that, Mike? It might just give him a heart attack, waking up like that."

"Hm, you might have a point there. How about I let loose with a couple blasts from outside? It won't be quite as funny, but it should do the trick."

With that, Mike got one of his emergency air horns and blasted two long bursts just outside the window of the room Bill was sleeping in. It worked. Not only did it wake him up, but he jumped to his feet like he had a springboard under him.

"What the hell was that? Are you trying to give me a stroke or something? I about jumped outta my skin. Holy crap! Is the room spinning, or is it just me?"

"Nope. It's you. Too much pie, I guess, huh? I think we're all feeling a little hungover. Get yourself some coffee, and we'll figure out what to do today."

With that, the three slowly began to stir about, each suffering from the effects of Rick's apple pie moonshine. A good, greasy breakfast would solve the queasiness. After breakfast, while enjoying the coziness of the wood stove in a semi-comatose state, Matt's cellphone let out an alert like an air raid siren, shocking them out of their comas.

"What the hell was that? I can't take too many more shocks to my system."

Bill was only half joking; his hungover had a firm grip on his physical state. Between Mike's improvised alarm clock, Matt's cell phone siren, and his body struggling with mild alcohol poisoning, he felt like his heart was working double time.

"Holy shit! It's the tracking alert from the trap we set yesterday. Something's taken the bait and is on the move."

Mike and Bill sat there, dumbfounded.

"Really? Are you fucking kidding me?"

"It's right here. The tracking app is showing that the geo-tracker has been deployed and is on the move. It looks like it's heading north, back towards the lake, but it's not going very fast. It almost seems to be meandering a little."

"Maybe it's stalking something, or maybe it's not our Shoo."

"I don't know. There aren't too many other things that would go after a free meal the size of a dead deer this time of year. Bears are hibernating, and otters or fisher cats aren't big enough to spring the trap. I think we'd better contact Rick and get out there. We need to see the trap to make sure."

"Yeah, just keep a close eye on that phone and make sure whatever it is doesn't double back on us. We don't need to be running into this thing in the middle of nowhere."

It was as if they all were suddenly healed from their respective hangovers, moving like firefighters woken by the alarm. They scarfed down breakfast, guzzled their coffee, and headed out the door. Mike called Rick to let him know what was happening and told him to meet them at the trailhead.

"What're you doing? We gotta go!"

Mike had headed back inside. "I'm grabbing my rifle. There's no way I'm going in those woods now without some protection. Either of you want a firearm? I have a couple different choices."

Matt and Bill seemed conflicted. Not that they weren't comfortable with guns; they both hunted and were very familiar with firearms. It was just that, in this case, they really wanted to try and take the Shoo alive, but self-preservation is a strong motivator. Bill thought it a good idea, but Matt refused.

"Let's see what you have. Matt, you want to take one?"

"I don't think so. I have a tranquilizer rifle in my car. I think I'll take that."

"Suit yourself. It's your ass out there."

With that, they piled into Mike's truck, armed with an assortment of firearms, and headed to the trail head of the Two Hearted River.

Mike's words hit home for Matt. It *was* his ass on the line, but he was determined to stay the course in his scientific mission. He would trust his tranq rifle to do the job. After all, he had developed the special concoction just for the Shoo, and what better way to show confidence in his abilities than to literally put his ass on the line to prove them.

"Man, whatever picked up the tracker is moving *fast*. Looks like it's sticking to the water and heading back to the lake."

The adrenaline surging through Mike's body reminded him of all those times working as a police officer when things would get serious. The senses become heightened, vision clearer, and time seems to slow as the brain works in hyper speed. The sensation is euphoric. Mike was used to the feeling and knew what to expect from it and how to use it to his advantage, but Bill and Matt weren't accustomed to the rush, and it was evident in their movements and elevated chatter.

"Do you think it's the Shoo? Could it be an otter or something? I mean, bears aren't out this time of year, and they don't move that fast, do they? Wow, this is exciting. We could be on the verge of a major scientific discovery."

Matt couldn't separate his mouth from his brain, and everything that crossed his mind spewed out. Mike found it mildly funny and a little irritating. Bill, at least, had had some limited exposure to the feeling. Working as a forensic science, he had had many instances where he needed to visit a crime scene to collect samples or observe the context of the scene. His life may not have been on the line, but the situation triggered the same adrenaline reaction. But, even with his limited experience, he would also have trouble controlling his thoughts and actions during the ride to the Two Hearted trailhead, and Mike needed to focus on driving the icy curves of the road.

"Would you two get ahold of yourselves? I can't concentrate on driving with you guys yammering on like little school girls. Focus on the issue at hand! Just keep an eye on the tracker and keep the speculations to yourselves. We'll know soon enough what the tracker hooked onto once we inspect the trap. But I'd be ready for anything."

That seemed to snap Bill and Matt back out of their chatter fest, and they settled into a more professional reaction to the situation.

"It's slowing down. Looks like it's only a few yards from the lake."

Rick was already waiting at the trailhead when they pulled up. He looked ready for war. He was carrying one of his rifles, wearing a sidearm, and had a military-style rucksack on his back.

"Holy shit, Rick. You sure you have enough firepower there?"

"Better to have it and not need it than to need it and not have it. What's the story on the tracker thing?"

"Well, whatever it's hooked to moved very fast upstream, but it slowed when it got close to the lake. It looks like it's just waiting, there."

"Maybe. Or maybe the tracker came off."

Matt hadn't considered that. If the tracker came off, where and when would be the questions. Matt was uneasy at the thought of being in the woods with the Shoo and not being able to see its movements with the tracker made him even more nervous; maybe he should've brought more than a tranquilizer gun.

"Only one way to tell. First, we need to check the trap and see if we can identify what tripped it. If it was our friend, and the tracker did break loose, we'll need to walk the riverbanks to see if there are any tracks coming out. It's gonna be a little hard going between the snow and the thick brush. You guys up for that?"

Mike was prepared for the hike, and so was Matt. After all, Matt was used to doing some field work and had the proper footwear and was in decent shape. Bill, however, was more used to desk work and was a little out of shape. Plus, his boots were not really suited for the terrain around the Two Hearted.

"I don't think I should go, guys. I'd just slow you down. I'll stay here and keep an eye on the vehicles, if that's okay."

Rick respected people who knew their limitations and didn't risk others by playing macho. He felt Bill made the right decision.

"Good idea, Bill. I was hoping someone would watch the cars. Don't need anyone pokin' around them, you know."

With that, Rick, Mike, and Matt started up the snow-covered hill and then down towards the trap, each wondering what they would find. Only Rick had an idea of what might lie ahead, so he had taken the lead.

Bill watched as the three men disappeared over the rise. He suddenly felt very alone. The winter scene of shades of gray and clean, white snow made him feel colder than it was, and he noticed a heavy silence in the air. Snow hushes sound, and silence can feel like pressure closing in. It made him uneasy, so he quickly got into Mike's truck and locked the doors. He looked around, and suddenly felt silly at his nervousness, but he still kept the doors locked. He started the truck, turned the heater on low, and turned the radio volume down, just loud enough to break the silence. Then he cracked his window so he could hear any gunshots or unusual sounds. He looked at the shotgun he had chosen from Mike's gun safe and hoped he wouldn't need it. Then he leaned back in the seat and slowly drifted off to sleep, the effects of the previous night's indulgence still haunting him, his body needing to recover.

Making their way as stealthily as they could through the thick, snow-covered brush towards the trap was difficult. Their tracks in the snow from the day before had been all but erased by a fresh five inches overnight. The area they chose to place the trap was overgrown and had numerous small trees on the ground, remnants from the many storms that blew through the Great Lakes each year, and the snow hid them well. They were like booby traps, lying in wait for the untrained eye and unsuspecting foot to entangle in their twisted branches.

"Son of a bitch!"

Matt's outburst was the first words any of them had spoken since they had started this trek, and it was because he had stepped on one of the icy, snow-covered logs, and it laid him flat on the ground.

"You okay, Matt?"

"Yeah. But I'm going to need a hand getting up. It's fuckin' slippery. Damn, that snow is cold when it gets shoved down your shirt."

Matt's fall was a well-timed break in the otherwise tense hike. They all had a little laugh. Fortunately, he wasn't hurt. Every year, hikers and snowshoers took similar tumbles due to the hidden obstacles under the snow, resulting in everything from mild sprains to compound fractures.

"Try to stay upright for the rest of the hike, please."

Rick was poking a little fun at Matt, but it was both teasing and a concern. He didn't want to have to deal with an injured part of the team *and* a hungry Shoo, and they were getting close to the trap.

"How's the tracker looking?"

"Well, it's still in the same general place as before. Doesn't seem to be moving much, but it is moving. Looks like it's moving in a circle."

"Okay, guys. We're getting pretty close. Let's fan out towards the right."

Rick was taking the lead, and Mike and Matt were fine with that. This was a dangerous moment, as well as a potentially historic one, but Rick would treat this more like a military maneuver, positioning the others to be able to repel an attack if one should come. Mike, too, was familiar with the tactic, one he had used many times while assigned to the Coeur d'Alene's SWAT team, and he moved deftly into his position.

Matt, however, was a little lost and relied on the other two to direct him. They would do this by using a variety of hand signals, so as not to make any unnecessary noise that may alert their prey, as if Matt's fall hadn't already done that. As they crept forward, Rick in the lead, followed by Mike, with Matt bringing up the rear, they advanced in a crescent formation, making sure not to be in each other's line of fire, if it came down to that. When they were within fifty feet or so of the trap location, Rick stopped and crouched down so he could survey the scene. He stayed motionless for what seemed an eternity before standing and signaling the others to move up.

"Well, whatever hit the trap sure made a mess of it. The deer's gone, and I don't think the trap held it for very long. The gate's all twisted up, so I'm guessing it wasn't no otter."

Rick made his way closer to what was left of the trap while Mike and Matt stared on in disbelief. Mike had seen live-capture bear traps that weren't built as sturdy as this one, and even the largest bears couldn't make a mess like this. He was starting to think they were greatly outmatched.

"I can't believe what I'm seeing. That trap was designed to hold together even if it was hit by a truck going forty-five miles an hour. This thing must have tremendous power, especially being able to do this kind of damage in a confined space."

Matt went to examine the carnage while Mike stood watch, scanning the thick underbrush for any movement that might be the Shoo. He wasn't convinced that the tracker was still attached to it; with the exception that it seemed to be moving in a circle, it really hadn't moved away from where Matt last recorded its position on the tracking app. Mike was thinking it came off somehow and was caught on something else.

"It's our friend, all right. Look at those tracks. They're huge. Judging by the lack of any drag marks, it carried that deer carcass off like it was nothing. I'm thinking we need to find out if that tracker is still on it."

Matt looked at Rick, then at the tracks, then back at Rick. Fear had ahold of him, a fear he'd never felt. Fight or flight? Hell, he couldn't even move or make a sound. He just stared at Rick with a blank look, unable to comprehend Rick's words.

"You okay, Matt? Matt? Matt! Snap out of it!"

Rick's words shuddered Matt back to consciousness. "Sorry, I'm just stunned, and I hate to admit I'm pretty damn scared about what I'm seeing. I thought for sure the trap would hold it."

"Well, it didn't. Sometimes things just don't work like we want 'em to, so you can't worry about that now. At least the tracker deployed like it was supposed to. Let's hope it's still stuck to it."

"Yeah, I'm concerned about that. Now the tracker looks like it's stopped moving in circles, looks static. You'd think that if it dislodged from it, the river current would keep it moving downstream. It's not so heavy that it would stay still. I guess we're going to find out."

The three followed the tracks until they disappeared into the river. They would be relying on the tracker and their own eyes from that point on. Rick took the lead, with Mike behind him. Matt would bring up the rear. If the Shoo was still in the river and decided to attack, Matt's tranquilizer gun was the last thing they wanted to fend off the creature with.

"It's on the move again. And it's moving fast. It's heading to the lake."

"You sure it's not just being pushed out by the current?"

"It's definitely moving faster than the river. I think the tracker is still attached. Man, it's really moving."

On one hand, Mike was hoping they wouldn't have to face this thing in these thick and snow-covered woods. Advantage: Shoo. But, at the same time, he was curious to see it for himself. Rick, however, was anxious to put an end to the Shoo's hunting. He picked up the pace, and the others were having a hard time keeping up, but they didn't say a word; they just kept moving.

"Looks like this is where it went back into the water. No more tracks. What's your app show? How far?"

"Looks like about a quarter mile, but it's moving faster than we can. It won't be long until it's back in the lake. I think we should see what the tracker does once it gets there. If it stops again, or seems to be staying in one place for a long time, that might indicate that it has fallen off, and we'll just have to hope it hits the other trap and picks up that tracker. I don't think we can follow it, especially since it's in the water."

"We're only about a mile from the lake. Why don't you two head back to the truck. I'm gonna follow this river out to the lake and see if I can get an eyeball on it, or maybe if the tracker came off, I can find it. Let me have your phone so I can see what the movement on it is. I'll call you guys if I see anything. Meet you back at the trucks when I can—probably an hour or so."

Mike wasn't too sure Rick should head out after the Shoo on his own, especially since they weren't sure if it still had the tracker attached, but Matt was cold and wet and more than happy to agree to Rick's plan.

"I'm going with you, Rick. I know you're the big, bad, hunter-tracker, but you might need a little backup if you run into this thing. But Matt, you need to get warm, so head on back to the truck. I'm sure Bill is getting a little antsy."

There was a little more conversation about Mike slowing Rick down and the merits of one person stomping through the woods as opposed to two, but Mike wasn't having any of it, so Rick agreed to have him go with him while Matt headed back.

Matt was fine walking back to the truck alone, at least until he lost sight of the others. He suddenly felt cold and helpless. All he had was a tranquilizer gun and no cellphone in case of trouble. He was almost a quarter mile from the trucks in some of the thickest brush and forest he'd ever been in, not to mention the snow cover. It was easy enough to follow their footprints back out, but that was no consolation if he were to fall again and get hurt. He would either have to wait for Mike and Rick to come back, or crawl out over all the buried branches and small shrubs. Neither of those options appealed to him, so he moved slowly and made sure of each step.

He suddenly realized how much he had become reliant on technology. What did people do before cellphones and GPS? He stopped and looked around at his surroundings. He knew there was a fairly well-traveled road just to the south, he knew Lake Superior was to his north, and he knew the trucks were to the west. But, if he didn't have the footprints to guide him, would he know which way was which? After all, most days during winter in this part of the Upper Peninsula didn't have much sunshine; it was mostly gray. So, using the sun for direction was out.

He stood there in the blanket of silence the snow created and felt small and insignificant. His body shuddered at the cold, and he refocused on getting back to the truck. When he came to where the trap was, he took some time to study the damage more closely. The frame of the cage had held up fairly well, just some minor deformation; the gate and lock had suffered the most damage. The locking mechanism had completely failed, tearing away from the frame like paper, the gate was mangled, and the trap had been moved about six feet.

Then Matt saw something in the mud. It was barely visible and blended in with the surroundings. It only caught his attention because there was just the tiniest amount of blood on it. The red didn't fit in with the browns, grays, and white of the landscape. Only one or two inches protruded from the mud, but when Matt pulled it out, it was closer to eight inches. It was some kind of boney spike, similar to the spikes on a stegosaurus tail. The find made him forget about being wet and cold, and he frantically looked for something to put the specimen in to protect any DNA evidence. He had nothing to place it in, so he decided to carry it back to the truck as carefully as possible. He knew there were some Ziplock bags in the truck, and they would have to do. He hoped his insulated neoprene gloves would keep the sample relatively uncontaminated.

"Bill, wake up! Do I have something to show *you*."

Matt's excited wake-up alarm just about gave Bill a heart attack. He had fallen into one of those deep sleeps where all time and space is erased. It took Bill a few seconds to realize where he was and what day it was.

"What the hell, Matt? Are you trying to kill me? Geez, I was out."

"I think your heart just might get another jolt when you see what I found. Quick, grab one of those large Ziplocks Mike keeps in the back. I need to get this in it as quickly as possible."

"Holy crap! What the hell is *that*?"

"I'm not sure. But one thing's for certain—it's from the Mishipeshu."

Mike kept storage box in his truck filled with all manner of items. He called it the if-I-only-had-a-whatever box. Among the large assortment were batteries, flashlights, extra boots, socks, rubber gloves, snacks, and several sizes of Ziplock bags, to list just a few of the items. Each item had been put in the box after some situation where he needed it but didn't have it. It started when he was just a rookie police officer, when he wished he had some rubber gloves to search a filthy homeless man. The collection had come in handy many times over the years.

"Are you kidding me? Did you see it? Where's Mike and Rick?"

"We didn't see it. The trap was completely destroyed. I'm guessing the Mishipeshu lost this while it was trying to escape the trap. Mike and Rick went after the tracker to find out if it's still attached or not. They took my phone to monitor it on the app."

"Damnit! I really hoped the trap would hold it. I guess we'll just have to wait here until they call or get back. At least it's warm in the truck."

Matt carefully placed the spike in a Ziplock and sealed it, making sure to remove as much air from the bag as possible. He and Bill then took turns studying the item, careful not to puncture the plastic. Where the spike had broken off from the Mishipeshu, there were jagged edges, and they didn't want those edges to break through.

"Maybe we should double-bag it. Less chance of exposing it to contaminants."

After thirty minutes or so, the adrenaline rush from the from finding the spike, along with the hangover and fatigue from being wet and cold, Matt settled back into his seat and closed his eyes. It wasn't long before he was asleep, and Bill wasn't far behind. While Bill and Matt were enjoying some much-needed rest, Mike and Rick were fighting through the thick brush and difficult footing as they closed in on the tracker's signal.

"What's that?"

Mike saw something sticking out often the frozen water, mixed in with a tangle of debris piled up close to shore.

"Looks like the deer carcass from the trap. Either the Shoo got it tangled in this mess and couldn't get it out, or he let go of it for some reason, and it floated to here. I kinda doubt that creature wouldn't be able to snatch it from that tangle. He must've let go."

Mike felt a chill course through his body. He sensed something watching them, sizing them up for an attack. Maybe the Shoo let go of the deer because there was a better meal coming right to it.

"Rick, I have a bad feeling."

"I know. Me, too. Watch our backside and keep one eye on the water. What's the tracker showin'?"

Mike looked at the app on Matt's phone, his hands shaky, then his heart skipped when he saw the tracker information.

"It's not moving. It's completely still."

"What? Where is it? How close?"

"Looks like it's just ahead about forty yards, close to that bend in the river right there."

Rick and Mike instinctively raised their rifles and pointed them in the direction of the river bend, searching the dark, icy waters for anything that could be the Shoo. There was nothing they could see, and the only sound was the gurgling water as it flowed over and around rocks, submerged logs, ice, and the debris it picked up as it moved downstream towards Lake Superior.

The water was tinted dark brown by the tannic acid leaching out of the many oak trees that lined its banks; it would be impossible to see anything beneath the surface. They stood there, motionless, staring at the water, trying to find anything out of the ordinary that could be their target. Nothing, but neither man moved a muscle, both transfixed on that spot.

There was no change in the water's flow—no surge of bubbles, no indication that there was anything there let alone something the size of the Mishipeshu. But that part of the river had a deep spot, a hole carved out of the soft, sandy river bottom where there was a finger of bedrock. The current had pushed out the sand and left only the bedrock, leaving a pool about fifteen feet deep. It also had a large pile of debris caught on a tree that had fallen across the river, leaving a gap of only five or six inches between it and the water rushing under it. It was a natural dam, collecting anything that was large enough to snag on the tree. It was the perfect place for the Mishipeshu to view what was following it. Its dark coloring made the perfect camouflage to disappear into the debris.

When it smelled the deer carcass in the trap, it had quickly made its way upstream to gather the easy meal. It bit down on the carcass with its saber-like teeth and started to back out of the trap, pulling the carcass with it and releasing the tracker deployment system and engaging the spring and closing the door on the trap. The flaw in the system was that all this happened *after* the bait was taken. The delay allowed the Shoo to partially exit the trap before the gate had fully closed. If the trap had been designed to operate like a live-capture trap used by animal control officers, where the gate is closed before the animal even reaches the bait, the Mishipeshu may very well have been trapped, and the hunt would be over.

Instead, the gate closed on the spike-filled tail of the Shoo, enraging it, and it thrashed about trying to destroy the trap, breaking one of its spikes off in the melee. Fortunately, the tracker deployed as planned and was firmly attached to the Shoo's back.

The Mishipeshu had dragged the deer carcass from the trap and had started to head back downstream when it caught the scent of humans in the woods. Even though it was an opportunistic eater, scavenging large carcasses when it came across them, it preferred fresh meat, and humans were is favorite. Humans were soft and easy to kill—no antlers, claws, or sharp teeth to injure it. Rarely did it come across a human that put up any kind of fight after it had one in its jaws. So it let go of the carcass in favor of a potential, fresh kill. It swam in circles to kick up more silt and debris, making it even harder to be seen in the dark waters. It sat still among the broken branches and small logs that had snagged on the fallen tree crossing the river; only its eyes and snout stuck out of the water, but with its natural coloring, it was nearly invisible. So, there it would wait for the humans to get close enough for it to lunge out of the water and kill its prey.

"Somethin' doesn't feel right. I got that somethin's-watchin'-us feeling."

Rick's gaze was fixed on the tangle of debris at the river bend and the fallen tree. He raised his rifle to look through its scope to see better. He turned the magnification from three, where he usually kept it, to six. This allowed him to view the debris pile as if he were six times closer to it.

"Yeah, me too. There's something out there, and pretty close, if this tracker thing is right."

Mike raised his rifle too, hoping that between the two of them, if the Shoo was just ahead, one of them would spot it. The Mishipeshu was watching, too, and it recognized the rifles from its encounter with one from the previous winter. It might not have known what they were, but it knew they caused pain, and it was already in some pain from losing a spike. It watched for a few moments, then quickly spun and submerged, making its way towards the lake and the safety of the ice.

"There!"

No sooner than Rick had yelled, Mike let loose three quick shots from his Browning 7-mm magnum rifle, piercing the silence of the woods with its booming reports.

"Holy shit, Rick! I didn't know you brought a shoulder cannon with you. I about jumped out of my skin."

"Did you see it? I saw its eyes, just above the water behind that snag of crap at the bend. I shot as soon as I knew what I was seeing. Don't know if I hit it, but I sure let it know we're here."

"All I saw was a huge splash right before you shot. After that, nothing. But the tracker shows it's moving, and moving fast. If you hit it, I don't think you did much damage."

None of Rick's shots found the Mishipeshu. It had started to submerge milliseconds before Rick fired his first round. By the time the bullets reached where it had been, it had made it ten yards farther downstream and was under the frozen river and on its way out to the lake, leaving Rick and Mike to take in all that had just happened.

"I can't believe something that big can disappear so fast and stay unseen. I could tell it was huge by the large splash it made, but I never really got a look at the creature itself."

"Well, I may have hit it, so I'm going to look for any signs of blood."

Mike and Rick scoured the area where the Shoo had been but found no signs that it had been hit. They did see where two of the rounds hit a birch tree behind the river bend, and they nearly cut that tree in two.

"Wow! Those rounds really do some damage. Small little entry holes, but the backside is decimated."

"I load my own rounds, and I put the maximum charge the shells and rifle can handle. Special delivery for the Shoo."

"Well, looks like our friend is in the lake and heading towards the point. We better get back to the trucks and head towards town so we can be ready if it shows."

Mike and Rick made their way back to the trucks where they found Bill and Matt fast asleep. They never even heard Rick's shots. Snow-covered branches make great soundproofing material; people have been much closer and not heard gunshots in the forest due to the snow absorbing the sound waves.

"Well, looks like you guys were really worried about us. Worn out from all that concern, right?"

"We knew you could handle yourselves. No need to waste energy worrying about things."

"Thanks, Bill. What a pal."

Mike and Bill's joking broke the tension from the day's events. But it was time to get back to the task at hand. Rick wasn't much for useless chatter.

"I hate to break up this party, but we've got a monster on the loose. What's the tracker showin'?"

"Looks like it's offshore about three hundred yards or so, heading north towards the point, and moving fast."

"I say we head that way and keep an eye on where it looks like it might go. Maybe we can ambush it, but we're gonna have to move fast too."

"So, the tracker's still attached? Did you get a look at it?"

Matt had almost forgotten about his trophy.

"Not really, but Rick fired off some shots from that shoulder cannon of his, but it looks like he missed. I can't believe you didn't hear the shots. My ears are still ringing."

"Well, we didn't come out completely empty-handed. I found this by the trap."

Bill, Mike, and Rick were excited to see the item. They took turns examining the spike, but it was Rick that noticed the obvious.

"It's not hollow. I thought it would be hollow. You know, like a rhinoceros horn, but it's more like an antler, solid."

"Like the thagomizer on a stegosaurus."

"Okay, Matt, now you're just making shit up. What the hell is a thagomizer?"

Matt was a dinosaur nerd; he had collected just about every dinosaur toy there was as a kid, and the stegosaurus was one of his favorites.

"The thagomizer was the term the *Far Side* cartoonist, Gary

Larson, gave to the stegosaurus' spiked tail, and it stuck. Science hadn't given that part of the stegosaurus an official name until Larson's cartoon. Anyway, the tail spikes were solid and thought to be for defense. I'm guessing the Shoo has the same feature on its tail. Hell, it may even be a throwback to the Jurassic or Albian period, the same time frame as the stegosaurus."

"Well, throwback or not, it's alive and well here in Paradise, and I plan on making it extinct. I don't really care about its history, only that we make it history. We need to get a move on and try and get ahead of it. No tellin' how secure that tracker is, or how long we'll have a signal. What's the battery life on that thing, anyway?"

Scientific discovery be damned. Rick was a man of singular focus when it came to the Shoo. Matt and Bill understood his thinking, even though they really wanted to capture it for study; they knew the chances were slim to none, especially since their best chance of capture had been handily destroyed. There was one other trap, but it had the same setup as the first and, looking at the spike, X figured it would meet the same fate, if the Mishipeshu even fell for the bait again. Their best chance of a successful capture rested in Matt's tranquilizer formula, and that was untested.

"You're right, Rick. We need to get back on its trail. The battery should last a couple of weeks, so let's hope we get to it before it runs out. There's four of us. We could spread out along its path, or split into two teams of two."

"There's plenty of daylight for us to spread out thin. I don't think it moves inland unless it uses a waterway or it's dark enough to move unnoticed. But if we haven't had contact with it during the day, we should team up so we all have backup in case it's needed. Matt, since you have the tracking app, I think you should stay somewhere in the middle. Keep the others posted on its location. We will move one way or the other based on that info. There's a lot of real estate in Chippewa County, so we need to be able to move quickly. Rick, how many snowmobiles do you have?"

"How many do I have, or how many do I have that run? I've got two ready to go and one I can have ready in a couple hours. I just need to swap out some parts from the half dozen wrecked ones I keep for parts."

"Okay, why don't you get that done while we keep an eye on this thing. After this morning, I'm thinking it might be a little cautious about coming right back out onto land. When you get finished, let us know, and we'll decide on where to meet. Do you need any help?"

"Nope. Help would just slow me down. I'll gas 'em up and get them loaded on the flatbed. Should be about two and a half, three hours."

Rick wasted no time getting started. Without so much as a "see you later," he was off, leaving the others to put together their plan.

They decided they needed to spread themselves from White-fish Point to the north, all the way to the intersection of State Highway 28 and Michigan 133 to the south, with one person positioned in the middle around the Curly Lewis Scenic Byway. The middle person would be Matt as he was most familiar with the tracking app. He would signal any major shifts in the Mishipeshu's movement via Mike's handheld radios. Cellphone service was hit and miss in this area, but Mike's handhelds had a range of thirty miles in this terrain. Mike had made friends with one of the volunteers at the Whitefish Point bird observatory, so he was able to get Bill set up inside that facility.

They would need to pick up Matt's car from Rick's cabin from the previous night's revelry. Once Rick got the snowmobiles ready, the four of them would regroup in Paradise to plan their next move. It was the beginning of snowmobile season, and the Wheelhouse restaurant was a popular sled head hangout, so having sleds on a trailer in that parking lot wouldn't seem unusual.

As soon as Mike had a signal on his cellphone, he called Sarah to update her on current plans. He assured her they would know where the Shoo was as long as the tracker stayed attached, and that he would try to be there when she got home to help her unload her car. But the real reason he wanted to be there was to get her inside as quickly as possible, just in case. The surreal atmosphere of the situation engulfed him. Just a few short months ago, he and Sarah were starting their retirement adventure in a place called Paradise, and it was Paradise for so many reasons. But Paradise soon turned into a sort of hell. How in the world did it get this far out of whack? A literal monster of the lake terrorizing the shores of Lake Superior, and it seemed it had been for ages. If he had been told the stories of the Mishipeshu before they moved, he would have called it nonsense. But, here he was, right in the middle of the nightmare.

"Radio check. Mike, do you read me?"

Bill was set up in the observatory, making sure his radio was connected to the others.

"Gotcha, Bill. Matt? You in place yet?"

"Just getting to the first pull-in spot. So far, the tracker still seems attached."

"Good deal. Keep us updated on any changes. I've got to head to my place to get Sarah secured. I'll radio when I'm done."

With Mike, Bill, and Matt in position, and Rick getting the sleds ready, they seemed prepared to monitor and, hopefully, eliminate the threat the Shoo posed to their community. In the meantime, the Shoo was cruising the far side of the shelf ice that ran the full length of Lake Superior and into Whitefish Bay. To Matt, it looked as if it was looking for targets of opportunity, moving back and forth from the entrance to Whitefish Bay at

Whitefish Point, all the way towards the towns of Brimley and Bay Mills to the south. These areas were sparsely populated but full of out-of-town thrill-seekers riding the remote snow-covered trails, oblivious to the danger that may be near. Its movements were almost mechanical, very little variance in cadence and direction. Matt was impressed by the speed of the Mishipeshu, making the circuit from the northernmost point then back to its southernmost point in about twenty-five minutes.

Assuming calm water and little wind, a boat of similar size traveling at twenty-five knots would take around thirty minutes to do the same route. This meant the Mishipeshu was traveling close to thirty knots, consistently. Matt had been tracking it for close to two hours when it changed its focus, seemingly narrowing its hunting area. Its northernmost route brought it to the edge of Paradise, and the southernmost shifted to just the other side of the river mouth. It must have smelled something that made it dial in on that area.

"Man, am I glad you're home. Things are really heating up with this Shoo thing."

Sarah had made it home, and Mike helped her get the groceries in and got her locked in before things got any worse.

"Me, too. I kept looking at the water every time I could see it, or scanning the edge of the wood lines all the way home, half expecting to see the damn thing pounce out in front of me at any minute. I'm scared, Mike. What if...?"

Before Sarah could finish her question, Matt's voice broke through in the radio.

"Guys! It's changing its pattern. We need to shift, now!"

Mike looked at Sarah's worried face, knowing she had good reason to be worried. Hell, he was worried, too. They really didn't know exactly how to handle the problem, only that they needed to try. Men like Mike and Rick were a rare breed becoming rarer, men of action and principal. Matt and Bill shared their traits but lacked experience in the practical applications. It would be up to the two experienced men to guide the others in order to be successful in their endeavor without losing anyone.

"I'm sorry, honey. I've got to go. Stay inside and keep your phone with you, just in case. I love you."

"I love you, too. Be careful, Mike."

With that, Mike was out the door.

"What's it doing, Matt?"

"It seems to be narrowing its search pattern. Looks like it's focused between town and the Curly Lewis Highway. I'll stay where I am, but you and Bill need to relocate. Rick? You on the radio?"

Rick had been frantically working to get the second snowmobile running and had shut the radio off so he could focus. He hadn't heard about the change in the Mishipeshu's movements, but he would find out shortly. He managed to get the second snowmobile running, gassed up, and loaded onto his trailer along with the other sled. He switched on the radio just in time to hear Bill acknowledge the need to shift locations. He was going to head into Paradise with Mike, moving to the river mouth.

"Hey, guys. Rick here. I got the second sled up and running, and both are loaded and ready. I'm heading into town and will let you know when I'm there."

Mike was extremely happy to hear Rick's voice come over the radio and that both sleds were ready. Now the team needed to determine where to deploy them, and that would have to wait for the Shoo to dial in its search. Maybe they would get lucky, and it would go for the second trap, or at least head into the Tahquamenon River, where it might be easier to corner in the shallower waters.

"Good news, Rick. I'll meet you at the Wheelhouse and get a plan together."

It looked as if all their planning and research was about to pay off. While heading into town to meet Rick, Mike was running through all the steps they'd taken to reach this point. Looking back, Mike felt like they'd been working on this for a year or so, but it had only been five months. Five months filled with disbelief, discovery, and determination. Five months he had thought he would be using to get their cabin redone. Five months he thought he'd be enjoying all the outdoor activities the area offered. Hiking, fishing, four-wheeling, and maybe some camping. Instead, he had spent most of those five months in cop mode, digging into the lore and history of the Mishipeshu, all the missing person reports, and anything that might give him insight into the Shoo. To be honest, it felt good to use his skills for such a different type of challenge. If it wasn't for the fact that this challenge involved him and Sarah, he might even say he was enjoying the mental and physical workout. Little did he know just how much of a workout those faculties would get.

15

THE SCENT

It had been up this river many times throughout its lifespan, but it had never come across such an easy meal. It entered what it perceived as a tangle of branches holding a meal of dead deer. But when the door of the trap slammed down on its back, the feel of steel made it realize this was nowhere it wanted to be, and it thrashed and clawed and bit at everything it touched. It never felt the spike that secured the tracking device on its back, but it knew this meant danger to it, so it started back downstream and back to the lake, where it felt safe.

That's when it caught scent of something in the woods approaching the area. It recognized the smell as food, and it would move to hide in the deeper part of the river where it could watch from the shadows. It's sat there, waiting and watching, tasting the air for the scent of prey. It caught a whiff of something familiar, a scent it had smelled before. It crouched lower in the water, focusing all its senses in the direction of the scent. It remembered this smell, and it was a memory that brought it pain. It still bore the scar from the encounter with the creature that carried that scent. It knew this was no ordinary meal; it was like it was a hunter, but with a fearsome weapon that brought noise and pain.

It would wait for the opportunity to escape into the deep waters of its domain. The scent came closer and seemed to the Mishipeshu that this hunter knew where it was, and for the first time in as long as its memory could draw on, it felt fear. It associated this scent with pain. It may be a primitive creature, but it does learn, and what it knew was that there was easier food than this; it would give this meal a wide berth. Just as it dove and turned towards the lake, it heard the loud reports from Rick's rifle as the bullets struck the trees just above it. It was the sound he remembered from before, so it dove and stayed underwater all the way to the lake and under the ice shelf until it reached the frigid waters on the other side. It would turn and head to the food-filled lands to the south.

That's where it caught the scent. It was very familiar with the smell of exhaust, sweat, and leather all blended together. It always sought out this scent, because it usually meant an easy meal. The prey was always so focused on the trails, it ignored the surrounding woods and ponds, so it was easy to get close to the food and easier to take it. It would follow the scent. As it cruised the waters on the lake side of the shelf ice, it kept its snout in the air, not just smelling but actually tasting the scent. The stronger the taste, the closer the prey. It swam fast, moving down the coastline then back up, zeroing in on the freshest scent. It caught the scent of its prey somewhere near the river waters where it spilled into the bay; it would focus on that area. But something caught its attention, not up river, but farther out on the lake. It would change course once again, and head out into the bay.

The scent seemed to stay, not moving like most, so it slowed down to get close. The ice was the only cover for it this far out, so it would need to stay submerged until right on the scent. It had hunted this far into the bay before, but it wasn't as successful over the long run—not as much food as on the land—but because of its close call earlier, it decided to take this chance and stay off the land, at least for now. As it closed the distance between it and the scent, it started to hear the sounds of its prey and began its stealthy move to attack. There was more than one meal on the ice; there were two. It was hungry now, so it would eat one now and take the other to its lair for storage. It was the middle of the afternoon by the time it made its attack, so there was still plenty of daylight. It would have to attack through the ice and quickly disable its prey before it could escape. Circling below the ice, it waited for both of them to be close enough to hit in one blow.

It was over before the two victims knew what happened. Of course, the fact that they had both been drinking all day slowed their thinking and reflexes, allowing the Shoo to make quick work of them. First, it swung its spiked tail up and through the ice, creating a massive collapse of ice and men into the frigid waters. Not even the shock of the cold water was enough to sober them up. Then it snapped the neck of one man with a powerful bite and gored the other with its tail, pinning him to the ice until he quit moving. It was over in less than a minute. It would consume the smaller meal first, taking the larger one to its cache.

Brothers Mark and Larry McFadden had ice fished this part of Whitefish Bay most of their lives. Born and raised in the small town of Eckerman, Michigan, they spent their adult lives doing odd jobs all over Chippewa County, everything from clearing trees to home repairs; they eked out a living for themselves. It was a modest life, but one that allowed them to pursue their love of hunting and fishing the vast woodlands and expansive waterways. Their family owned twenty acres just off highway M123, and Mark and Larry had small mobile homes on that property. It wasn't much, but they were happy. When winter came, about the only things for them to do was plowing snow and fishing; of course, that also allowed them time for their other favorite pastime, drinking.

On those long days when they spent the entire day and into the night ice fishing, drinking gave them something to do while they waited for their tip lines to trip. During these times, they mostly told the same old jokes, the same old stories, and had the same old arguments, which never really amounted to more than one of them calling the other an idiot or a dumbass. They stayed out of trouble, never married, and never had much ambition to do anything other than just squeak by; it was the life they chose, as many who lived in these remote areas did.

They never paid income tax on the money they earned, because they only accepted cash or trade for payment. The property taxes for their land and mobile homes was less than $1,000 a year, and they easily made that in a week of hard work. They lived simply, but they would die violently. The only clue that there was anything in the water other than the whitefish they were fishing for was a surge of water from the Shoo's pass by that splashed up through their ice holes. They barely had time to wonder what made that splash before all hell descended upon them. First, the ice exploded all around them, dumping the two men into the frigid water. Larry watched in horror as the Shoo emerged from under the ice and grabbed Mark by the throat, nearly severing his head as its powerful jaws clamped down. Before Larry could move, the spikes on the Shoo's tail gored him and pinned him to the ice. He watched his lifeblood flow onto the ice along with parts of his intestines as he faded into darkness.

The Shoo finished its meal and left with Larry's body, leaving a horror show of blood and entrails strewn across the ice. With the broken ice, it almost looked like an explosion had occurred, ripping the men's bodies apart.

It wouldn't take long for the Mishipeshu to reach its cache, deposit the body, then return to its hunting grounds. All this time, it was unaware of the hitchhiker attached to its back sending its location to the app on Matt's phone—information that until now had been just a rumor or unproven theory. But the discovery of the Mishipeshu itself used to be an unproven theory and rumor.

16

CHANGE OF DIRECTION

"Damnit! It's going out into the lake. What the hell is it doing?"

Matt watched the movements of the Shoo. To him, they seemed off. He had seen its movements along the shoreline become shorter and shorter then more confined to a specific area, then all of a sudden change course to a more easterly track. It slowed, then stopped, then quickly headed towards the deep waters of Lake Superior. Not only was it moving very fast, it wasn't deviating from its course; it was a straight track heading towards Michipicoten Island, its rumored home. He radioed the others to let them know.

"What are you saying, Matt? Is it still on the same course?"

Mike was wondering if it was still heading towards Michipicoten. He remembered the story about it being where Native Americans said it lived. But it was also in the supposed Lake Inferior. If so, why would it be going back now? After all, as far as they knew, there hadn't been any attacks since they came upon it early that day.

"Yep. It's making a beeline for Michipicoten Island. Either it got spooked and is running home, which I doubt, or it had a successful hunt and is done for the day. I don't like it."

"Maybe we should check out the area it was in just before it changed course. Might give us some more info. Rick, what can you tell us about the area?"

"Well, if it was off the river mouth, it's pretty shallow for the most part, but there's deeper holes around there where ice fishing is pretty good. The ice gets thick out there, thick enough for the sleds."

Mike had never gone out on any ice before. He didn't trust it, let alone going out on a thousand-pound snowmobile. But it was the only way to know for sure if there was any reason for the Mishipeshu to suddenly change course. He and Rick would head to the river mouth and start a search of the area while Matt and Bill kept tabs on the Shoo through the app.

Rick wasted no time getting to the river mouth to offload the snowmobiles. He had them off and running by the time Mike arrived. They couldn't help but notice a lone beat-up Ford F150 at the edge of parking lot. There was a snowmobile trailer hooked up to it but no sleds, just the tracks of two snowmobiles heading out onto the ice in the direction where the Shoo had been.

"Well, that doesn't look good. I think we better see where these tracks go. It might be nothin', but it might be somethin'."

"Yeah, I think you're right, Rick. If we don't find anything out of the ordinary, we can at least try to warn whoever's out there, if they don't think we're crazy."

The two men loaded their sleds with some water, snacks, their rifles, and a first aid kit. Mike tried to be prepared for any possibility. They didn't say much as they mounted the sleds and prepared to venture out on the ice.

Only Mike spoke. "You sure this ice is thick enough to hold us?"

Rick just looked at Mike with a wry little smile and took off onto the ice. Mike watched for a few seconds, just to make sure, then made his way onto the frozen surface.

Mike found it surprisingly smooth riding on the ice. He half expected a lot of bumps from the chunks of ice that tended to pile up close to shore. But they were half a mile offshore, where it was free from the shelf ice phenomenon. They had been traveling on it for thirty minutes when they caught sight of something in the distance, so they picked up the pace. As they got closer, they saw the remnants of an ice fishing shack. There were two snowmobiles parked a few yards from the debris, and blood was everywhere. Rick stopped his snowmobile and motioned for Mike to do the same.

"I don't want to risk getting too close to that mess. I can see a large hole in the ice, and it might not be stable enough for our sleds. We need to walk up."

The two men shouldered their rifles and carefully stepped onto the ice. A distinct cracking sound from the ice let Mike know things were about to get real. For the first time in years he felt the familiar rush of adrenaline course through his body bringing all his senses to that heightened level that helped him focus on the task at hand.

"What the hell was that? Is this ice going to hold us?"

"It's normal. The ice makes that sound all the time. It's the popping sound you need to worry about, and you'd know it if you heard it. Sounds like a gun goin' off."

That didn't really make Mike feel any better, but Rick was moving forward in a way that seemed to show he wasn't too worried about the ice, so Mike kept moving too.

"Geez! Looks like our little creature has been here, for sure.

Look at those gouges in the ice. Those are claw marks. I know those sleds. They belong to the McFadden brothers. Kinda loner types. So, I'm guessin' they both bought the farm here."

Mike had seen crime scenes and messy vehicle accidents many times in his career, but nothing like this. Blood had spewed from obvious arterial wounds as far as ten feet from the scene, and there were small bits of tissue and, likely, innards.

"I don't get it. It couldn't have eaten both men in such a short time, could it? That's a lot to swallow, bones and all. It must be storing some of the victims for later. That could explain the lack of sightings throughout the year. Could be it only hunts in the winter months."

"I don't know nothin' about that, but I do know it's taken two more people. We've got to kill this damn thing, and we better find a way soon. Peak snowmobile season is just around the corner, and there'll be plenty of food for it then, *and* it will be harder for us to corner it."

"I hear you, Rick. But I guess right now, we need to notify the police."

"I'm not sure that's a good idea. These two brothers are barely seen in winter. They stick to themselves, and they ain't got no family except each other. Not tryin' to sound cold, but no one's gonna miss them, at least not for a while. We call the cops in, no offense, and word's gonna get out we got some kind of monster eatin' tourists, and that probably ain't good for business, if you know what I mean. If we hadn't been trackin' this thing, no one would ever know nothin' about what happened here. Unless, of course, some sledder or ice fisherman stumbled on this mess, but that's unlikely. We have weather comin' in, and it'll erase all this evidence in just a couple hours. I say we focus on our plan and let Mother Nature do what she does."

Mike was concerned about not notifying the authorities, but

he saw Rick's point. But not letting the authorities know what happened could end up biting them in the butt. They needed to tell someone what they found, if not for anything else but to keep the McFaddens from becoming just another missing person report.

"We have to tell someone, Rick. We can't just let this go. I say we tell Jim Harrison. He's a rescue diver, right?"

"Yeah, so?"

"Well, he's aware of our little problem, and he's got a vested interest in this town's business, and as a rescue diver, he would have to investigate things like boats sinking and the occasional submerged snowmobile. We could give him the coordinates where the brothers disappeared. The sleds are bound to go under sooner or later. He could say he got an anonymous call or something about someone seeing a snowmobile under the water. After all, the water's pretty clear, and it's not that deep here, right? What is it, fifteen feet or so?"

"About that, yeah."

"Well, a snowmobile could be seen from a boat at that depth, so it's not that far-fetched. At least this way, we won't be spooking the tourists, and those brothers will be counted as drowned or something, and hopefully we can stop this thing before it kills again."

"Okay, I guess I'm good with that. Let's just hope some other sledder doesn't come across this before the weather gets here. Our sled tracks are out here, too. People might think them brothers were killed by some other sled heads."

Before heading back to the river mouth, Mike took several pictures on his cellphone so they would have a record of the scene to show the others what they found. Then they headed back in, making sure to take a slightly different route so they wouldn't have their tracks go straight to the kill sight then straight back, making it look more like a random route than a deliberate one.

They reached the river mouth, loaded the sleds, and headed to the Wheelhouse to inform Jim of their discovery. The two men didn't say a word as they made the three mile trip into town. The only break in the silence was Mike radioing Matt and Bill to meet them there. Neither of them could get the kill site out of their heads, but neither was willing to let the other know their concerns about it. Rick was hoping they had the firepower to kill it, never really considering that they just left the scene of the horrible deaths of two fellow Yoopers. It was just a fact that couldn't be changed to him.

Mike, on the other hand, wasn't comfortable with that, but he understood it. His worries were more personal. This thing had already killed on *his* property, and now he had a picture in his head of what that might've looked like, and that scared him. He wasn't used to being scared, but this wasn't a fear for his own safety, but for Sarah. He couldn't bear the thought of such a sweet soul having to face such a primal evil. He was now more determined to destroy this creature than ever.

Matt and Bill were waiting for them in the parking lot when they arrived. By the looks on their faces, Mike could tell they were anxious to hear what they had to report, and he wasn't looking forward to the conversation.

"How was your little excursion onto the ice? I bet it was interesting being that far offshore. Did you see anything out there?"

Mike gave Bill a blank stare, the kind of look that meant your thoughts were focused on something other than the immediate conversation, and Bill knew that whatever Mike was going to tell them wasn't good.

"Well, looks like our creature has struck. It was a pretty gruesome sight to see—violent, bloody, and vicious. It looked like the ice just exploded and shredded whoever was on it. There were two men, to the best of our knowledge, taken by it. Rick recognized the sleds parked close to the scene. There was little left of their bodies, remnants mostly. Rick can fill you in on the details. I'm going inside to see if Jim is around. I need to discuss this with him."

Matt and Bill hadn't expected to hear about victims. They thought maybe some tracks or something, but the story brought them back to reality; their idea of capturing it might not be possible. Rick filled them in on their decision not to call the authorities and why, while Mike went inside the Wheelhouse.

"Are you shittin' me? Jesus, Mike, what the hell do you expect me to do about this? I'm not part of the sheriff's department, you know. This could blow up on you, you know. Leaving the scene like that is a big deal."

"You're not telling me anything I don't know, Jim, but this wasn't a car accident or a crime scene. It was an animal attack with no bodies to be examined. But more importantly, it was the Shoo that did it. This town doesn't need something like that being blasted all over the media. It would kill the snowmobile season, no pun intended, and it may ruin the town for future tourism. There's supposed to be a storm coming in tonight. It should clean up the scene so we can keep it under wraps while my team and I try to deal with this. I marked the location of the attack on my GPS so you, in an official act as a rescue diver, can investigate an anonymous concerned citizen's call about seeing a snowmobile under the water in the spring."

"I see your point. It just seems a little sketchy. A lot could go wrong if everything that you think will happen doesn't happen. I want you to understand that if someone finds out about your little secret, I'll have to play stupid about it. Okay? I can't afford to have a big state police investigation messing up my business or my dive status. It might be a good time to bring Sheriff Baxter in on this.

After all, if the shit hits the fan, he's gonna be the one gettin' sprayed."

"Do you think he'll play along, or just laugh us off? I mean, if I was the Sheriff, I'd probably call the men in the white coats."

"Oh, Lester Baxter is a good man. It'll take some convincing, but I think he'll keep an open mind. He's lived up here most of his life, and he's heard the stories. Hell, he's probably known some of those that went missing. Besides, if it comes to it, he's got some assets available to him that may come in handy in a fight. Let's get the rest of your team in here and see what they think. First round is on me."

Mike was just about to go get the others, when they entered the restaurant. Matt and Bill had that look of fear and desperation on their faces, and Rick just looked pissed off.

"What's going on, fellas, besides what we already know?"

"The tracker quit working. It just... fell off the radar."

"Are you kiddin' me? The battery couldn't have died already. It's only been six or seven hours since it activated. It should last for days, right?"

"Yeah. That's what I don't understand. There's a battery indicator on the app, and it barely shown any usage. The tracker just doesn't draw that much juice. It makes no sense."

"Well, fuck! We need to figure out what we're going to do now. Jim wants to meet to go over our ideas. I guess the timing of this couldn't have been better. He's buying the first round, but go easy on the drinks, guys. I have a feeling things are gonna get busy."

With that, the four joined Jim upstairs in his office to get him up to speed. It would be good to have him as part of the group. He knew everyone in town, and a few good people to know outside of Paradise as well. He could be a real help to the mission.

"So, when did the signal drop?"

"It was right about here, just before it reached Michipicoten Island. The signal just vanished, like something swallowed it up."

Matt was showing the group the map grid on the app when the signal suddenly reappeared on the screen. It was moving back towards Paradise.

"What the hell? There must be some sort of glitch."

"Did the signal come back exactly where it stopped?"

Jim had a look that was a mix of excitement and disbelief.

"Yeah, pretty much, as far as I can tell. Why?"

Jim quickly turned and went to his file cabinet. Opening one of the drawers, he pulled out a worn-out piece of a map. On the upper left corner were the words *Isle Maurepas*. He rolled the map out on the table.

"You see this? It's the original hand-drawn map of that area, drawn by French explorer, Sir Duluth, in 1679. He claims to have found a lake *under* Lake Superior he called Lac d'Enfer, or Lake of Hell. It's supposed to have an entrance somewhere around Michipicoten Island. I know it sounds crazy, but I've been diving the area for years tryin' to find it. Problem is, the island is in the Canadian part of Lake Superior, so it's not that easy to just take a boat over and go for a dive. There's so much of the area around the island I haven't searched. What if the Shoo goes there? That could explain the loss of your signal."

"Yeah, I found reference to this lake under the lake too. They called it Lake Inferior. If there *is* an underwater lake, the Shoo might be using it as its den. That could explain how it's stayed hidden for so long."

"Are you telling me there's a lake *under* Lake Superior? I've never heard of anything like that. It seems a little too fanciful to me."

"Well, there's been references to it since the late sixteen hundreds. It's just that mainstream science never put forth any serious expeditions to search for it. Most of the research has been done by amateurs like myself with little or no funding. The water can be seven hundred feet deep and extremely cold around the island, so it's a difficult endeavor. But there has been some documentation of this lake from some fairly serious explorers in the past. It's just that their findings were lost to history, except the map I have from Duluth, but it's not complete."

"That's all great stuff and all, but do I need to remind you guys that it's winter? Even if it is using some sort of underwater lake for its hiding place, there's absolutely nothing we can do about it. At least not until the ice melts."

Matt's voice had a tone of frustration. He had a possibly perfect place to trap the Mishipeshu alive, but no way of getting there. If they weren't able to capture it, they would, most likely need to kill it to keep it from taking human lives. The age old paradox—man invades habitat, native species see man as a threat or food source and behave accordingly, man feels threatened and kills the native species. It's not the species fault; it's man's fault, but man is the apex predator, so anything that preys on man must be eliminated to keep the status quo.

The five of them huddled there at Jim's desk and studied the map while watching the tracker on Matt's phone. It was making a beeline back towards Paradise. As the signal crossed over from Canadian waters and into the American part of Whitefish Bay, Jim noted something that hadn't crossed anyone else's mind yet.

"It's making pretty much a straight line from the island back to its hunting grounds. Shortest distance between two points. I think it hurries from its home back to where it hunts and then carries the kill back in the same straight line. That gives us the potential to know where it's going to be after a kill and where it might return to when it comes back."

"Jesus, Jim. That means we have to have victims to plot it. That's a little morbid, don't you think?"

Matt was saying what the others were thinking, except Mike. He understood the reality of their situation. Preventing the loss of another human life might not be possible, but they could use the tracker to see if the Shoo was returning to its lair or not, allowing the group to get ahead of it before it made it to the safety of the ice.

"It's not like I'm *hoping* for someone to be killed. I'm just saying we need to watch this pattern. At least we might have something we can use, at least while the tracker's working."

"It looks like it's heading for the river mouth again. There's a lot of sled heads that ride the frozen river. Could be one of its spots."

"You know, now that I think about it, I usually have to dive a couple times each winter for someone that went through the ice. Only once did I find a body. Could be that was the only one that actually broke through. Maybe the rest were from the Shoo."

"Unless anyone's got a better idea, I say we see if Jim's hunch is right. Any other ideas? Since no one's saying anything, I'll take that it a yes. It's going to be difficult to know exactly where it might come ashore, but we know it will somewhere. Rick, is the ice between shore and the shelf ice safe to ride?"

"Usually. The water's not very deep along the shore, so it freezes pretty solid. Even if you broke through, it won't be much deeper than your chest."

"Well, I think Rick and I should use the sleds to patrol back and forth on that ice between shore and the shelf ice, while you two monitor the Shoo's movement. If it comes ashore, we should see its tracks. Maybe we'll get lucky and see it before it gets to shore. Jim, if you want to call sheriff Baxter and fill him in on things, I think that might be a good idea. He knows you. He might just think this was all a prank or something, coming from us. I've got to call Sarah and tell her what we're doing and to be ready just in case."

The group had a plan, and it looked as though they had a real shot at stopping the Mishipeshu from using their town as its food source, but the plan had to work, or it would just move to another area to hunt. It had done it before many times in its life. It had been found out by the Ojibwe Tribe in the winter of 1797 in what is now called Bay Mills, and the tribe hunted the Mishipeshu all winter, losing many of its members to it before it moved north. The following winter, the Mishipeshu stayed away from the Bay Mills area, focusing on the Keweenaw Peninsula for the next few years. This pause in hunting more fertile grounds resulted in the Mishipeshu fading into tribal legend instead of being an actual threat. The Mishipeshu learned, remembered, and adapted to that information.

As more and more humans came to inhabit once virgin lands, it became easier for it to stay undiscovered, moving from populated area to populated area in a more random pattern. As time passed, the area up to the Keweenaw that would be known as Paradise would become its preferred hunting area. There were enough prey animals in those areas to fulfill its needs, but not so many as to make it difficult to move unseen among them.

As the human population grew, it would once again have to change its patterns. The area that would become known as Chippewa County would eventually become its preferred hunting ground. Sparsely populated with huge tracts of forests along with numerous waterways snaking through them, would provide ample ambush locations that would keep it concealed from view, rarely needing to expose itself in the open. As humans developed more advanced methods of accessing these remote tracks, more and more areas became fruitful for the Mishipeshu.

Almost since its founding in 1925, Paradise and the surrounding woodlands and waters have been a Mecca for outdoor enthusiasts of all types. Snowmobilers, cross-country skiers, snowshoers, and all manner of water sportsmen have enjoyed what the area has to offer. This diversity of activity has allowed the Mishipeshu to stay largely unseen. Only a few have caught a glimpse of this massive creature, but their stories, if told, were relegated to drunken misidentifications or campfire tales.

The endeavor by these men was the first of its kind since the Ojibwe Tribe sent its warriors out to hunt it down in the eighteenth century, but unlike the Ojibwe, who rallied the entire tribe for the cause, this hunt was limited to just these few men, their immediate family, and those close to them.

As man has become more secular and less spiritual, the demons that were once openly spoken of and prepared for have become myths, legends, and the concoctions of the less enlightened, stories to be ridiculed and ignored instead of respected and honored. No matter the outcome of this mission, the locals would have a better grasp of what they'd been living with for ages.

17

ICE PATROL

M ike nervously moved out onto the ice, expecting it to give way under the weight of the snowmobile. Nothing. It was as solid as being on land.

"Now, you gotta be careful driving along on this type of ice. It can be smooth as glass one minute, then full of chunky ice the next. Hit that chunky shit too fast, and you might flip if you ain't careful, so take it easy until you get a feel for the ice. I'm goin' down towards the river mouth and south. You head north up to the point. This should be pretty close to halfway, so let's make this our meet-up spot. If I ain't here when you get here, wait, and I'll do the same. We should be able to see each other coming, as long as we maintain similar speeds. Good luck and be careful."

"Will do. You, too."

Mike knew why Rick wanted the southern run; it was the best chance of coming in contact with the Shoo, and Rick wanted it bad. He was more than a little nervous about running into it alone, and Rick had had some experience with it, so Mike wasn't about to argue about his assignment.

"Matt, we're starting our runs. Any change in its track?"

"Nope. Still heading straight in. Looks like about ten miles out, but it's closing fast. You guys keep your head on a swivel. I'm not sure how accurate this tracker is. After being submerged for so long, it could be off by a couple hundred yards or so, but it's all we have."

"Ten-four."

One official-type mission, and Mike had reverted back to cop mode. He was shaking his head at himself for using the universal ten-four for roger or okay. He could almost hear the others laughing.

As Mike traversed the frozen waters along Whitefish Bay's shoreline, he was amazed at how smooth most of the ice was. Just a few weeks earlier, these waters were churning with waves generated by the gales the area was known for. But as the waters cooled, the water had turned to slush, then to blocks of ice, and finally freezing solid. The nearly constant wind blowing across the bay smooths out the ice to glass-like finish. It's a mesmerizing process. It was easy to get lost in the serene nature of the lake this time of year.

The lake is closed to shipping this time of year, so there are no ships, no small craft, and few residents living along the icy shore. The only sound is the occasional buzz of snowmobiles zipping down Whitefish Point Road as they head to the many trailheads that intersect this thoroughfare.

The only sound Mike could hear was the engine of the snowmobile he was riding. Most sled heads wore special snow suits to keep them warm as the frigid air blasts their bodies as they ride. Mike had no such gear, so he loaded up on his layers. Thermal underwear, insulated overalls, a winter parka, insulated gloves, and a wool scarf—usually plenty of insulation for an average day of snow shoveling and the like, but not quite good enough for riding a snowmobile. Mike was cold but not freezing, and he could handle being a little uncomfortable.

For almost two hours, Mike and Rick made their rounds, meeting almost exactly where they started at each turn. Sarah was somehow comforted to see her husband zipping by on the ice just outside their cabin. It had been a long, lonely stretch of Mike being so involved with this quest, but she was used to it. There were long stakeouts, extended days due to working nights or evenings and then having to be in court to testify during the day, not to mention the undercover operations he had been a part of on occasion. Those could last months or even years with no normal eight-hour day. At least she could see him go by their window or know he would be home sometime during the day or night. Still, knowing he was patrolling so close to home because of a creature that sought human flesh made her nervous.

The days are short this time of year, and the sun sets early. It was already 3:30 and starting to get dark. In about an hour, it would be total darkness. Mike started thinking the Shoo knew this and timed its arrivals for just after sunset, and he got that feeling he used to get when he felt there was a threat somewhere close by. Police officers call it situational awareness. Some feel it's mostly experience that programs their subconscious to recognize sights, sounds, smells, and even random thoughts as alerts to dangers. Whatever the cause, it had served Mike well, usually raising his adrenaline and making him more focused, more aware, but in this situation, it made him feel uneasy. He didn't like it.

"Matt, where is it now?"

Mike wanted reassurance it wasn't lurking just out of his line of sight, waiting for him.

"It's getting close, maybe a mile out, but it's slowed down. Maybe it hears your snowmobiles and wants to take a look."

The thought of the Shoo being attracted to their activity made

Mike question their tactics. What if, instead of trying to intercept it, they were actually baiting it in? It gave Mike an idea.

"Rick, head back towards me. I want to run something by you."

"Ten-four, good buddy."

Mike had to shake his head and laugh over Rick's nod to his earlier ten-four response.

It was only about ten minutes before Rick made it to where Mike was parked.

"What's on your mind, Mike?"

"I was just thinking that we might actually be attracting this thing to us with our sledding back and forth. Matt says it looks like it's slowed down and is only about a mile or so out. I hate to say it, but what if we could use that to our advantage? You know, bring it to us instead of trying to figure out where it might go. The battery on that tracker isn't going to last the rest of the winter, so I say we try to speed up the process."

"That all sounds fine and dandy, but I'm not sure I like being bait."

"Me neither. I don't believe what I'm about to suggest, but I think we should bring it into my cabin."

"Are you fuckin' crazy? Even if we survived its attack, that thing might tear your place apart."

"I know, I know. But we rigged up those bombs between the cabin and the water. With any luck, we can keep it from getting to the cabin. There's a lot of trees on the property that could provide a good vantage spot to hang a tree stand, which I have in my garage. It might just give us the edge we need. I think it's our best chance, assuming we can bring it in."

"Better let the others know what's on your mind, and quick. We ain't got much time to set this one up."

"Yeah, but the real problem is Sarah. She's not going to be happy about this, especially since I'm going to get her out of here so she's safe. I'll take care of that right away and grab the tree stand. You pick out a good tree."

Mike was right that Sarah wouldn't be happy; she was furious at the thought of her home being in the middle of a battlefield with her husband as bait for some giant prehistoric creature. But Mike was adamant that she leave and go to the Wheelhouse to be safe. He assured her everything would be fine and that he would call her as soon as it was over. Of course, inside Mike's head was the reality that the chance of everything being fine was slim.

"What the hell are they thinking? That's the craziest idea I've ever heard, and it might just get them killed."

Bill was saying what everyone else was thinking about Mike and Rick's idea to lure the Shoo in. Rick had radioed their plan to the others, making sure they understood that for the plan to have a chance, they had to make it look like Mike was alone on the ice. The others could wait just down the road, but they were not to enter Mike and Sarah's property unless called in. The others were listening in on the radio call, including Sheriff Baxter and Jim, and they all had a look of disbelief at what they were hearing.

"I'm not sure I can allow this to happen, Jim. Not on my watch."

"I understand what you're sayin', Les, but you gotta let this play out, at least this one time, or we may have more people go missing around here. Let's just be ready to help if they need it."

"I don't like it, Jim. Remember, I am the sheriff, the only regular law presence in this town. The state police barely even drive through here. If this thing goes south, and people find out I was aware of what was happening, it'll be my damn head on a platter."

"That's why we're keeping this confined to such a small group. Besides, we just clued you in on this a few minutes ago. So, anything that happens tonight, your hands are clean."

"Maybe. But I'm gonna sit in my patrol car at the Magnusen like I'm watching for speeders. That way I'm close by if needed."

"Thanks, Les. Let's hope it all goes as planned."

After the sheriff left the restaurant, Jim approached Bill and Matt to figure out what they were going to do. Mike didn't want them at his cabin, but there wasn't anything said about being parked on Whitefish Point Road.

"I say we park about two or three lots lawn from Mike's cabin. There's a couple of vacant lots we can park on, and the cabin between them is empty this time of year. No one will bother us, and we'll be able to be at Mike and Sarah's in seconds. Hey, look. Here comes Sarah. Better let her know our plan so she can have a little peace of mind. She's gotta be worried sick."

Sarah walked into the room with her gaze fixed on the group with a look mixed with hopelessness and anger. Before she got far into the restaurant, Bill walked towards her and guided her outside and onto the deck.

"I know what you're feeling, Sarah. We all feel the same way. Mike called and told us what he and Rick were going to do, but we have to keep this under wraps. I'm sorry I dragged you out here, but I could tell by the look on your face that you were going to say something, and the place is packed with tourists. This town can't afford the panic something like this could bring. Rest assured, we aren't going to let those guys down. The sheriff's aware of the situation, and we're all headed out to be close by, seconds away, if they need our help."

"That's all well and good, Bill, but it's my husband out there. So if you're going, so am I. There's no damn way I'm sitting in there by myself just waiting to hear something. You got that?"

By the time Bill and Sarah had finished their conversation, the others had joined them on the deck. Their small group had big plans, and it was time to set things in motion. Sheriff Baxter would position his cruiser along the shoulder of Whitefish Point Road, with Jim riding shotgun. They would be just about a quarter mile from Mike and Sarah's cabin. Matt, Bill, and Sarah would park in the vacant lot just three lots from the cabin. So as not to make too much noise setting up, they would coast into the lot with the headlights off.

Sarah sent Mike a text to let him know what they were doing in the hopes he would feel a little better knowing she and his friends were close.

At the cabin, Rick had found a suitable tree to hang the tree stand, and he and Mike were about to get into their respective positions—Rick in the tree, with Mike parked out on the ice sitting on his snowmobile. Hopefully, the Shoo would see Mike as an easy meal and come in close enough for the two men to end its use of the Upper Peninsula as its own private hunting preserve.

Rick was settled in his perch high above the property with his Browning 7-mm magnum rifle, hand-loaded with his personal rounds, his night vision scope, and the control panel to detonate the explosives they had buried. They were as ready as they could be. Mike radioed one last time to Matt to verify the Shoo was still in the area. It was. According to Matt, it looked as though it was swimming along the shelf ice about half a mile offshore, slowly cruising up and down as fine-tuning where its next meal might be. The path it was swimming took it right past his cabin; it seemed the Shoo was looking for Mike. He had left the snowmobile idling on the ice while he and Rick got set up in the hopes the sound would keep it interested. It looked like that ploy might worked. From this point on, there would be no radio contact between the men, only texts with the phones on silent. It was game on.

Mike made his way out to his snowmobile, half expecting the Shoo to come flying over the ice any minute. He would have to trust Matt's updates so he could make his escape off the ice and, hopefully, lead the Shoo into the kill zone before it reached him. He had his cellphone on vibrate so he'd know if he was getting any texts with updates on its position. He was all set to appear as a broken-down snowmobiler. He had just one more to do.

Sarah looked down at the text Mike had just sent her. "I love you" was all it said, but that was enough for Sarah; Mike wasn't known for being wordy.

Mike looked up at Rick's position, but the sun had set, and the moon hadn't come up yet. It was dark, very dark, and that worried Mike. He wouldn't be able to see anything moving out on the ice until the moon provided some light, and that could be a while. He felt his phone buzz and looked at the message; it was Sarah saying she loved him too, and to be careful. The text coming through made his heart skip; he thought it was Matt telling him the Shoo was coming, but Sarah's message calmed him a bit, but not for long.

His phone buzzed again, and this time, it *was* Matt. The Shoo seemed to be zeroing in on Mike's position. It was moving slowly but straight at him. Mike could feel his sphincter tighten, and a cold chill coursed through his body. This was it.

Matt had sent Rick the text too, and he was on alert. He racked a round into the chamber and took the safety off. He, too, was anxious about how this would play out. He had seen this thing up close and knew it was going to be tough to kill, but he had faith in the plan, such as it was. The Shoo might survive his rifle, but he felt there was no way it could survive the bombs. The trick would be not to shoot too early, to let it get in the blast zone.

Mike would have to move fast to a safe place before Rick set off any explosives, and that safe place was between the cabin and Mike's shop, about thirty-five yards from the blast zone, but before Mike even got to the blast zone, he would have to travel almost forty yards over a frozen lake and up some pretty icy steps. It was going to be close.

The Mishipeshu smelled a human, and it moved in closer to set up an attack run. It reached the outermost shelf ice and slowly raised its head above the crest of what Mike and Sarah called ice mountains. They stood about seven feet out of the water at this point, and the water was only twelve feet deep, so the Mishipeshu had no trouble pulling itself up to investigate. When it scanned the ice in front of it, it recognized the cabin as a place of a successful hunt, and it salivated over the prospect of another kill. It saw the human out on the ice only a few hundred yards away. At full speed, it could close the distance in less than a minute, but there was something about what it was seeing that made it cautious. Call it intuition or recall, but the scent was familiar, and there was a faint, second human scent not far off that was familiar as well. This was not unusual to the Mishipeshu; many times, it took its prey while other humans were close by, but it did make it more difficult. It decided to move slowly, cautiously, across the ice, using the secondary ice shelf closer to shore as cover.

Mike looked at his cellphone. Another text. It was closing in on his position. Mike felt his legs get weak as the fear of confronting the Shoo became almost certain. He would have to lure it off the ice and into the blast zone, but he couldn't run. Through his research and the experiences that Rick and the team had had so far, they felt it had some intelligence, even if it was just knowledge gained by ages of close calls, so they had decided that Mike would try to act as though he didn't know it was there, walking away from the snowmobile and up the stairs that accessed the beach, and then to the area behind his cabin. It would be a fast walk, but it was a walk none the less. They hoped this would bring the Shoo in close.

It was almost time for Mike to make his move, and it took all his nerve not to look out at the ice. Then Mike noticed something, a horrible stench. A stench that seemed to be a combination of rotten fish and decaying flesh. It was putrid and almost made him gag. He remembered the reports that the Shoo smelled of rotting fish, and he knew the Shoo was getting close; it was time to move. He turned and headed towards the beach, focusing on the stairs ahead. He told himself, "Don't look back, don't look back..." as he made his way across the ice. He imagined the Shoo breathing down his back, and he wanted to run. Mike had been in numerous dangerous situations before, but none frightened him saso much as this. His heart pounded as if about to burst out of his chest.

He reached the bottom of the steps when he heard the ice cracking behind him, and he knew the Shoo was closing in. Still, he moved as if there was nothing wrong, and he hoped Rick was ready. He counted the steps as he climbed; there were fifteen steps to the top. "One... two... three... four..." Time seemed to slow to a snail's pace, and the pounding from his heart was deafening. "... eight... nine... ten..."

He glanced up to Rick perched high in the large white pine that overlooked the target zone. He could barely make out the dark outline of Rick with his rifle trained on the ice behind him, and it calmed him. "Thirteen... fourteen... *fifteen*." He had made it to the top. Now he needed to make it to the space between his cabin and the shop, and that was a long thirty-five yards away. *Don't speed up. Rick's got this. He hasn't shot yet, so it must not be that close yet.* He counted the yards to the shed...*Five yards down...* "Eight... ten..."

Rick's rifle let loose a deafening blast. *Boom!* Then another. *Boom!* Instinctively, Mike dove for the ground.

Rick had watched the Shoo move stealthily across the ice, closing the distance between it and Mike. He was amazed how quietly something that big could move across the ice, and it was a little unnerving.

Mike had just made it to the stairs when the Shoo had closed to within fifty yards. He could hear the ice cracking under the weight of the Shoo's mass.

Rick knew he had to wait until the last possible moment to shoot so he wouldn't spook it back out into the lake. This was, most likely, the only chance they would have where they were set up before the Shoo came, instead of after an attack.

Mike had made it to the top of the stairs, but the Shoo was just ten yards from the bottom step. Mike would never make it to the safe spot before the Shoo was on him.

Rick waited as long as he could before he fired; by then, the Shoo had climbed the steep bank next to the staircase and was focused on Mike.

Rick waited for the Shoo to be completely over the edge and almost on top of one of their explosive devices before taking his shot. The Shoo was a mere ten yards from Mike when he fired. The bullet struck the Shoo in its neck, close to where its windpipe should be. It let out a roar that shook the earth, and Rick felt it, even in his perch. But it didn't fall. It didn't even act affected, so he shot again. This time, he aimed for the right eye. If that didn't put it down, maybe it would cripple its abilities somehow. The Shoo reeled from the shot, staggering further into the blast zone. Rick quickly looked to see where Mike was, then he flipped the switch on the bomb closest to the creature.

Boom! The blast shook the surrounding area like an earthquake. The concussion shattered the two windows closest to the explosion. It also caused Rick to lose his grip on the detonator panel, and it fell to the ground. Rick could see that the Shoo was wounded, but it was still on its feet. But the worst thing was that it seemed to be looking in his direction, as though it knew where

Rick was. Then the Shoo started to move in Rick's direction. Rick's rifle only held three rounds in its chamber, and he had already used two. He started his internal rant on government interference with firearms capacities. He quickly realized how futile his mental ranting was and refocused on his situation, and it was dire.

Through his night vision scope, he saw the Shoo clearly and the damage done to it. He could see blood pouring from just above its right eye; his shot had hit, and the wound was bleeding profusely. Even though he had missed his intended target, the wound had accomplished the results Rick wanted; the Shoo had a hard time seeing through all the blood. But the Shoo didn't need its eyesight to be perfect. Its sense of smell was intact, and it could locate Rick with that alone. Rick also noticed the Shoo had a large, gaping wound just behind its right shoulder that was also bleeding. He figured the explosive charge would have been more successful if he hadn't dropped the control panel.

Mike had been stunned by the blast but was starting to refocus on his surroundings. *Where is it?* He got to his feet and turned in the direction of the lake. There it was, mere yards from where he stood, but it wasn't coming towards him. It was moving in Rick's direction. Mike looked up at Rick's perch to see if he could see him. The moon was cresting over the bay, and there was just enough light to make him out. Rick was motioning with one hand, pointing down, and Mike looked where he was pointing and saw the control panel. "Shit!" Here he was, just a few yards from the Shoo—a wounded Shoo, at that. He only had his .45 auto pistol, and he knew that wasn't enough firepower to do anything but piss it off, and there was Rick without the control panel.

Mike knew, if they were to survive this, they needed that panel. Knowing there was no way he could reach it without going past the Shoo, Mike decided to try and draw its attention away from Rick and onto him. He drew his pistol and fired a round just in front of the Shoo. It hit the ground and sprayed dirt and sand into the Shoo's face. It turned in Mike's direction and let out another roar as it slowly changed direction to come to him. Mike's plan seemed to be working, but now he was on the Shoo's menu.

Mike slowly backed into the breezeway that connected the cabin to the shop, hoping to lure the Shoo in his direction. It would be out of the blast zone, but Rick should be able to get down and retrieve the detonator. Maybe Mike could work it around to re-enter the zone before it got Mike in its grip.

Rick slowly maneuvered out of the stand and quietly made his was down the tree. The Shoo didn't pick up on him, and grabbed the panel and slowly backed into the shrubs—a small bit of cover form the Shoo's sight.

Now it was up to Mike to figure out a way to lure it back into the zone, while being able to escape it himself. Mike made his way through the breezeway with the Shoo closing in. As he made it to the opposite side of the breezeway, in the few seconds Mike was out of the Shoo's sight, he made a mad dash to the far side of the cabin, where he planned to circle out back to the lakeside and into the bomb-laden part of their yard. At his age, it was more like a fast trot.

As he made the final turn around the cabin, he glanced back over his shoulder. The Shoo was closing in and within twenty feet of Mike; he hoped Rick was ready as he ran straight across the line of bombs. Just as Mike reached the far corner of the cabin, he dove around the corner as the Shoo lunged at him. It never reached him.

Boooom!

Rick had set off bomb number two and followed up quickly with bomb number three.

Boooom!

Mike was still crawling away from the blast zone as Rick set the bombs off. It was close. Mike lay there, covered in dirt, sand, and Shoo carnage. He rolled over on his back and sat up, making sure to move slowly in case he was injured. He could see the Mishipeshu lying there, gaping wounds along its belly. Blood poured out of its body, and it breathed its last breath.

Mike sat there, in awe of its massive size and a little ashamed that they had possibly destroyed something that was the last of its kind. He took stock of his body, and everything seemed okay—just a few scratches, and a nail stuck in his calf from the bombs. All in all, it had gone better than he had hoped. He could see Rick running towards him yelling something, but Mike's hearing had been deadened from the explosions; it looked like Rick was yelling something like, "We did it! It's dead!"

Rick closed in on the Mishipeshu and put the final round from his rifle into its brain. The coup de grâce. The magnitude of what just happened and the shear relief of surviving the ordeal hit Rick pretty hard. He collapsed to his knees and started crying, something he thought he was incapable of. The shear emotion boiled out uncontrollably and his legs shook from running and adrenaline, he couldn't even stand up.

The rest of the team heard the gunshots and explosions, and Sarah started crying uncontrollably over the thought of her husband facing such a monster. She wanted to rush home and be with Mike, but Bill kept her in the car.

Time slows when the fight or flight kicks in, and it seemed like an eternity between the first shots and explosions and the final explosions; everyone felt something must have gone terribly wrong.

Sheriff Baxter wasn't waiting any longer and sped out onto Whitefish Point Road, lights flashing and siren blaring, and raced to Mike and Sarah's cabin. Bill didn't waste any time either. Once the sheriff headed out, he immediately got his car moving too. The patrol car had barely come to a stop before Baxter and Jim jumped out, rifles at the ready. Bill pulled in right behind him, and they hesitated for just a few seconds as they viewed the scene before them.

It was a mess. There were pieces of the Shoo strewn about. Rick was standing over it with his rifle. Although it was empty, he still had it aimed at its head. And there was Mike, still lying on the ground. They all feared the worst, assuming Mike was dead or seriously injured.

Sarah started towards her husband and saw him turn his head to look back at the group that had just arrived. He had a huge grin on his face, and Sarah knew he was all right. She dropped down and held him tighter than he'd ever felt her hug him before.

"Hell, woman, I feel like I'm being squeezed by an anaconda."

She didn't care, and neither did he. It was pure joy and relief all rolled into one explosion of emotion. The group stood in silent awe at the sheer mass of the Mishipeshu, and, truth be told, there was quite a bit of guilt running through them. Yes, this creature had been preying on humans, and had been for ages, but it was the last of its kind, a connection to the prehistoric past.

Even though it had sustained fatal wounds, it was still a mostly intact specimen, and Matt was already trying to come up with a way to study it.

"Not to shift the gears here, but how do we get this thing outta here without drawing too much attention? This thing is *huge*. It's not like we can just toss it in the back of my pickup, and there ain't no way I can get my flatbed back here."

Rick was always one step ahead of the rest of them when it came to planning, but this was a different situation all together.

Sheriff Baxter came up with a possible solution. "Well, you can get your flatbed over to the river mouth, right?"

"Yeah, so?"

"I say we get a tractor over here and use it to roll the damn thing down the hill there and get it back on the ice. From there, we could tie it to a couple snowmobiles and slide it to the boat launch. The ice is thick enough to hold the weight all the way there, then you could winch it up on the flatbed. But we gotta get moving if that's the plan. It's good and dark, and chances are, we can do it before daylight if we hurry. That way, no one's gonna see it. At least the chances of someone seeing it will be slim."

"That's all fine and dandy, sheriff, but what do I do with it then? Have the world's biggest barbecue?"

"I think I know what to do with it, Rick. Deliver it to the university. That way, we can study it and learn more about how this thing was able to adapt and survive for so long."

With Matt offering up a solution, the team mobilized once again and worked to move the Shoo onto the ice and to Lake Superior State University. Jim had a tractor, so they didn't have to bring anyone else in on their secret, and Rick's snowmobiles were attached to it once it was on the ice. From there, it was a slow but easy tow to the river mouth. It all went off without any issues and, as far as they could tell, no one saw them.

Once again, Rick pointed out the obvious. "What about the damn blood trail leading all the way here? Won't that raise a few questions?"

"Well, maybe that snowstorm they predicted will get here soon. It was supposed to have hit by now. The wind is picking up. Maybe that's the start of it."

Predicting the weather on the Great Lakes is always tricky. It's not just about the sky and air temperature; it's the temperature of the lakes that really drives the weather, and the winter storm that was predicted for earlier that night had been slowed by the temperature inversion over Lake Superior. That created a buildup of additional moisture, and the eight to ten inches of snow would turn out to be over a foot, a fortuitous set of circumstances for the team. By the time they reached the boat launch at the river mouth, it had started to snow.

The next day, Jim smiled to himself when he heard patrons talking about hearing explosions in the night and what sounded like gunfire. When Sheriff Baxter was questioned about this, he said the explosions were military jets breaking the sound barrier over the lake, and as far as the gunshots went—happens all the time. People target-shooting or popping off a round or two at skunks or raccoons. Nothing to see here.

Over the next few weeks, Matt and his team of student researchers worked around the clock on dissecting the Mishipeshu and recording everything they found. Keeping the project a secret was almost impossible; everyone involved had to sign non-disclosure agreements, and there were no cellphones, and, except for the university's equipment, there would be no recording devices in the examination hall. Matt handpicked his team, but human nature being what it is, word eventually got out, and the university received quite a bit of media attention over the find. But the story of how they came into possession of it would never be revealed. Matt had concocted a story of finding it floating in Whitefish Bay during one of his research outings; obviously, it had been struck by one of the many freighters that crossed its waters, which explained the damage to it.

Mike and Sarah repaired the damage to their cabin from the explosions, mostly replacing broken windows and siding. They had Rick remove and take the buried explosives home with him for disposal. Bill went back to Idaho with great memories and a small souvenir, the scale that Rick had. Rick had a new one. He had taken one of the Mishipeshu's spikes.

Not one law enforcement agency even paid attention to the dramatic drop in missing person reports, simply putting it down to their patrols and public safety announcements. They just figured the public was finally heading their message.

There were a few inquiries from local tribal leaders, and Matt gave them private viewings of the Mishipeshu. After all, it had been a part of their folklore for centuries, and they deserved an opportunity to validate their history.

Jim and Matt formed a friendship that would see them plotting and planning a search for the legendary Lake Inferior. With the data Matt had from the tracking app, they narrowed the search field to within just a few hundred yards. Over the winter, they worked to gather a crew, obtain all the necessary permits, and gather funding. Of course, with the discovery of the Mishipeshu, Matt was able to make some contacts who wanted in on the expedition. They would set off after the ice melted.

The reign of silent terror that had gone on for ages had come to a violent end for the Mishipeshu. Time and technology had caught up with the elusive creature, or so it seemed. The Mishipeshu had hunted these waters and its bordering lands since the age of dinosaurs, a single creature of purpose.

How, then, does one animal survive for tens, or even hundreds of thousands, of years? The answer is quite simple. It doesn't. In the grand scheme of things, God created the Earth and all that dwell on it. He gave life on Earth the ability to adapt to their ever-changing environment, even to the point of reproduction. The Mishipeshu was one of a kind, alone on this planet with no other being like it, so it had developed a limited ability to reproduce through a process known as parthenogenesis, or the ability to reproduce without the need of a mate. In the Mishipeshu's case, it could lay an egg—one single egg that would provide an heir of sorts to the parent.

So, deep below the surface of Whitefish Bay, just offshore from Michipicoten Island's Schafer Bay, there lies a secret. A large meteor struck the area long before the Great Lakes were formed, long before the age of man. A relatively small hole was created in the rock on the side of the crater, leading to a large cavity that would eventually become known as Lake Inferior. The ice age would come, and in its retreat, the meltwaters filled what would become known as the Great Lakes, but before Lake Superior was filled, water trickled into that small hole, partially filling the cavity until the water above it overran the opening, stopping the steady flow in and creating an access point for what would become known as the Mishipeshu. Fresh water would be let in to Lake Inferior through this hole—large enough for small amounts to be let in, but too small to let enough in to fill the cavity. It was akin to turning a milk jug upside down, only allowing milk to pour out in glugs instead of all at once. This would be the perfect home for the Mishipeshu and its offspring.

When the time was right in the Mishipeshu's life, an egg would form inside its massive body, and as has been through all its history, it lay it just prior to its exit from its warm-weather lair. As the Mishipeshu returned with the bodies of its victims, it would pile them around the egg, a morbid incubator of sorts, and at the end of winter, when its time to hunt was done, it too would lie next to the egg and die. When the egg hatches about six weeks later, all the food needed to feed the new Mishipeshu would be close by, including the previous protector of the lake. By the time the following winter set in, this new Mishipeshu would be able to fend for itself and learn to hunt as its parent did, having the genetic code and instincts needed to become the silent hunter its lineage demanded and adding to the lore of its kind, once again proving that in the Upper Peninsula of Michigan, winter kills.

ABOUT M.C. PEAK

I've been an avid outdoorsman most of my life. I spent many years hiking and camping in the Blue Ridge Mountains of Virginia before moving to North Idaho, where I continued to pursue my love of the outdoors. The wildlife was bigger and more dangerous, but also more majestic, and I thoroughly enjoyed the moose that overwintered on our property. The many Bigfoot sightings in that area, the ongoing Bigfoot research that went on, and the many Native American historical accounts of sightings, as well as some personal experiences, are what inspired me to write the book *Hoodoo*.

I have since retired and moved to the Upper Peninsula of Michigan to be closer to family, but I continue to enjoy the great outdoors in a town aptly named Paradise. I also continue to write. Who would have thought there would be a high Bigfoot presence here in the UP? My interest in the Native American understanding of nature and our place in it has inspired another book, about a

little known cryptid in and around Lake Superior that will, hopefully, be coming out soon.

I hope you enjoyed reading *Hoodoo*. Thank you.

AFTERWORD

Go to hangarıpublishing.com to learn more about the Authors and stay up to date with their newest releases.

www.ingramcontent.com/pod-product-compliance
Lightning Source LLC
Chambersburg PA
CBHW060138150626
46550CB00015B/1582